Kathleen Raine

Norman MacCaig

Derick Thomson

D0297205

Robert

Hugh MacDiarmid   T.S. Eliot

Gerard Manley Hopkins

W.S. Graham

Alasdair Gray

John Hedderwick

R.L. Stevenson

Douglas Dunn

Derek Mahon

Basil Bunting

Tony Harrison

Sir Walter Scott

...is MacNeice

Robert Southey

Norman Nicholson

John Dalton   John Earl

William Wordsworth   Andrew Marvell

Sidney Keyes   Harold Massingham

Andrew Young

Stephen Spender

John Dyer   Ted Hughes

Richard James   Emily Brontë

Anne Ridler

Charles Kingsley   W.H. Auden   Stevie Smith

Tobias Hill

Gerard Manley Hopkins   William Allingham   Philip Larkin

D.H. Lawrence

Elizabeth Jennings   James Bisset

A.E. Housman   Christopher North

R.S. Thomas

Katherine Pierpoint

William Shakespeare

Derek Walcott   Michael Drayton

W. Langland

Henry Vaughan   Edward Thomas   George Eliot   Michael Hofmann   George Crabbe

E. Barrett Browning   William Cowper   Rupert Brooke

...liam Barnes   A. Motion   William Whitehead

Idries Davies   Ivor Gurney   Alexander Pope   William Strode   John Clare   Robert Bloomfield

Gillian Clarke   Glyn Maxwell   Charles Tomlinson

Edmund Spencer   J. Milton   Robert Lloyd   John Scott

...iam   Anne Finch   James Thomson   Thomas Gray

...per   Oliver Goldsmith   Patrick Hannay   Fred Downie

...asefield   Louis MacNeice   J. Betjeman   Oscar Wilde   U.A. Fanthorpe

Gilbert White   William Morris

John Keats   Geoffrey Hill   Philip Sidney   ...nach Palmer

Thomas Hardy   V. Sackville-West

Hilaire Belloc   Christopher Fry   Matthew Arnold

William Barnes   William Blake   John Davidson

A.C. Swinburne

Rudyard Kipling

THE FABER BOOK OF LANDSCAPE POETRY

The Faber Book of
LANDSCAPE POETRY

edited by KENNETH BAKER

ff

faber and faber

First published in 2000
by Faber and Faber Limited
3 Queen Square London WC1N 3AU
Published in the United States by Faber and Faber, Inc.,
an affiliate of Farrar, Straus and Giroux, New York

Photoset by Wilmaset Ltd, Birkenhead, Wirral
Printed in England by Clays Ltd, St Ives plc

Kenneth Baker is hereby identified as editor of this
work in accordance with Section 77 of the Copyright,
Designs and Patents Act 1988

A CIP record for this book
is available from the British Library

ISBN 0-571-20071-0

10 9 8 7 6 5 4 3 2 1

for our grandchildren, Tess, Oonagh and Conrad

Editor's Note

The dates of birth and death of each of the poets are
included in the index. I have tried to identify the places
described in each poem, and I am grateful for the assistance
that Christopher Reid and I have had from several poets.
Some of the poems are too general to be identified with a
specific place. This task was not made easier by changes in
county boundaries over the centuries and by the
disappearance of traditional names and the appearance of
new and, on the whole, rather less attractive ones. If any
readers have different views or other placenames, I would be
glad to hear from them.

I would like to thank Christopher Reid, formerly the
Poetry Editor at Faber, for all his help and guidance,
particularly in fashioning the shape of this anthology.

My thanks are also due to Arthur Freeman, for directing
me to some of the lesser-known poets of the eighteenth
century, and finally to my secretary, Kathy Hubbard, for her
help in marshalling this book.

Contents

Introduction xxi

The Tables Turned WILLIAM WORDSWORTH 1

Walks and Surveys

from L'Allegro JOHN MILTON 3
Grongar Hill JOHN DYER 5
The Naturalist's Summer-Evening Walk GILBERT WHITE 9
from The Shepherd's Calendar ('October') JOHN CLARE 11
from Aurora Leigh, Book I ELIZABETH BARRETT
   BROWNING 12
Cotswold Ways IVOR GURNEY 14
Poem in October DYLAN THOMAS 14
The Mayo Tao DEREK MAHON 17
On Westwell Downs WILLIAM STRODE 18

Mountains, Hills and the View from Above

from Gnomic Verses WILLIAM BLAKE 20
from Gnomic Stanzas ANONYMOUS (WELSH) 20
from Reflections on Having Left a Place of
   Retirement SAMUEL TAYLOR COLERIDGE 21
Under the Mountain LOUIS MACNEICE 22
Hilles Edge GLYN MAXWELL 23
Looking Down on Glen Canisp NORMAN MACCAIG 24
Scafell Pike NORMAN NICHOLSON 25
from The Prelude, Book I WILLIAM WORDSWORTH 26

Rivers and Streams

from Prothalamion EDMUND SPENSER 28
from To the City of London WILLIAM DUNBAR 29
from Fresh Water ANDREW MOTION 30
The River Humber STEVIE SMITH 31
Five Rivers NORMAN NICHOLSON 32
'Stones trip Coquet burn' BASIL BUNTING 34
'Says Tweed to Till' ANONYMOUS 35
Afton Water ROBERT BURNS 35
from Britannia's Pastorals WILLIAM BROWNE 36
On Sturminster Foot-bridge THOMAS HARDY 37
The Water-Fall HENRY VAUGHAN 38
The Brook ALFRED, LORD TENNYSON 39
Rising Damp U. A. FANTHORPE 41

Lakes, Floods, Marshes and Fens

An Irish Lake W. R. RODGERS 43
Daffodils WILLIAM WORDSWORTH 44
from Poly-Olbion MICHAEL DRAYTON 45
from Brent, a Poem WILLIAM DIAPER 46
from Eclogue II JOHN SCOTT 47
Flooded Meadows THOM GUNN 47
Saltmarsh and Skylark KATHERINE PIERPOINT 48

Sea and Coast

Dover Beach MATTHEW ARNOLD 50
Winter Seascape JOHN BETJEMAN 51
from King Lear, Act IV WILLIAM SHAKESPEARE 52
Blackberrying SYLVIA PLATH 53
North Wind: Portrush DEREK MAHON 54
The Peninsula SEAMUS HEANEY 56
St Columba's Island Hermitage ANONYMOUS (IRISH) 57

Moors, Heaths and Barren Places

from Sir Gawain and the Green Knight THE 'PEARL'
  POET 59
'Loud without the wind was roaring' EMILY BRONTË 61
To S. R. Crockett ROBERT LOUIS STEVENSON 63
Rannoch, by Glencoe T. S. ELIOT 64
Whinlands SEAMUS HEANEY 64
from The Mores JOHN CLARE 65

Wind and Rain

Summer Rain HARTLEY COLERIDGE 67
Rain TED HUGHES 67
Rain SEAMUS O'SULLIVAN 69
'O rain of July pouring down from the heavens' IDRIS
  DAVIES 70
The Rainbow D. H. LAWRENCE 70
from To The Wind DAFYDD AP GWILYM 71
Wind TED HUGHES 72
The Storm HENRY VAUGHAN 73
from The Favourite Village, Book III JAMES HURDIS 74
'High waving heather, 'neath stormy blasts bending'
  EMILY BRONTË 74

The Hours and the Seasons

'Weeping oaks grieve, chestnuts raise' BASIL BUNTING 76
Spring GERARD MANLEY HOPKINS 76
The Heat of Noon JOHN CLARE 77
A Nocturnal Reverie ANNE FINCH, COUNTESS OF
  WINCHILSEA 77
In Teesdale ANDREW YOUNG 79
Digging EDWARD THOMAS 80
Burning the Stubble JON STALLWORTHY 80
Song ALFRED, LORD TENNYSON 81

The Burning of the Leaves LAURENCE BINYON 82
A Snowy Day ANONYMOUS (WELSH) 83
Winter in Wensleydale HAROLD MASSINGHAM 85

Order and Wilderness

The Garden ANDREW MARVELL 87
from The Task, Book III WILLIAM COWPER 89
On the Late Improvements at Nuneham WILLIAM
    WHITEHEAD 90
Gardeners DOUGLAS DUNN 91
from The Old Mansion-House ROBERT SOUTHEY 92
from A Forsaken Garden ALGERNON CHARLES
    SWINBURNE 94
Tall Nettles EDWARD THOMAS 96
Thistles JON STALLWORTHY 96
Inversnaid GERARD MANLEY HOPKINS 97
from A True and Natural Description of the Great Level of
    the Fenns SIR JONAS MOORE 98

Trees and the Deaths of Trees

King Edward's Flora U. A. FANTHORPE 99
from The Description of Cooke-ham AEMILIA LANYER 100
from Yardley Oak WILLIAM COWPER 101
Last Laugh DOUGLAS YOUNG 104
Aspens EDWARD THOMAS 105
Binsey Poplars GERARD MANLEY HOPKINS 106
Felling a Tree IVOR GURNEY 107
The Trees Are Down CHARLOTTE MEW 110
The Hurricane and Charlotte Mew AMY CLAMPITT 111
from 'O sweete woods the delight of solitarines'
    SIR PHILIP SIDNEY 112
from The Mink War GENE KEMP 113
In a Wood THOMAS HARDY 115

Rocks and Stones

Rock Face NORMAN NICHOLSON 117
Stone on High Crag KATHLEEN RAINE 117
Cairn JOHN FULLER 118
In Praise of Limestone W. H. AUDEN 119
from On a Raised Beach HUGH MACDIARMID 122

Ruins and Great Houses

The Ruin ANONYMOUS (OLD ENGLISH) 124
from Upon Appleton House ANDREW MARVELL 125
Lament over the Ruins of the Abbey of Teach
    Molaga JAMES CLARENCE MANGAN 126
from The Ruined Cottage WILLIAM WORDSWORTH 129
from Rokeby, Canto V SIR WALTER SCOTT 130
from To Penshurst BEN JONSON 131
Blenheim Palace ALEXANDER POPE 133
Sissinghurst V. SACKVILLE-WEST 133

Churches and Churchyards

The Belfry R. S. THOMAS 135
Elegy Written in a Country Churchyard THOMAS GRAY 135
Hughley Steeple A. E. HOUSMAN 139
The Mountain Chapel EDWARD THOMAS 140
Highland Graveyard KATHLEEN RAINE 142
At Briggflatts Meetinghouse BASIL BUNTING 143
The Earthen Lot TONY HARRISON 143

Death in the Countryside

from Windsor-forest ALEXANDER POPE 145
The Gallows EDWARD THOMAS 146
The Hunting of the Hare MARGARET CAVENDISH,
    DUCHESS OF NEWCASTLE 147

from The Seasons ('Autumn') JAMES THOMSON 150
from Reynard the Fox JOHN MASEFIELD 151
from The Year of Seeds: Section XL EBENEZER ELLIOT 152
Coming Down through Somerset TED HUGHES 152

Pastoral and Realism

from The Faerie Queene, Book VI EDMUND SPENSER 154
from Henry VI, Part III, Act II WILLIAM SHAKESPEARE 155
from The Sun's Darling THOMAS DEKKER 156
from The Task, Book I WILLIAM COWPER 158
from The Village, Book I GEORGE CRABBE 159
from The Villa by the Sea JAMES HEDDERWICK 161
from As You Like It, Act II WILLIAM SHAKESPEARE 162

Working the Land

The Foddering Boy JOHN CLARE 164
The Great Hunger: Section XIII PATRICK KAVANAGH 165
A Peasant R. S. THOMAS 166
Washing the Coins DOUGLAS DUNN 167
from The Land ('Winter') V. SACKVILLE-WEST 169
from The Favourite Village, Book IV JAMES HURDIS 170
Crow Hill TED HUGHES 172
In Time of 'The Breaking of Nations' THOMAS HARDY 173

Ownership and Dispossession

The Land RUDYARD KIPLING 174
On Buying OS sheet 163 U. A. FANTHORPE 177
from The Deserted Village OLIVER GOLDSMITH 178
Remembrances JOHN CLARE 179
The Common a-Took In WILLIAM BARNES 182
The Clearances IAIN CRICHTON SMITH 183
A man in Assynt NORMAN MACCAIG 184

Dead Fires GEORGE MACKAY BROWN 187
Gin the Goodwife Stint BASIL BUNTING 188

Industrialization

Croydon of the Charcoal Burners PATRICK HANNAY 189
from The Fleece JOHN DYER 189
from Ramble of the Gods through Birmingham
    JAMES BISSET 191
North Country D. H. LAWRENCE 193
from A Descriptive Poem, Addressed to Two Ladies, at their
    Return from Viewing the Mines, near Whitehaven
    JOHN DALTON 194
From Feathers to Iron: Poem 12 C. DAY LEWIS 196
National Trust TONY HARRISON 197
East Moors GILLIAN CLARKE 198

Violation of Nature and the Landscape

from The Deserted Village OLIVER GOLDSMITH 200
Nutting WILLIAM WORDSWORTH 201
The Pylons STEPHEN SPENDER 203
from 'The summer holds: upon its glittering lake'
    W. H. AUDEN 204
The Planster's Vision JOHN BETJEMAN 205
Going, Going PHILIP LARKIN 205
The Green Man's Last Will and Testament
    JOHN HEATH-STUBBS 207

Villages and Small Towns

The Village R. S. THOMAS 210
Our Village – by a Villager THOMAS HOOD 211
'The village of Fochriw grunts among the higher hills'
    IDRIS DAVIES 214
The Small Towns of Ireland JOHN BETJEMAN 215

Tewkesbury IVOR GURNEY 216
Armagh W. R. RODGERS 218

Ambiguous Terrain

The Cit's Country Box ROBERT LLOYD 220
from London Rurality GEORGE COLMAN,
    THE YOUNGER 224
Flat Suburbs, S.W., in the Morning D. H. LAWRENCE 225
Love in a Valley JOHN BETJEMAN 225
Lines Written on Richmond Park JAMES THOMSON 226
The Park LOUIS MACNEICE 227
Allotments: April BERNARD SPENCER 228
Draining the Grand Union TOBIAS HILL 229
Her Garden FREDA DOWNIE 231

Cities

'As one who, long in rural hamlets pent' SYDNEY SMITH 232
Composed upon Westminster Bridge, September 3, 1802
    WILLIAM WORDSWORTH 232
In the Isle of Dogs JOHN DAVIDSON 233
Symphony in Yellow OSCAR WILDE 235
from The Earthly Paradise ('Prologue') WILLIAM
    MORRIS 236
Birmingham LOUIS MACNEICE 236
Durham ANONYMOUS (OLD ENGLISH) 238
from Marmion, Canto IV SIR WALTER SCOTT 239
Ode to Swansea VERNON WATKINS 240
from Manchester's Improving Daily ANONYMOUS 241

Road and Rail

Roads EDWARD THOMAS 244
The Roman Road THOMAS HARDY 246
The Rolling English Road G. K. CHESTERTON 247

Devonshire Roads SAMUEL TAYLOR COLERIDGE 248
The White Road up athirt the Hill WILLIAM BARNES 249
Midsummer: Poem XXXV DEREK WALCOTT 250
From a Railway Carriage ROBERT LOUIS STEVENSON 251
Express WILLIAM ALLINGHAM 252
The Whitsun Weddings PHILIP LARKIN 253

History

from Iter Lancastrense RICHARD JAMES 257
'On Wenlock Edge the wood's in trouble'
    A. E. HOUSMAN 258
Puck's Song RUDYARD KIPLING 259
Chalk Horse MICHAEL BALDWIN 260
Lollingdon Downs JOHN MASEFIELD 261
Millom Old Quarry NORMAN NICHOLSON 262
Toome SEAMUS HEANEY 263
The Threefold Place EDWIN MUIR 264
Battlefield CHRISTOPHER NORTH 264
Wessex Guidebook LOUIS MACNEICE 266
The Laurel Axe GEOFFREY HILL 267
Four Quartets: 'East Coker', Part I T. S. ELIOT 268

Divinity

from Milton WILLIAM BLAKE 270
'The world is too much with us; late and soon'
    WILLIAM WORDSWORTH 270
'And now the trembling light' SAMUEL PALMER 271
Hurrahing in Harvest GERARD MANLEY HOPKINS 272
Harvest CHARLES TOMLINSON 273
Harvest and Consecration ELIZABETH JENNINGS 274
from The Boy with a Cart, Act I CHRISTOPHER FRY 275
Lewis in Summer DERICK THOMSON (RUARAIDH
    MACTHÓMAIS) 277
Salmon-Taking Times TED HUGHES 277

The Clay-Tip Worker JACK CLEMO 278
Moorland R. S. THOMAS 280

Visions and Mysteries

The Cliff of Alteran ANONYMOUS (IRISH) 281
from Piers Plowman WILLIAM LANGLAND 281
from Jerusalem WILLIAM BLAKE 283
Four Quartets: 'Little Gidding', Part I T. S. ELIOT 284
from Briggflatts, Part V BASIL BUNTING 286

Spirits and Ghosts

Resolution and Independence WILLIAM WORDSWORTH 289
from The Scholar Gipsy MATTHEW ARNOLD 294
La Belle Dame sans Merci JOHN KEATS 299
Beeny Cliff THOMAS HARDY 301
The Sands of Dee CHARLES KINGSLEY 302
Ha'nacker Mill HILAIRE BELLOC 303
The Way through the Woods RUDYARD KIPLING 304
The Fakenham Ghost ROBERT BLOOMFIELD 305

The Poet's Shadow

'Look through the naked bramble and blackthorn'
    JOHN CLARE 308
William Wordsworth SIDNEY KEYES 308
Worldsworth STEPHEN SPENDER 309
Emily Brontë TED HUGHES 313
The Last Signal THOMAS HARDY 314
Hopkins in Wales ELIZABETH JENNINGS 314
Myopia in Rupert Brooke Country MICHAEL HOFMANN 316
from Aurora Leigh, Book I ELIZABETH BARRETT
    BROWNING 316
The Reader Looks Up ARTHUR FREEMAN 318
Skald's Death HUGH MACDIARMID 319

Sounds

from The Deserted Village OLIVER GOLDSMITH 320
The Ecchoing Green WILLIAM BLAKE 321
The Eolian Harp SAMUEL TAYLOR COLERIDGE 322
from Poems on the Naming of Places WILLIAM
   WORDSWORTH 324
In Romney Marsh JOHN DAVIDSON 325
Waterfalls VERNON WATKINS 326
Windharp JOHN MONTAGUE 327
from To Autumn JOHN KEATS 328
Telegraph Wires TED HUGHES 328
On Hearing the Full Peal of Ten Bells from Christ Church,
   Swindon, Wilts. JOHN BETJEMAN 329

Birds and Birdsong

from The Shepherd's Calendar ('March') JOHN CLARE 330
from Campaspe JOHN LYLY 332
On the Death of a Nightingale THOMAS RANDOLPH 332
Ode to a Nightingale JOHN KEATS 333
'Yes it was the mountain Echo' WILLIAM WORDSWORTH 336
The Dying Swan ALFRED, LORD TENNYSON 337
The Wild Swans at Coole W. B. YEATS 338
The Darkling Thrush THOMAS HARDY 339
Adlestrop EDWARD THOMAS 340
The Herons FRANCIS LEDWIDGE 341
Bempton Cliffs ANNE RIDLER 341
from There Was a Boy WILLIAM WORDSWORTH 342

Colour and the Painter's Eye

Pied Beauty GERARD MANLEY HOPKINS 344
A Meditation on John Constable CHARLES TOMLINSON 344
Green WILLIAM BARNES 346
Dun-Colour RUTH PITTER 347

from Christmas Eve ROBERT BROWNING 348
And Light Fading P. J. KAVANAGH 350

Sustained by Nature

Lines Composed a Few Miles above Tintern
   Abbey WILLIAM WORDSWORTH 351
Retirement HENRY VAUGHAN 356
from Fears in Solitude SAMUEL TAYLOR COLERIDGE 357
from As You Like It, Act II WILLIAM SHAKESPEARE 358
'There was a dreamer in the mining town' IDRIS DAVIES 358
Landscape and I NORMAN MACCAIG 360
Field Day W. R. RODGERS 361

Childhood

from Ode on a Distant Prospect of Eton College
   THOMAS GRAY 362
from The Prelude, Book I WILLIAM WORDSWORTH 363
Sonnet to the River Otter SAMUEL TAYLOR COLERIDGE 365
from Brother and Sister GEORGE ELIOT 365
Fern Hill DYLAN THOMAS 366
Childhood EDWIN MUIR 368
Loch Thom W. S. GRAHAM 369
Carrickfergus LOUIS MACNEICE 370
Tyne Dock FRANCIS SCARFE 372
Mercian Hymns: VI, VII GEOFFREY HILL 373

Nature's Influence on Character and Mood

from The Lay of the Last Minstrel, Canto VI
   SIR WALTER SCOTT 375
Scotland SIR ALEXANDER GRAY 376
On the South Coast of Cornwall JOHN GRAY 377
To Dean-bourn, a Rude River in Devon ROBERT
   HERRICK 378

A Northern Suburb JOHN DAVIDSON 379
'The heart is hard in nature...' WILLIAM COWPER 380
Introduction to a Landscape ELIZABETH JENNINGS 381

Pride, National and Local

from Richard II, Act II WILLIAM SHAKESPEARE 382
from Fears in Solitude SAMUEL TAYLOR COLERIDGE 382
A Charm RUDYARD KIPLING 383
By Severn IVOR GURNEY 384
Northumbrian Place-names JOHN EARL 385
Scotland Small? HUGH MACDIARMID 386
Hallaig SORLEY MACLEAN (SOMHAIRLE
   MACGILL-EAIN) 387
Stony Grey Soil PATRICK KAVANAGH 389
Ulster Names JOHN HEWITT 390
Broagh SEAMUS HEANEY 392
Reservoirs R. S. THOMAS 393

Secret and Special Places

This Lime-Tree Bower My Prison SAMUEL TAYLOR
   COLERIDGE 395
My Orcha'd in Linden Lea WILLIAM BARNES 397
from The Prelude, Book I WILLIAM WORDSWORTH 398
from The Bothie of Tober-na-Vuolich ARTHUR HUGH
   CLOUGH 399
At 'The Angler' BERNARD SPENCER 401
Silent Noon DANTE GABRIEL ROSSETTI 402
The Lake Isle of Innisfree W. B. YEATS 402
The Combe EDWARD THOMAS 403
Bog JOHN FULLER 404
Summer Farm NORMAN MACCAIG 404
Settings: xxiv SEAMUS HEANEY 405

Homesickness and Wanderlust

Home-Thoughts, from Abroad ROBERT BROWNING 406
In Springtime RUDYARD KIPLING 407
from Verses Written in the Chiosk of the British Palace,
    at Pera LADY MARY WORTLEY MONTAGU 408
from The Old Vicarage, Grantchester RUPERT BROOKE 409
Song IVOR GURNEY 410
'Into my heart an air that kills' A. E. HOUSMAN 411
My Heart's in the Highlands ROBERT BURNS 411
Kerr's Ass PATRICK KAVANAGH 412
from Don Juan, Canto II GEORGE GORDON, LORD
    BYRON 413
from The Seafarer ANONYMOUS (OLD ENGLISH) 413
from Epistle to My Brother George JOHN KEATS 414
Audley Court ALFRED, LORD TENNYSON 414

Acknowledgements 419
Index of Poets 423
Index of Places 425

Introduction

The two greatest assets that we have in our country are its language and its landscape. This book attempts to celebrate the landscape through the eyes, sensibilities, imagination and, of course, the language of poets over the last thousand years. Over that time both the landscape and the language have changed dramatically. The English language, spoken then by fewer than a million people, has developed from its Celtic and Anglo-Saxon roots to become the immensely rich language of today, spoken by over eight hundred million around the world. It was created not by grammarians but from the usage of ordinary people coming into Britain as waves of immigrants – Celts, Angles, Saxons, Romans, Jutes, Germans, Vikings, Normans, Jews, Asians and West Indians.

Over that same period the landscape has been changed out of all recognition by the actions of those same people: the great forests have disappeared; moors, meadows, downland, heaths have all shrunk; hamlets have become cities, and estuaries ports. Man has shaped nature and the countryside: the simple assertion of William Cowper that 'God made the country and man made the town' was not true even in the eighteenth century. The landscape is both natural and artificial, and the poems I have chosen reflect this dual heredity.

There are thirty-seven sections in this anthology, each dealing with a different aspect of our landscape. The first six contain poems about the natural features which have not changed much over the centuries: *Walks and Surveys*, *Mountains Rivers Lakes* and *Marshes*, the *Sea Coast* and *Moors*, followed by other sections on the man-made environment, *Villages and Small Towns*, *Cities*, *Road and Rail*. These are poems principally of description, and I've let the poets themselves 'draw the landskip bright and strong'. For the most part, they are poems of enjoyment in which the poets single out the particular pleasures that give them their greatest joy: for Milton it was the brightness of a Spring morning; for William

Cowper it was the sight of 'animals running free'; for Coleridge it was the exhilaration of climbing a mountain. Emily Brontë so loved her wild and windswept Yorkshire moors that she makes you feel that you are walking with her over them. These experiences sink deep into the memory, never to be forgotten: as Robert Louis Stevenson lay dying in Samoa he pined to see again the hills of home in Scotland and feel the winds 'austere and true'.

The built environment also has its champions. They write lovingly of the intimacy of villages, and of their pride in their towns and cities – as in the street ballad of the 1820s which proudly proclaimed that 'Manchester's improving daily'. I also thought it right to include some poems about those places that are neither completely in the country or in the town, *Ambiguous Terrain* – those places which are a borderland like the suburbs, or patches in a city like parks and allotments, which are deliberate attempts to create an element of the country in an urban landscape. While few would claim that roads are things of beauty, they can provide moments of happiness – as for Hardy walking with his mother along a Roman road, or Chesterton revelling in the reeling, rolling English road 'that rambles round the shire'. Edward Thomas loved the country roads:

Whatever the road bring
To me or take from me,
They keep me company
With their pattering,

Crowding the solitude
Of the loops over the downs,
Hushing the roar of towns
And their brief multitude.

Britain does not have mountain ranges on the scale of the Alps or the Pyrenees but it does have heath and moorland, which may appear gentler, but can be just as remote and savage. Much of this has now been lost or tamed by the enclosures of the common land from the seventeenth to the nineteenth centuries. In the section *Ownership and Dispossession*, John Clare in the 1820s mourns the fencing and enclosure of the common land in Northamptonshire, which took away time-honoured traditional freedoms: 'Inclosure like a Buonaparte let not a thing remain'. In Scotland the clearances were more brutal, leaving scarred landscapes, empty hovels and centuries of bitterness. William Barnes in the 1840s in Dorset regretted the loss of freedom and gaiety as men, women, children and cattle were stopped from roaming freely when 'The Common a-Took In':

> Girt banks do shut up ev'ry drong,
> An' stratch wi' thorny backs along
> Where we did use to run among
>   The vuzzen an' the broom.

Ownership of land changes all the time, and the defenders of enclosure would claim that it led to greater agricultural prosperity – by which they meant a smaller number of people got higher prices for a greater share of the crops. But the land itself could remain stubbornly unchanged; it has a continuity of its own, as Kipling recognized when he recorded how the cunning of several generations of peasants defied the successive efforts of the Romans, the Saxons, the Normans, and even the enclosing landowners of the eighteenth century, to drain a meadow.

The role of the peasant in shaping the landscape has not been fully acknowledged, and that is why I have included a section on *Working the Land*. Too wet in winter, too hot in summer, the climate ensures that it is a constant struggle to make the land yield its crops: medieval manuscripts are full of pictures of peasants ploughing, sowing, harrowing, shepherding, foddering and harvesting, because the monks, who copied the texts in question, knew that these village labourers were vital. The Irish poet Patrick Kavanagh is in no doubt of their importance:

> *There* is the source from which all cultures rise,
> And all religions,
> *There* is the pool in which the poet dips
> And the musician.
> Without the peasant base civilisation must die,
> Unless the clay is in the mouth the singer's singing is useless.

A few generations back all our ancestors either worked on the land or serviced those who did. The habits and practices of these peasant-farmers led to the formation of village communities, which shaped their local landscape. In many of the great landscape paintings it is the small figure of a farm worker which brings the whole scene to life – he is just as much part of the landscape as the trees, the river or the clouds. Like Hardy's man harrowing the clods, he goes 'onward the same / Though dynasties pass'.

This sense of what time has done to the environment is reflected in the section on *History*. In the countryside one is haunted by the past; reminded at every turn of some past event; conscious that what one sees happening has happened countless times before. Nature keeps its own record of that wheel which turns forever in the grooves of death and regeneration. This is T. S. Eliot in 'East Coker':

> In my beginning is my end. In succession
> Houses rise and fall, crumble, are extended,
> Are removed, destroyed, restored, or in their place
> Is an open field, or a factory, or a by-pass.
> Old stone to new building, old timber to new fires,
> Old fires to ashes, and ashes to the earth
> Which is already flesh, fur and faeces,
> Bone of man and beast, cornstalk and leaf.

It is impossible in the countryside to repudiate the past as there are constant reminders of the flow of time. As you move up a river, like the Thames, you move back through history – from the estuary and from the wharves of the busy trading city, past the rebuilt Globe and on to Windsor and Oxford, and finally to the little streams bubbling up in the Cotswolds much as they have done for thousands of years. Then there are the great white horses cut into the chalk downs signifying perhaps the extent of some tribe's territorial authority, or some other myth bound up with the land – 'We walk our shadows astride / Those shimmering flanks at sunset'.

Then there are ruins like Tintern Abbey, torn down and desecrated by Henry VIII in 1539 and which inspired Wordsworth's

great poem, or the still visible circular forts of the Celts at
Holmbury Hill, or the 'loam, flints, musket-balls, / fragmented
ware, / torcs and fish-bones' that are to be found in Seamus
Heaney's alluvial mud. Ruins covered in ivy and bathed in moon-
light were not a Victorian romantic invention. I was glad to come
across Richard Hamer's translation of a twelfth-century English
poem 'The Ruin' which reminds us that however strong and
splendid the ramparts may be 'the works / Of giants crumble'.

The spirit of a country is found in its history and in its landscape.
In the section *Pride, National and Local*, Ivor Gurney made a bid for
his beloved Severn valley to be the true heart of England:

> If England, her spirit lives anywhere
> It is by Severn, by hawthorns, and grand willows.

National pride has its roots deep in the soil and earth of one's country –
Kipling's 'Take of English earth as much / As either hand may rightly
clutch'. And Hugh MacDiarmid expresses his love for Scotland also
through the things that grow in its earth – in this case all the little wild
plants that are found on a Scottish heather moor. In R. S. Thomas's
poem it is the violation of Welsh earth to provide a reservoir for
England which provokes his anger. In Ulster, John Hewitt finds his love
and pride in the placenames of the land:

> The names of a land show the heart of the race;
> they move on the tongue like the lilt of a song.
> You say the name and I see the place –
> Drumbo, Dungannon, Annalong.
> Barony, townland, we cannot go wrong.

The tradition of pastoral poetry, which started with Edmund
Spenser's *Shephearde's Calendar* in 1579, celebrated a rustic ideal,
where people 'hating the tradeful citys hum' fled from the insinuating
corruption of the courtly life to find peace, harmony and the pleasure of
simple things, and where a contented peasantry went about their ways
with a bucolic jollity. The first few poems in *Pastoral and Realism*
describe this escapism but it was all to come to a sharp end in the middle
of the eighteenth century. The Agricultural Revolution and Enclosure

led to the calamities recorded in Goldsmith's *The Deserted Village* and there was a general change of tone first shown in the harsh realism of George Crabbe. In his Suffolk, the lot of the folk who lived on the land or on the sea was one of miserable poverty, ill-health and early death: a view which Hazlitt thought led to an 'unvaried note of unavailing woe'.

The way of looking at the countryside also changed. In 1770 William Gilpin published his *Observations on the River Wye and several parts of South Wales* in which he set about 'not barely examining the face of a country, but examining it by the rules of picturesque beauty'. Two years later there followed his guide to the picturesque scenery of *The Mountains and Lakes of Cumberland and Westmoreland* and in 1777 Paul Sandby published his engravings, *A Collection of Landscapes*, from which people south of the border could appreciate the grandeur and isolated beauty of the Highlands of Scotland. The Romantic movement had been born: henceforth the appeal of natural beauty was to lie in rugged mountains shrouded in clouds, windswept moors, shadows, caves, darkness, moonlight, dawn and twilight. With the publication of the *Lyrical Ballads* in 1798 Wordsworth and Coleridge established a new and different way of describing the beauty of nature and the landscape, and the effect they could have upon the human spirit.

However it is not just the grandeur of majestic scenery or the wildest elements that can stir the spirit. It is often in those *Secret and Special Places* that a poet will find the greatest contentment. For Coleridge it was his Lime-tree bower:

> Henceforth I shall know
> That Nature ne'er deserts the wise and pure,
> No plot so narrow, be but Nature there,
> No waste so vacant, but may well employ
> Each faculty of sense, and keep the heart
> Awake to love and beauty!

For Wordsworth it was when he broke away from his fellow ice-skaters to find 'a silent bay'; for William Barnes it was his Orchard in Linden Lea; for Yeats it was 'The Lake Isle of Innisfree' and for Norman MacCaig a Summer Farm:

I lie, not thinking, in the cool, soft grass
Afraid of where a thought might take me –
This grasshopper with plated face
Unfolds his legs and finds himself in space.

But not every prospect pleases and not every vista affords delight. Wordsworth's leech-gatherer worked in a lonely moorish muddy pond, and Keats's Knight at Arms is doomed to loiter on a cold hillside 'though the sedge is withered from the lake and no birds sing'.

In the two sections *Visions and Mysteries* and *Spirits and Ghosts*, I have chosen poems that deal with mysticism in nature. Woods, rivers, mountains, ravines, cliffs and great trees are infused with memories and associations that have over the centuries assumed a mystical and mythical quality. There are things that cannot be explained rationally but survive in folklore, in custom and tradition, in stories handed down from one generation to the next, and a historic sense that the destiny of man is bound up with the spirits of Nature. William Cowper's poem 'The Yardley Oak' was popular in the nineteenth century because its growth from an acorn to its full stature and to its dying from its top downwards was seen as a parallel to the decay of England – the spirit of the tree was intertwined with the spirit of Albion. William Blake's vision of the golden pillars built over the fields from Islington to Marylebone is a victory over the druid past, and Derek Mahon finds in a forest clearing that:

It is here that the banished gods are hiding,
    Here they sit out the centuries
        In stone, water
    And the heart of trees,
Lost in a reverie of their own natures [...]

Of zero-growth economics and seasonal change
    In a world without cars, computers
        Or chemical skies,
    Where thought is a foundling of stones
And wisdom a five-minute silence at moonrise.

Our country is full of haunted landscapes, and even a poet as down-to-earth as Kipling conjures up the magic of the ghostly woman rider 'Steadily cantering through / The misty solitudes', of the vanished Way through the Woods.

In his preface to the re-printing of the *Lyrical Ballads* in 1805 Wordsworth said, 'Poetry is the spontaneous overflow of powerful feeling: it takes its origins from emotion recollected in tranquillity'. That emotion often has at its heart a spiritual experience. The landscape is often best enjoyed alone, perhaps on a walk through the countryside, when one is surrounded with the beauty of nature and immersed in the atmosphere of the place so that one's enjoyment becomes a source of refreshment and one can be aware of a presence greater than oneself. For some that presence is God, for others some pagan deity or some universal spirit, through which one hears 'The still sad music of Humanity'. In the section *Divinity* poets reveal their spiritual experiences. Many of these occurred as the stillness of evening approached, or in the celebration of one of the perennial activities of the countryside like the bringing in of the harvest. Gerard Manley Hopkins in 'Hurrahing in Harvest' 'glean[s] our Saviour ... And the azurous hung hills are his world-wielding shoulder / Majestic'. Another Catholic, Elizabeth Jennings, welcomes the harvest as a guarantee of resurrection:

> I spoke of Mass and thought of it as close
> To how a season feels which stirs and brings
> Fire to the hearth, food to the hungry house
>   And strange, uncovered things –
> God in a garden then in sheaves of corn
> And the white bread a way to be reborn.

The sections *Sustained by Nature, Nature's Influence on Character and Mood* and *Childhood* reveal the crucial impact of the environment upon the poet and the human spirit in general. The landscape of childhood can never be forgotten or obliterated from one's memory for its formative power is just as persistent and influential as any genetic link. We all carry with us memories from our childhood of certain events, whose vividness is as fresh as if they had happened yesterday because they are rooted in a specific place. Wordsworth's poetry derived from, and drew its sustenance from, a handful of such incidents which he experienced as a boy in the hills of Cumbria; just as Dylan Thomas found his inspiration from playing in the farms and along the seashore of South Wales. The rugged Cornish fishermen of John Gray, the Highland Scots of Sir Alexander Gray, and the suburban dweller of John Davidson have all had their inner landscapes shaped by the outer landscapes in which they had lived. In the section on *Homesickness and Wanderlust* we are reminded that the pull of those happy places from the past is a love that cannot be denied.

No poet starts with a completely clean slate. Each carries his or her memories of earlier poets who in one way or another have had some influence upon them, and they generously express their admiration of those who left their mark on the very landscape they wrote about. In the section *The Poet's Shadow*, John Clare readily acknowledges his debt to William Cowper; Ted Hughes writes lovingly of Emily Brontë; and Stephen Spender, taken as a boy by his parents to the Lake District during the First World War to avoid a Zeppelin raid in London, honours Wordsworth:

> Rhythms I knew called Wordsworth
> Spreading through mountains, vales,
> To fill, I thought, the world.
> '*Worldsworth*', I thought, this peace
> Of voices intermingling –
> 'Worldsworth', to me, a vow.

Over the centuries man has hungered to bring nature under control and to impose some tidy order over the chaotic confusion and wildness of the natural world. Such attempts to tame nature are usually temporary victories. The section *Order and Wilderness* deals with man's repeated attempts to subdue nature through gardening – where wild grass is mowed to produce a smooth lawn; hedges clipped into unnatural shapes; weeds eradicated and natural growth is limited. Despite the creation of some ravishly beautiful gardens poets are for the most part deeply suspicious of the arts of the gardener: Cowper castigated Capability Brown and Marvell regretted that "Tis all enforced – the Fountain and the Grot; while the sweet Fields do lye forgot'. But Nature has a way of winning: in time most gardens revert to the wild and the weeds win.

Man has a lot to answer for when it comes to spoiling the environment. Much of the damage the landscape has suffered has resulted from the need to cope with the increase in population, which rose dramatically in the fifty years from 1740 to 1790 from 6 million to 8 million and went on to reach 41 million by 1900. Over a period of 200 years an essentially pastoral economy was transformed into an industrialized one – 1851 was the year when the census revealed that more people worked in towns than on the land. The sections on *Violation of Nature and the Landscape* and *Industrialization* show how what we have come to think of as a pastoral Paradise was lost: the result of many forces, some deliberate, and some almost accidental. Until the latter years of the twentieth century developers and industrialists had scant regard for the consequences of their actions and the results were polluted rivers, slagheaps, pylons, urban villas taking the place of ancient forests, and concrete everywhere.

In his poem 'Going, Going', which was commissioned in 1972 at the request of Robert Jackson, later an MP and a member of a government enquiry into the 'Human Habitat', Philip Larkin saw that all he loved most around him was slipping away under concrete and tyres. A sense of angry regret prevails. But that was not the view of poets such as John Dyer and John Dalton, writing in the early eighteenth century; they welcomed the Industrial Revolution, 'for industry brings all her honey to the hive'. Blake was certainly opposed to industrialization, but his 'dark Satanic mills' refer, it is now thought, not to the belching chimneys of the wool and cotton mills in Yorkshire and Lancashire, but to either the Church of England or the Newtonian system. There has always been a conflict of interest between industrial development and the beauty of the landscape. When a steel works like East Moors closes, the gain, as Gillian Clarke points out, is fresher air and cleaner washing on the line, but the loss is the idle men left to potter at home.

The lovers of the countryside must share some of the blame.

Wordsworth, forever frank, describes how as a boy going nutting, he came upon a hazel tree that no one else had found, and gleefully stripped it bare. Farmers too, the very custodians of the countryside, should recognize their responsibility for the devastation of the bird population over the last twenty years. In that time it has been estimated that the number of skylarks has fallen from over 4 to 1 million; sparrows from over 7 to less than 3 million; and grey partridges from half a million to under 100,000. The techniques of intensive farming – the use of herbicides, the grubbing up of hedges, the draining of wetlands – have destroyed the habitat of these birds. Weedkillers eradicate not only the weeds among the crop, but also the weeds and wild flowers at the edge of the fields. Thistles, the staple winter food for linnets and yellowhammers, are heedlessly cut down; the planting of winter crops immediately after the harvest has made the stubble, which was the foraging ground for the skylark in winter, unavailable. It is not surprising that birdsong is now heard much less: it has become the victim of the need for cheaper food. The only birdsongs recognized by most young people today are the distinctive cry of the cuckoo and the hooting of owls, and that is a tragedy. The poems in the section on *Birds and Birdsong* describe how the ravishing beauty of birdsong can crystallize a unique moment: it is a blackbird in Edward Thomas's 'Adlestrop' which makes that railway halt on a summer day so memorable, and it is Hardy's old and gaunt Darkling Thrush which utters a sound so ecstatic that it carries with it some hope for all humanity.

The most vulnerable assets in the countryside are its trees. The four great forests of England of a thousand years ago, Sherwood, Arden, the Forest of Dean and the New Forest, have all but disappeared, the victims of the need for timber for fuel, for housing and, up to the nineteenth century, for the building of ships. Our concern about the loss of trees is not just a concern of the twentieth century, for laws were passed in the eighteenth century to save woodlands which were considered essential for the country's economy. Trees, too, have been lost in great storms: we all remember the ravages of the storm of 1987, but John Evelyn recorded that in the great storm of 1703, 3,000 great oaks in the

Forest of Dean and 4,000 in the New Forest had been uprooted. In the section *Trees and the Deaths of Trees* Hopkins expresses his personal agony when his beloved poplars at Binsey were felled, and Charlotte Mew, when she saw the great plane trees coming down at the end of her garden, pleaded 'Hurt not the trees'. Francis Nowell Mundy, who was a Derbyshire magistrate and country gentleman, published a poem in 1776 called 'Needwood Forest' in which he makes a great oak speak out against the axe. The only dissenting voice that I have come across was Ivor Gurney's. He lived much closer to poverty than most of the other poets and he was proud of felling a tree which was to provide the 'fuel for the bright kitchen – for brown tea, against cold night'.

As a result of positive government intervention and tax incentives more trees are planted each year than are felled. But the love of trees is not simply a matter of protecting the landscape but also the recognition of a much more elemental pull that they have upon the human imagination. Great oaks became symbols of stability and national endurance, and the greenwoods were the sanctuaries for free men standing out against oppressive tyrannies. Forests and woods are part of a primeval past, impregnated with mystery and myth, places where solemn rites were performed, where sacrifices were made, where outlaws lived and where wild animals hid for security. In the eighteenth century James Hall, the Scottish antiquarian, trained saplings in the shape of arches to prove his conviction that gothic architecture was derived from the perpendicular alley formed by trees: to him the tree was a symbol of the resurrection of man.

I hope that this book will lead you to enjoy more intensely the beauty of our landscape. All of the poets have tried to capture the spirit of the places they describe, asking you to share their feelings as if you had been there with them. They also remind us that the unique natural beauty of our country is under constant threat. As we celebrate the beginning of a new millennium we have to recognize how much has been lost over the last 1,000 years. The Highlands of Scotland have recently been designated as the last Wilderness of Europe, which is a matter both for regret and for hope. But it is also a reminder that we must do much more in the future to protect and to preserve our natural environment, for once a place of beauty is lost it is lost for ever. We are the losers now but the greater losers are the generations yet to come.

WILLIAM WORDSWORTH

The Tables Turned

Up! up! my Friend, and quit your books;
Or surely you'll grow double:
Up! up! my Friend, and clear your looks;
Why all this toil and trouble?

The sun, above the mountain's head,
A freshening lustre mellow
Through all the long green fields has spread,
His first sweet evening yellow.

Books! 'tis a dull and endless strife:
Come, hear the woodland linnet,
How sweet his music! on my life,
There's more of wisdom in it.

And hark! how blithe the throstle sings!
He, too, is no mean preacher:
Come forth into the light of things,
Let Nature be your Teacher.

She has a world of ready wealth,
Our minds and hearts to bless –
Spontaneous wisdom breathed by health,
Truth breathed by cheerfulness.

One impulse from a vernal wood
May teach you more of man,
Of moral evil and of good,
Than all the sages can.

Sweet is the lore which Nature brings;
Our meddling intellect
Mis-shapes the beauteous forms of things: –
We murder to dissect.

Enough of Science and of Art;
Close up those barren leaves;
Come forth, and bring with you a heart
That watches and receives.

Alfoxden, Somerset

Walks and Surveys

JOHN MILTON

from L'Allegro

Come, and trip it as you go
On the light fantastic toe,
And in thy right hand lead with thee,
The mountain nymph, sweet Liberty;
And if I give thee honour due,
Mirth, admit me of thy crew
To live with her, and live with thee,
In unreproved pleasures free;
To hear the lark begin his flight
And singing startle the dull night
From his watch-tower in the skies,
Till the dappled dawn doth rise;
Then to come, in spite of sorrow,
And at my window bid good-morrow
Through the sweetbriar, or the vine,
Or the twisted eglantine:
While the cock with lively din
Scatters the rear of darkness thin
And to the stack, or the barn-door,
Stoutly struts his dame before:
Oft listening how the hounds and horn
Cheerly rouse the slumbering morn,
From the side of some hoar hill,
Through the high wood echoing shrill;
Sometime walking, not unseen,
By hedge-row elms, on hillocks green,
Right against the eastern gate
Where the great sun begins his state

Robed in flames and amber light,
The clouds in thousand liveries dight;
While the ploughman near at hand,
Whistles o'er the furrowed land,
And the milkmaid singeth blithe,
And the mower whets his scythe,
And every shepherd tells his tale
Under the hawthorn in the dale.
Straight mine eye hath caught new pleasures
Whilst the landscape round it measures;
Russet lawns, and fallows gray,
Where the nibbling flocks do stray;
Mountains, on whose barren breast
The labouring clouds do often rest;
Meadows trim with daisies pied,
Shallow brooks, and rivers wide;
Towers and battlements it sees
Bosomed high in tufted trees,
Where perhaps some beauty lies,
The cynosure of neighbouring eyes.
Hard by, a cottage chimney smokes
From betwixt two aged oaks,
Where Corydon and Thyrsis met,
Are at their savoury dinner set
Of herbs, and other country messes
Which the neat-handed Phillis dresses;
And then in haste her bower she leaves
With Thestylis to bind the sheaves.

Horton, Buckinghamshire

JOHN DYER

Grongar Hill

Silent Nymph, with curious eye!
Who, the purple ev'ning, lie
On the mountain's lonely van,
Beyond the noise of busy man,
Painting fair the form of things,
While the yellow linnet sings,
Or the tuneful nightingale
Charms the forest with her tale;
Come with all thy various hues,
Come, and aid thy sister Muse;
Now while Phœbus riding high,
Gives lustre to the land and sky,
Grongar Hill invites my song.
Draw the landskip bright and strong;
Grongar, in whose mossy cells,
Sweetly-musing Quiet dwells;
Grongar, in whose silent shade,
For the modest Muses made,
So oft I have the evening still,
At the fountain of a rill,
Sate upon a flow'ry bed,
With my hand beneath my head,
While stray'd my eyes o'er Towy's flood,
Over mead, and over wood,
From house to house, from hill to hill,
Till Contemplation had her fill.
    About his chequer'd sides I wind,
And leave his brooks and meads behind,
And groves, and grottoes where I lay,
And vistoes shooting beams of day:
Wide and wider spreads the vale,

As circles on a smooth canal:
The mountains round, unhappy fate!
Sooner or later, of all height,
Withdraw their summits from the skies,
And lessen as the others rise:
Still the prospect wider spreads,
Adds a thousand woods and meads,
Still it widens, widens still,
And sinks the newly-risen hill.
   Now I gain the mountain's brow,
What a landskip lies below!
No clouds, no vapours intervene,
But the gay, the open scene
Does the face of nature show
In all the hues of heaven's bow!
And swelling to embrace the light,
Spreads around beneath the sight.
   Old castles on the cliff arise,
Proudly tow'ring in the skies!
Rushing from the woods, the spires
Seem from hence ascending fires!
Half his beams Apollo sheds
On the yellow mountain-heads!
Gilds the fleeces of the flocks;
And glitters on the broken rocks!
   Below me trees unnumber'd rise,
Beautiful in various dyes:
The gloomy pine, the poplar blue,
The yellow beech, the sable yew,
The slender fir, that taper grows,
The sturdy oak, with wide-spread boughs,
And beyond the purple grove,
Haunt of Phillis, queen of love!
Gaudy as the op'ning dawn,
Lies a long and level lawn
On which a dark hill, steep and high,

Holds and charms the wand'ring eye!
Deep are his feet in Towy's flood,
His sides are cloath'd with waving wood,
And ancient towers crown his brow,
That cast an awful look below;
Whose ragged walls the ivy creeps,
And with her arms from falling keeps;
So both a safety from the wind
On mutual dependence find.
　　'Tis now the raven's bleak abode;
'Tis now th'apartment of the toad;
And there the fox securely feeds;
And there the pois'nous adder breeds,
Conceal'd in ruins, moss, and weeds;
While, ever and anon, there falls
Huge heaps of hoary moulder'd walls.
Yet time has seen, that lifts the low,
And level lays the lofty brow,
Has seen this broken pile compleat,
Big with the vanity of state:
But transient is the smile of fate!
A little rule, a little sway,
A sunbeam in a winter's day,
Is all the proud and mighty have
Between the cradle and the grave.
　•　And see the rivers how they run
Thro' woods and meads, in shade and sun,
Sometimes swift, and sometimes slow,
Wave succeeding wave, they go
A various journey to the deep,
Like human life to endless sleep!
Thus is nature's vesture wrought,
To instruct our wand'ring thought;
Thus she dresses green and gay,
To disperse our cares away.
　　Ever charming, ever new,

When will the landskip tire the view!
The fountain's fall, the river's flow,
The woody vallies, warm and low;
The windy summit, wild and high,
Roughly rushing on the sky!
The pleasant seat, the ruin'd tow'r,
The naked rock, the shady bow'r;
The town and village, dome and farm,
Each gives each a double charm,
As pearls upon a Æthiop's arm.
    See on the mountain's southern side,
Where the prospect opens wide,
Where the ev'ning gilds the tide;
How close and small the hedges lie!
What streaks of meadows cross the eye!
A step, methinks, may pass the stream,
So little distant dangers seem;
So we mistake the future's face,
Ey'd thro' hope's deluding glass;
As yon summits soft and fair,
Clad in colours of the air,
Which, to those who journey near,
Barren, brown, and rough appear;
Still we tread the same coarse way;
The present's still a cloudy day.
    O may I with myself agree,
And never covet what I see.
Content me with an humble shade,
My passions tam'd, my wishes laid;
For while our wishes wildly roll,
We banish quiet from the soul:
'Tis thus the busy beat the air;
And misers gather wealth and care.
    Now, ev'n now, my joys run high,
As on the mountain turf I lie;
While the wanton Zephyr sings,

And in the vale perfumes his wings;
While the waters murmur deep;
While the shepherd charms his sheep;
While the birds unbounded fly,
And with musick fill the sky,
Now, ev'n now, my joys run high.
   Be full, ye courts, be great who will;
Search for Peace with all your skill:
Open wide the lofty door,
Seek her on the marble floor.
In vain you search, she is not there;
In vain you search the domes of care!
Grass and flowers Quiet treads,
On the meads and mountain-heads,
Along with Pleasure, close ally'd,
Ever by each other's side:
And often, by the murm'ring rill,
Hears the thrush, while all is still,
Within the groves of Grongar Hill.

   Grongar Hill, by Llandeilo, Carmarthenshire

GILBERT WHITE

The Naturalist's Summer-Evening Walk

When day declining sheds a milder gleam,
What time the may-fly haunts the pool or stream;
When the still owl skims round the grassy mead,
What time the timorous hare limps forth to feed;
Then be the time to steal adown the vale,
And listen to the vagrant cuckoo's tale;
To hear the clamorous curlew call his mate,
Or the soft quail his tender pain relate;
To see the swallow sweep the dark'ning plain

Belated, to support her infant train;
To mark the swift in rapid giddy ring
Dash round the steeple, unsubdued of wing:
Amusive birds! – say where your hid retreat
When the frost rages and the tempests beat;
Whence your return, by such nice instinct led,
When spring, soft season, lifts her bloomy head?
Such baffled searches mock man's prying pride,
The God of Nature is your secret guide!

   While deep'ning shades obscure the face of day,
To yonder bench leaf-sheltered let us stray,
Till blended objects fail the swimming sight,
And all the fading landscape sinks in night;
To hear the drowsy dor come brushing by
With buzzing wing, or the shrill cricket cry;
To see the feeding bat glance through the wood;
To catch the distant falling of the flood;
While o'er the cliff th' awakened churn-owl hung
Through the still gloom protracts his chattering song;
While high in air, and poised upon his wings,
Unseen, the soft, enamoured woodlark sings:
These, Nature's works, the curious mind employ,
Inspire a soothing melancholy joy:
As fancy warms, a pleasing kind of pain
Steals o'er the cheek, and thrills the creeping vein!

   Each rural sight, each sound, each smell, combine;
The tinkling sheep-bell, or the breath of kine;
The new-mown hay that scents the swelling breeze,
Or cottage-chimney smoking through the trees.

   The chilling night-dews fall: – away, retire;
For see, the glow-worm lights her amorous fire!
Thus, ere night's veil had half obscured the sky,
Th' impatient damsel hung her lamp on high:
True to the signal, by love's meteor led,
Leander hastened to his Hero's bed.

   Selborne, Hampshire

JOHN CLARE

from The Shepherd's Calendar ('October')

Nature now spreads around in dreary hue
A pall to cover all that summer knew
Yet in the poets solitary way
Some pleasing objects for his praise delay
Somthing that makes him pause and turn again
As every trifle will his eye detain
The free horse rustling through the stubble land
And bawling herd boy with his motly band
Of hogs and sheep and cows who feed their fill
Oer cleard fields rambling where so ere they will
The geese flock gabbling in the splashy fields
And qua[c]king ducks in pondweeds half conseald
Or seeking worms along the homclose sward
Right glad of freedom from the prison yard
While every cart rut dribbles its low tide
And every hollow splashing sports provide
The hedger stopping gaps wi pointed bough
Made by intruding horse and blundering cow
The milk maid tripping on her morning way
And fodderers oft tho early cutting hay
Dropping the littering forkfulls from his back
Side where the thorn fence circles round the stack
The cotter journying wi his noisey swine
Along the wood side where the brambles twine
Shaking from dinted cups the acorns brown
And from the hedges red awes dashing down
And nutters rustling in the yellow woods
Scaring from their snug lairs the pheasant broods
And squirrels secret toils oer winter dreams
Picking the brown nuts from the yellow beams
And hunters from the thickets avenue

In scarlet jackets startling on the view
Skiming a moment oer the russet plain
Then hiding in the colord woods again
The ploping guns sharp momentary shock
Which eccho bustles from her cave to mock
The sticking groups in many a ragged set
Brushing the woods their harmless loads to get
And gipseys camps in some snug shelterd nook
Where old lane hedges like the pasture brook
Run crooking as they will by wood and dell
In such lone spots these wild wood roamers dwell
On commons where no farmers claims appear
Nor tyrant justice rides to interfere
Such the abodes neath hedge or spreading oak
And but discovered by its curling smoak
Puffing and peeping up as wills the breeze
Between the branches of the colord trees
Such are the pictures that october yields
To please the poet as he walks the fields

Helpston, Northamptonshire (in Clare's day, now Cambridgeshire)

ELIZABETH BARRETT BROWNING

from Aurora Leigh, Book I

Ofter we walked only two
If cousin Romney pleased to walk with me.
We read, or talked, or quarrelled, as it chanced.
We were not lovers, nor even friends well-matched:
Say rather, scholars upon different tracks,
And thinkers disagreed, he, overfull
Of what is, and I, haply, overbold
For what might be.
                        But then the thrushes sang,

And shook my pulses and the elms' new leaves;
At which I turned, and held my finger up,
And bade him mark that, howsoe'er the world
Went ill, as he related, certainly
The thrushes still sang in it. At the word
His brow wold soften, – and he bore with me
In melancholy patience, not unkind,
While breaking into voluble ecstasy
I flattered all the beauteous country round,
As poets use, the skies, the clouds, the fields.
The happy violets hiding from the roads
The primroses run down to, carrying gold;
The tangled hedgerows, where the cows push out
Impatient horns and tolerant churning mouths
'Twixt dripping ash-boughs, – hedgerows all alive
With birds and gnats and large white butterflies
Which look as if the May-flower had caught life
And palpitated forth upon the wind;
Hills, vales, woods, netted in a silver mist,
Farms, granges, doubled up among the hills;
And cattle grazing in the watered vales,
And cottage-chimneys smoking from the woods,
And cottage-gardens smelling everywhere,
Confused with smell of orchards. 'See,' I said,
'And see! is God not with us on the earth?
And shall we put Him down by aught we do?
Who says there's nothing for the poor and vile
Save poverty and wickedness? behold!'
And ankle-deep in English grass I leaped
And clapped my hands, and called all very fair.

Episode set fictionally in Shropshire, but description inspired by
Herefordshire (around Hope End, Colwall)

IVOR GURNEY

Cotswold Ways

One comes across the strangest things in walks:
Fragments of Abbey tithe-barns fixed in modern
And Dutch-sort houses where the water baulks
Weired up, and brick kilns broken among fern,
Old troughs, great stone cisterns bishops might have blessed
Ceremonially, and worthy mounting-stones;
Black timber in red brick, queerly placed
Where Hill stone was looked for – and a manor's bones
Spied in the frame of some wisteria'd house
And mill-falls and sedge pools and Saxon faces;
Stream-sources happened upon in unlikely places,
And Roman-looking hills of small degree
And the surprise of dignity of poplars
At a road end, or the white Cotswold scars,
Or sheets spread white against the hazel tree.
Strange the large difference of up-Cotswold ways;
Birdlip climbs bold and treeless to a bend,
Portway to dim wood-lengths without end,
And Crickley goes to cliffs are the crown of days.

Cotswolds, east of Gloucester

DYLAN THOMAS

Poem in October

It was my thirtieth year to heaven
Woke to my hearing from harbour and neighbour wood
And the mussel pooled and the heron
Priested shore

                    The morning beckon
With water praying and call of seagull and rook
And the knock of sailing boats on the net webbed wall
                    Myself to set foot
                        That second
          In the still sleeping town and set forth.

            My birthday began with the water-
Birds and the birds of the winged trees flying my name
          Above the farms and the white horses
                        And I rose
                    In rainy autumn
And walked abroad in a shower of all my days.
High tide and the heron dived when I took the road
                    Over the border
                        And the gates
          Of the town closed as the town awoke.

          A springful of larks in a rolling
Cloud and the roadside bushes brimming with whistling
          Blackbirds and the sun of October
                        Summery
                    On the hill's shoulder,
Here were fond climates and sweet singers suddenly
Come in the morning where I wandered and listened
                    To the rain wringing
                        Wind blow cold
          In the wood faraway under me.

          Pale rain over the dwindling harbour
And over the sea wet church the size of a snail
          With its horns through mist and the castle
                    Brown as owls
                    But all the gardens
Of spring and summer were blooming in the tall tales
Beyond the border and under the lark full cloud.
                    There could I marvel

My birthday
Away but the weather turned around.

It turned away from the blithe country
And down the other air and the blue altered sky
Streamed again a wonder of summer
With apples
Pears and red currants
And I saw the turning so clearly a child's
Forgotten mornings when he walked with his mother
Through the parables
Of sun light
And the legends of the green chapels

And the twice told fields of infancy
That his tears burned my cheeks and his heart moved in
  mine.
These were the woods the river and sea
Where a boy
In the listening
Summertime of the dead whispered the truth of his joy
To the trees and the stones and the fish in the tide.
And the mystery
Sang alive
Still in the water and singing birds.

And there could I marvel my birthday
Away but the weather turned around. And the true
Joy of the long dead child sang burning
In the sun.
It was my thirtieth
Year to heaven stood there then in the summer noon
Though the town below lay leaved with October blood.
O may my heart's truth
Still be sung
On this high hill in a year's turning.

New Quay, Cardiganshire (now Dyfed)

DEREK MAHON

The Mayo Tao

for Eugene Lambe

I have abandoned the dream kitchens for a low fire
    and a prescriptive
        literature of the spirit.
A storm snores on the desolate sea.

The nearest shop is four miles away.
    When I walk there
        through the shambles of the morning
for tea and firelighters
    the mountain paces me
        in a snow-lit silence.

My days are spent in conversation
    with stags and blackbirds;
        at night fox and badger
            gather at my door.

I have stood for hours watching
    a salmon doze
        in the tea-gold dark,
for weeks watching a spider weave
    in a pale light, for months
listening to the sob-story
    of a stone on the road –
        the best, most monotonous
sob-story I have ever heard.

I am an expert on frost crystals
    and the silence of crickets,
a confidant of the stinking shore,
    the stars in the mud.

(There is an immanence in these things
  which drives me, despite
    my scepticism, almost
  to the point of speech –
    like sunlight cleaving
  the lake mist at morning
or when tepid water runs cold at last from the tap.)

I have been working for years
  on a four-line poem
    about the life of a leaf.
I think it may come out right this winter.

  Co. Mayo, Ireland

WILLIAM STRODE

On Westwell Downs

When Westwell Downs I gan to tread,
Where cleanly winds the green did sweep,
Methought a landskip there was spread,
Here a bush and there a sheep:
    The pleated wrinkles of the face
    Of wave-swoll'n earth did lend such grace,
    As shadowings in imag'ry
    Which both deceive and please the eye.

The sheep sometimes did tread the maze
By often winding in and in,
And sometimes round about they trace
Which milkmaids call a fairy ring:
    Such semicircles have they run,
    Such lines across so trimly spun
    That shepherds learn whenere they please
    A new geometry with ease.

The slender food upon the down
Is always even, always bare,
Which neither spring nor winter's frown
Can aught improve or aught impair:
    Such is the barren eunuch's chin,
    Which thus doth evermore begin
    With tender down to be o'ercast
    Which never comes to hair at last.

Here and there two hilly crests
Amidst them hug a pleasant green,
And these are like two swelling breasts
That close a tender fall between.
    Here would I sleep, or read, or pray
    From early morn till flight of day:
    But hark! a sheep-bell calls me up
    Like Oxford college bells, to sup.

Cotswolds: near Burford, Oxfordshire

Mountains, Hills and
the View from Above

WILLIAM BLAKE

from Gnomic Verses

Great things are done when men and mountains meet;
This is not done by jostling in the street.

ANONYMOUS

from Gnomic Stanzas

[translated from the Welsh by Anthony Conran]

Mountain snow, everywhere white;
A raven's custom is to sing;
No good comes of too much sleep.

Mountain snow, white the ravine;
By rushing wind trees are bent;
Many a couple love one another
Though they never come together.

Mountain snow, tossed by the wind;
Broad full moon, dockleaves green;
Rarely a knave's without litigation.

Mountain snow, swift the stag;
Usual in Britain are brave chiefs;
There's need of prudence in an exile.

   Mountain snow, hunted stag;
Wind whistles above the eaves of a tower;
    Heavy, O man, is sin.

Mountain snow, leaping stag:
Wind whistles above a high white wall;
    Usually the calm are comely.

Mountain snow, stag in the vale;
Wind whistles above the rooftop;
There's no hiding evil, no matter where.

Wales

SAMUEL TAYLOR COLERIDGE

from Reflections on Having Left
a Place of Retirement

Low was our pretty cot: our tallest rose
Peeped at the chamber-window. We could hear
At silent noon, and eve, and early morn,
The sea's faint murmur. In the open air
Our myrtles blossom'd; and across the porch
Thick jasmines twined: the little landscape round
Was green and woody, and refreshed the eye.
It was a spot which you might aptly call
The Valley of Seclusion! Once I saw
(Hallowing his Sabbath-day by quietness)
A wealthy son of commerce saunter by,
Bristowa's citizen: methought, it calmed
His thirst of idle gold, and made him muse
With wiser feelings: for he paused, and looked
With a pleased sadness, and gazed all around,
Then eyed our cottage, and gazed round again,
And sighed, and said, it was a blessed place.
And we *were* blessed. Oft with patient ear
Long-listening to the viewless skylark's note
(Viewless, or haply for a moment seen
Gleaming on sunny wings) in whispered tones

I've said to my beloved, 'Such, sweet girl!
The inobtrusive song of happiness,
Unearthly minstrelsy! then only heard
When the soul seeks to hear; when all is hushed,
And the heart listens!'
                              But the time, when first
From that low dell, steep up the stony mount
I climbed with perilous toil and reached the top,
Oh! what a goodly scene! *Here* the bleak mount,
The bare bleak mountain speckled thin with sheep;
Grey clouds, that shadowing spot the sunny fields;
And river, now with bushy rocks o'erbrowed,
Now winding bright and full, with naked banks;
And seats, and lawns, the abbey and the wood,
And cots, and hamlets, and faint city-spire;
The channel *there*, the islands and white sails,
Dim coasts, and cloudlike hills, and shoreless ocean –
It seemed like Omnipresence! God, methought,
Had built Him there a temple: the whole world
Seemed imaged in its vast circumference,
No *wish* profaned my overwhelmed heart.
Blest hour! It was a luxury, – to be!

   Nether Stowey, Somerset

LOUIS MACNEICE

Under the Mountain

Seen from above
The foam in the curving bay is a goose-quill
That feathers ... unfeathers ... itself.

Seen from above
The field is a flap and the haycocks buttons
To keep it flush with the earth.

Seen from above
The house is a silent gadget whose purpose
Was long since obsolete.

But when you get down
The breakers are cold scum and the wrack
Sizzles with stinking life.

When you get down
The field is a failed or a worth-while crop, the source
Of back-ache if not heartache.

And when you get down
The house is a maelstrom of loves and hates where you –
Having got down – belong.

    Slievemore, Achill Island, Co. Mayo, Ireland

GLYN MAXWELL

Hilles Edge

A man has clambered up a hill so high
five counties hold their breath. There the air there is
is all his own and however far away
are farms and rivers they can all hear this.

He breathes again, his call unechoed. Winds
are pestering him with nothing. Soon enough
he takes a quarter-turn to look askance
and fixedly along the ridge, as if

to strike a balance between known and not,
between the dogged journey and the rest,
acknowledging the endlessness not yet,
scanning the close at hand for interest,

or at least a place to crouch in out of the wind
while the others scramble up. They will see in him
the mark of having seen. He will see in them
the awe he can now only understand.

near Stroud, Gloucestershire

NORMAN MACCAIG

Looking Down on Glen Canisp

The summer air is thick, is wads
that muffle the hill burn's voice
and stifle colours
to their cloudier selves – and
bright enough: the little loch
is the one clear pane
in a stained-glass window.

The scent of thyme and bog myrtle
is so thick
one listens for it, as though it might be
a drowsy honey-hum
in the heavy air.

Even the ravens
have sunk into the sandstone cliffs
of Suilven, that are dazed blue
and fuzz into the air around them –
as my mind does, till I hear
a thin far clatter and
look down to where two stags
canter across the ford, splashing up before them
antlers of water.

The Highlands

NORMAN NICHOLSON

Scafell Pike

Look
Along the well
Of the street,
Between the gasworks and the neat
Sparrow-stepped gable
Of the Catholic chapel,
High
Above tilt and crook
Of the tumbledown
Roofs of the town –
Scafell Pike,
The tallest hill in England.

How small it seems,
So far away,
No more than a notch
On the plate-glass window of the sky!
Watch
A puff of kitchen smoke
Block out peak and pinnacle –
Rock-pie of volcanic lava
Half a mile thick
Scotched out
At the click of an eye.

Look again
In five hundred, a thousand or ten
Thousand years:
A ruin where
The chapel was; brown
Rubble and scrub and cinders where
The gasworks used to be;

No roofs, no town,
Maybe no men;
But yonder where a lather-rinse of cloud pours down
The spiked wall of the sky-line, see,
Scafell Pike
Still there.

Scafell, at 3,210 feet the highest English mountain, is in Cumbria

WILLIAM WORDSWORTH

from The Prelude, Book I

One evening (surely I was led by her)
I went alone into a Shepherd's Boat,
A Skiff that to a Willow tree was tied
Within a rocky Cave, its usual home.
'Twas by the shores of Patterdale, a Vale
Wherein I was a Stranger, thither come
A School-boy Traveller, at the Holidays.
Forth rambled from the Village Inn alone
No sooner had I sight of this small Skiff,
Discover'd thus by unexpected chance,
Than I unloos'd her tether and embark'd.
The moon was up, the Lake was shining clear
Among the hoary mountains; from the Shore
I push'd, and struck the oars and struck again
In cadence, and my little Boat mov'd on
Even like a Man who walks with stately step
Though bent on speed. It was an act of stealth
And troubled pleasure; not without the voice
Of mountain-echoes did my Boat move on,
Leaving behind her still on either side
Small circles glittering idly in the moon,
Until they melted all into one track

Of sparkling light. A rocky Steep uprose
Above the Cavern of the Willow tree
And now, as suited one who proudly row'd
With his best skill, I fix'd a steady view
Upon the top of that same craggy ridge,
The bound of the horizon, for behind
Was nothing but the stars and the grey sky.
She was an elfin Pinnace; lustily
I dipp'd my oars into the silent Lake,
And, as I rose upon the stroke, my Boat
Went heaving through the water, like a Swan;
When from behind that craggy Steep, till then
The bound of the horizon, a huge Cliff,
As if with voluntary power instinct,
Uprear'd its head. I struck, and struck again,
And, growing still in stature, the huge Cliff
Rose up between me and the stars, and still,
With measur'd motion, like a living thing,
Strode after me. With trembling hands I turn'd,
And through the silent water stole my way
Back to the Cavern of the Willow tree.
There, in her mooring-place, I left my Bark,
And, through the meadows homeward went, with grave
And serious thoughts; and after I had seen
That spectacle, for many days, my brain
Work'd with a dim and undetermin'd sense
Of unknown modes of being; in my thoughts
There was a darkness, call it solitude,
Or blank desertion, no familiar shapes
Of hourly objects, images of trees,
Of sea or sky, no colours of green fields;
But huge and mighty Forms that do not live
Like living men mov'd slowly through my mind
By day and were the trouble of my dreams.

Ullswater and Black Crag

Rivers and Streams

EDMUND SPENSER

from Prothalamion

Calm was the day, and through the trembling air
Sweet-breathing Zephyrus did softly play
A gentle spirit, that lightly did delay
Hot Titan's beams, which then did glister fair;
When I, (whom sullen care,
Through discontent of my long fruitless stay
In princes' court, and expectation vain
Of idle hopes, which still do fly away
Like empty shadows, did afflict my brain,)
Walked forth to ease my pain
Along the shore of silver-streaming Thames;
Whose rutty bank, the which his river hems,
Was painted all with variable flowers,
And all the meads adorned with dainty gems
Fit to deck maidens' bowers,
And crown their paramours
Against the bridal day, which is not long:
   Sweet Thames! run softly, till I end my song.

There in a meadow by the river's side
A flock of nymphs I chanced to espy,
All lovely daughters of the flood thereby,
With goodly greenish locks all loose untied
As each had been a bride;
And each one had a little wicker basket
Made of fine twigs entrailèd curiously,
In which they gathered flowers to fill their flasket,
And with fine fingers cropped full feateously

The tender stalks on high.
Of every sort which in that meadow grew
They gathered some; the violet, pallid blue.
The little daisy that at evening closes,
The virgin lily and the primrose true,
With store of vermeil roses,
To deck their bridegrooms' posies
Against the bridal day, which was not long:
    Sweet Thames! run softly, till I end my song.

Thames Valley

WILLIAM DUNBAR

from To the City of London

Above all ryvers thy Ryver hath renowne,
    Whose beryall stremys, pleasaunt and preclare,
Under thy lusty walls renneth down,
    Where many a swanne doth swymme with wyngis fair;
    Where many a barge doth saile, and row with are,
Where many a ship doth rest with toppe-royall.
    O! towne of townes, patrone and not compare:
London, thou art the flour of Cities all.

Upon thy lusty Brigge of pylers white
    Been merchauntis full royall to behold [...]

Thames at London

ANDREW MOTION

from Fresh Water

This is a long time ago. I am visiting my brother, who is
    living
near Cirencester, and he says let's go and see the source of
    the Thames.
It's winter. We leave early, before the sun has taken frost off
    the fields,

and park in a lane. There's a painful hawthorn hedge with a
    stile.
When we jump down, our boots gibber on the hard ground.
Then we're striding, kicking ice-dust off the grass to look
    confident –

because really we're not sure if we're allowed to be here.
In fact we're not even sure that this is the right place.
A friend of a friend has told us; it's all as vague as that.

In the centre of the field we find more hawthorn, a single
    bush,
and water oozing out of a hole in the ground. I tell my
    brother
I've read about a statue that stands here, or rather lounges
    here –

a naked, shaggy-haired god tilting an urn with one massive
    hand.
Where is he? There's only the empty field glittering,
and a few dowager cows picking among the dock-clumps.

Where is Father Thames? My brother thinks he has been
    vandalised
and dragged off by the fans of other rivers – they smashed
    the old man's urn,
and sprayed his bare chest and legs with the names of rivals:

Trent, Severn, Nene, Humber. There's nothing else to do,
so I paddle through the shallow water surrounding the
    spring,
treading carefully to keep things in focus,

and stoop over the source as though I find it fascinating.
It is fascinating. A red-brown soft-lipped cleft
with bright green glass right up to the edge,

and the water twisting out like a rope of glass.
It pulses and shivers as it comes, then steadies
into the pool, then roughens again as it drains into the
    valley.

My brother and I are not twenty yet. We don't know who
    we are,
or who we want to be. We stare at the spring, at each other,
and back at the spring again, saying nothing.

A pheasant is making its blatant *kok-kok*
from the wood running along the valley floor.
I stamp both feet and disappear in a cloud.

  Source of the Thames

STEVIE SMITH

The River Humber

No wonder
The river Humber
Lies in a silken slumber.

For it is dawn
And over the newly warm
Earth the mists turn,

Wrapping their gentle fringes
Upon the river where it hinges
Upon the perfect sleep of perfected images.

Quiet in the thought of its felicity,
A graven monument of sufficiency
Beautiful in every line the river sleeps complacently.

And hardly the dawn distinguishes
Where a miasma languishes
Upon the waters' farther reaches.

Lapped in the sleeping consciousness
Of its waves' happiness
Upon the mudbanks of its approaches,

The river Humber
Turns again to deeper slumber,
Deeper than deeps in joys without number.

Yorkshire

NORMAN NICHOLSON

Five Rivers

Southward from Whitehaven, where cliffs of coal
Slant like shale to the low black mole,
The railway canters along the curving shore
Over five rivers, which slowly pour
On the steps of the shingle where the grey gulls bask
EHEN and CALDER, IRT and MITE and ESK.

The EHEN twists and flicks its fin
Red as rhubarb beneath the grey skin,
For its veins are stained with the blood of the ore
Of the mines of Egremont and Cleator Moor.
Here drill and navvy break the stone

And hack the living earth to the bone;
Blood spurts like water from the stricken rock.
Seeps into drain and gully and trickles to the beck.
Green herringbones of watercresses ride
On the tilt and tug of the red tide;
Bladderwrack, thrift and salty turf
Crust over cobbles at the edge of the pink surf.

The introspective CALDER hums to the pebbles
A memory of plainsong and choirboys' trebles,
Of collect and introit, creed and antiphon,
Of cistercians in the abbey of blood-red stone,
Where now tarpaulin and sheet lead shield
Groined roof and cloister and stoup from the wild
Weather of time, and the wall ferns spread
Where once the praying lamp hung before the holy bread.

The IRT comes from Wastdale, the land of the screes,
Of bracken up to your waist and ham-and-egg teas,
Of men who remember Will Ritson, the biggest liar
That ever lived, who sit by the fire
And laugh their inherited laughs at the talk
Of hounds with wings of eagles sniffing the lake.

The MITE, the tyke, lollops along
Like a blue-haired collie with a dribbling tongue,
The children's plaything as they ride the toy train
That runs beneath the rocks in a hawthorn lane,
Where dog-daisy, dogrose and stiff dog-grass
Bark at the wheels as the whistling truckloads pass.

But the ESK comes from the narrowest dale
Where statesmen meet at the Woolpack for a glass of ale
And a crack about herdwicks or a cure for the tick
And how some fool has broken his neck on the rock.
The ESK knows the stonechat and the parsley fern
And breaks like a bottle at every turn,
And bursts on the boulders and froths like beer,

Runs solid as glass and green and clear,
Till it mixes with MITE and IRT in the marsh,
Where roman cement and arches teach
Of the galleys that came to Ravenglass
Bearing the invaders with helmets of brass.
Where the plover creaks and the curlew whines,
The rivers ferret among the dunes,
Till the channels burst through a gap in the sand
Like a three-pronged pitchfork jabbed in the flank of the
    land.

Brown clouds are blown against the bright fells
Like celtic psalms from drowned western isles.
The slow rain falls like memory
And floods the becks and flows to the sea,
And there on the coast of Cumberland mingle
The fresh and the salt, the cinders and the shingle.

> The five rivers you meet (in this order) travelling south from
> Whitehaven in Cumbria

BASIL BUNTING

'Stones trip Coquet burn'

Stones trip Coquet burn;
grass trails, tickles
till her glass thrills.

The breeze she wears
lifts and falls back.
Where beast cool

in midgy shimmer
she dares me chase
under a bridge,

giggles, ceramic
huddle of notes,
darts from gorse

and I follow, fooled.
She must rest, surely;
some steep pool

to plodge or dip
and silent taste
with all my skin.

   Northumberland

ANONYMOUS

'Says Tweed to Till'

Says Tweed to Till,
What gars ye rin sae still?
Says Till to Tweed,
Though ye rin wi' speed
And I rin slaw,
For ae man that ye droun
I droun twa.

   ? Scottish Borders, Northumberland

ROBERT BURNS

Afton Water

Flow gently, sweet Afton, among thy green braes,
Flow gently, I'll sing thee a song in thy praise;
My Mary's sleep by thy murmuring stream,
Flow gently, sweet Afton, disturb not her dream.

Thou stock dove whose echo resounds thro' the glen,
Ye wild whistling blackbirds in yon thorny den,
Thou green crested lapwing thy screaming forbear,
I charge you disturb not my slumbering Fair.

How lofty, sweet Afton, thy neighbouring hills,
Far marked with the courses of clear, winding rills;
There daily I wander as noon rises high,
My flocks and my Mary's sweet cot in my eye.

How pleasant thy banks and green valleys below
Where wild in the woodlands the primroses blow;
There oft as mild ev'ning weeps over the lea,
The sweet scented birk shades my Mary and me.

Thy chrystal stream, Afton, how lovely it glides,
And winds by the cot where my Mary resides;
How wanton thy waters her snowy feet lave,
As gathering sweet flowerets she stems thy clear wave.

Flow gently, sweet Afton, among thy green braes,
Flow gently, sweet River, the theme of my lays;
My Mary's asleep by thy murmuring stream,
Flow gently, sweet Afton, disturb not her dream.

Ayrshire

WILLIAM BROWNE

from Britannia's Pastorals

As *Tavy* creepes upon
The Westerne vales of fertile *Albion*,
Here dashes roughly on an aged Rocke,
That his extended passage doth up locke;
There intricately 'mongst the Woods doth wander,
Losing himselfe in many a wry Meander:

Here amorously bent, clips some faire Mead;
And then disperst in Rils, doth measures tread
Upon her bosome 'mongst her flowery ranks:
There in another place beares downe the banks
Of some day-labouring wretch: here meets a rill,
And with their forces ioyn'd cuts out a Mill
Into an Iland, then in iocund guise
Survayes his conquest, lauds his enterprise:
Here digs a Cave at some high Mountaines foot:
There undermines an Oake, tears up his root:
Thence rushing to some Country-farme at hand,
Breaks o'er the Yeomans mounds, sweepes from his land
His Harvest hope of Wheat, of Rye, or Pease:
And makes that channell which was Shepherds lease.

Devon

THOMAS HARDY

On Sturminster Foot-bridge

(Onomatopœic)

Reticulations creep upon the slack stream's face
      When the wind skims irritably past,
The current clucks smartly into each hollow place
That years of flood have scrabbled in the pier's sodden base;
      The floating-lily leaves rot fast.

On a roof stand the swallows ranged in wistful waiting
  rows,
      Till they arrow off and drop like stones
Among the eyot-withies at whose foot the river flows:
And beneath the roof is she who in the dark world shows
      As a lattice-gleam when midnight moans.

Sturminster Newton, Dorset

HENRY VAUGHAN

The Water-Fall

With what deep murmurs, through time's silent stealth,
Doth thy transparent, cool, and watry wealth
      Here flowing fall,
      And chide, and call,
As if his liquid, loose retinue staid
Lingring, and were of this steep place afraid;
      The common pass,
      Where, clear as glass,
      All must descend
      Not to an end,
But quickned by this deep and rocky grave,
Rise to a longer course more bright and brave.

    Dear stream! dear bank! where often I
    Have sate, and pleas'd my pensive eye;
    Why, since each drop of thy quick store
    Runs thither whence it flow'd before,
    Should poor souls fear a shade or night,
    Who came (sure) from a sea of light?
    Or, since those drops are all sent back
    So sure to thee that none doth lack,
    Why should frail flesh doubt any more
    That what God takes He'll not restore?

    O useful element and clear!
    My sacred wash and cleanser here;
    My first consigner unto those
    Fountains of life, where the Lamb goes!
    What sublime truths and wholesome themes
    Lodge in thy mystical, deep streams!
    Such as dull man can never finde,
    Unless that Spirit lead his minde,

Which first upon thy face did move
And hatch'd all with his quickning love.
As this loud brook's incessant fall
In streaming rings restagnates all,
Which reach by course the bank, and then
Are no more seen: just so pass men.
O my invisible estate,
My glorious liberty, still late!
Thou art the channel my soul seeks,
Not this with cataracts and creeks.

The Ffrwdgrech Falls, near Brecon, Powys

ALFRED, LORD TENNYSON

The Brook

I come from haunts of coot and hern,
    I make a sudden sally
And sparkle out among the fern,
    To bicker down a valley.

By thirty hills I hurry down,
    Or slip between the ridges,
By twenty thorps, a little town,
    And half a hundred bridges.

Till last by Philip's farm I flow
    To join the brimming river,
For men may come and men may go,
    But I go on for ever.

I chatter over stony ways,
    In little sharps and trebles,
I bubble into eddying bays,
    I babble on the pebbles.

With many a curve my banks I fret
    By many a field and fallow,
And many a fairy foreland set
    With willow-weed and mallow.

I chatter, chatter, as I flow
    To join the brimming river,
For men may come and men may go,
    But I go on for ever.

I wind about, and in and out,
    With here a blossom sailing,
And here and there a lusty trout,
    And here and there a grayling,

And here and there a foamy flake
    Upon me, as I travel
With many a silvery waterbreak
    Above the golden gravel,

And draw them all along, and flow
    To join the brimming river,
For men may come and men may go,
    But I go on for ever.

I steal by lawns and grassy plots,
    I slide by hazel covers;
I move the sweet forget-me-nots
    That grow for happy lovers.

I slip, I slide, I gloom, I glance
    Among my skimming swallows
I make the netted sunbeam dance
    Against my sandy shallows.

I murmur under moon and stars
    In brambly wildernesses;
I linger by my shingly bars;
    I loiter round my cresses;

And out again I curve and flow
  To join the brimming river,
For men may come and men may go,
  But I go on for ever.

U. A. FANTHORPE

Rising Damp

*A river can sometimes be diverted but it is a very hard thing to lose it
altogether.* (J. G. Head: paper read to the Auctioneers' Institute, 1907.)

At our feet they lie low.
The little fervent underground
Rivers of London

(Effra, Graveney, Falcon, Quaggy,
Wandle, Walbrook, Tyburn, Fleet)

Whose names are disfigured,
Frayed, effaced.

These are the Magogs that chewed the clay
To the basin that London nestles in.
These are the currents that chiselled the city,
That washed the clothes and turned the mills,
Where children drank and salmon swam
And wells were holy.

They have gone under.
Boxed, like the magician's assistant.
Buried alive in earth.
Forgotten, like the dead.

They return spectrally after heavy rain,
Confounding suburban gardens. They infiltrate
Chronic bronchitis statistics. A silken
Slur haunts dwellings by shrouded

Watercourses, and is taken
For the footing of the dead.

Being of our world, they will return
(Westbourne, caged at Sloane Square,
Will jack from his box),
Will deluge cellars, detonate manholes,
Plant effluent on our faces,
Sink the city

(Effra, Graveney, Falcon, Quaggy,
Wandle, Walbrook, Tyburn, Fleet)

It is the other rivers that lie
Lower, that touch us only in dreams
That never surface. We feel their tug
As a dowser's rod bends to the source below

(Phlegethon, Acheron, Lethe, Styx).

   London

Lakes, Floods, Marshes and Fens

W. R. RODGERS

An Irish Lake

There in the hard light
Dark birds, pink-footed, dab and pick
Among the addery roots and marrowy stones,
And the blown waves blink and hiccup at the lake's
Lip. A late bee blares and drones on inland
Into a cone-point of silence, and I
Lying at the rhododendron's foot
Look through five fingers' grille at the lake
Shaking, at the bare and backward plain, and
The running and bending hills that carry
Like a conveyer belt the bright snail-line
Of clouds along the sky all day unendingly.

There, far from the slack noose of rumour
That tightens into choking fact, I relax,
And sound and sights and scents sail slowly by.
But suddenly, like delicate and tilted italics,
The up-standing birds stretch urgently away
Into the sky as suddenly grown grey.
Night rounds on Europe now. And I must go.
Before its hostile faces peer and pour
Over the mind's rim enveloping me,
And my so-frightened thoughts dart here and there
Like trout among their grim stony gazes.

? Northern Ireland

WILLIAM WORDSWORTH

Daffodils

I wandered lonely as a cloud
That floats on high o'er vales and hills,
When all at once I saw a crowd,
A host, of golden daffodils;
Beside the lake, beneath the trees,
Fluttering and dancing in the breeze.

Continuous as the stars that shine
And twinkle on the milky way,
They stretched in never-ending line
Along the margin of a bay:
Ten thousand saw I at a glance,
Tossing their heads in sprightly dance.

The waves beside them danced; but they
Out-did the sparkling waves in glee:
A poet could not but be gay,
In such a jocund company:
I gazed – and gazed – but little thought
What wealth the show to me had brought:

For oft, when on my couch I lie
In vacant or in pensive mood,
They flash upon that inward eye
Which is the bliss of solitude;
And then my heart with pleasure fills,
And dances with the daffodils.

Ullswater

MICHAEL DRAYTON

from Poly-Olbion

Of all the *Marshland* Iles, I *Ely* am the Queene:
For Winter each where sad, in me lookes freshe and greene.
The Horse, or other beast, o'rway'd with his owne masse,
Lies wallowing in my Fennes, hid over head in grasse:
And in the place where growes ranke Fodder for my Neat;
The Turffe which beares the Hay, is wondrous needfull Peat:
My full and batning earth, needs not the Plowmans paines;
The Rils which runne in me, are like the branched vaines
In humane Bodies seene; those Ditches cut by hand,
From the surrounding *Meres*, to winne the measured land,
To those choyce waters, I most fitly may compare,
Wherewith nice women use to blanch their Beauties rare.
Hath there a man beene borne in me, that never knew
Of *Watersey* the *Leame*, or th' other cal'd the *New*.
The *Frithdike* neer'st my midst, and of another sort,
Who ever fish'd, or fowl'd, that cannot make report
Of sundry *Meres* at hand, upon my Westerne way,
As *Ramsey mere*, and *Ug*, with the great Whittelsey:
Of the abundant store of Fish and Fowle there bred,
Which whilst of *Europes* Iles Great *Britaine* is the Head,
No *Meres* shall truely tell, in them, then at one draught,
More store of either kinds hath with the Net been caught:
Which though some pettie Iles doe challenge them to be
Their owne, yet must those Iles likewise acknowledge me
Their soveraigne. Nor yet let that Islet *Ramsey* shame,
Although to *Ramsey-Mere* shee onely gives the name;
Nor *Huntingdon*, to me thought she extend her grounds,
Twit me that I at all usurpe upon her Bounds.
Those *Meres* may well be proud, that I will take them in,

Which otherwise perhaps forgotten might have bin.
Beside my towred *Phane*, and my rich Citied seat,
With Villages and Dorpes, to make me most compleat.

The Fens

WILLIAM DIAPER

from Brent, a Poem

Happy are you, whom Quantock overlooks,
Blessed with keen healthy air and crystal brooks;
While wretched we the baneful influence mourn
Of cold Aquarius and his weeping urn.
Eternal mists their dropping curse distil
And drizzly vapours all the ditches fill:
The swampy land's a bog, the fields are seas
And too much moisture is the grand disease.
Here every eye with brackish rheum o'erflows
And a fresh drop still hangs at every nose.
Here the winds rule with uncontested right,
The wanton gods at pleasure take their flight;
No sheltering hedge, no tree or spreading bough
Obstruct their course, but unconfined they blow;
With dewy wings they sweep the watry meads
And proudly trample o'er the bending reeds.
We are to north and southern blasts exposed,
Still drowned by one, or by the other frozed.
Though Venice boast, Brent is as famed a seat,
For here we live in seas, and sail through every street;
And this great privilege we farther gain,
We never are obliged to pray for rain.
And 'tis as fond to wish for sunny days,

For though the god of light condense his rays
And try his pow'r, we must in water lie;
The marsh will still be such, and Brent will ne'er be dry.

    near Weston-super-Mare, Somerset

JOHN SCOTT

from Eclogue II

  Say, friends! whoe'er his residence might chuse,
Would these sweet scenes of sylvan shade refuse,
And seek the black waste of the barren wold,
That yields no shelter from the heat or cold?

  Dull are slow Ousa's mist-exhaling plains,
Where long rank grass the morning dew retains;
Who pastures there in Autumn's humid reign,
His flock from sickness hopes to save in vain.

  The bleak, flat, sedgy shores of Essex shun,
Where fog perpetual veils the wintry sun;
Though flattering Fortune there invite thy stay,
Thy health the purchase of her smiles must pay.

    Essex

THOM GUNN

Flooded Meadows

In sunlight now, after the weeks it rained,
Water has mapped irregular shapes that follow
Between no banks, impassive where it drained
Then stayed to rise and brim from every hollow.
Hillocks are firm, though soft, and not yet mud.

Tangles of long bright grass, like waterweed,
Surface upon the patches of the flood,
Distinct as islands from their valleys freed
And sharp as reefs dividing inland seas.
Yet definition is suspended, for,
In pools across the level listlessness,
Light answers only light before the breeze,
Canceling the rutted, weedy, slow brown floor
For the unity of unabsorbed excess.

KATHERINE PIERPOINT

Saltmarsh and Skylark

A man sits in a bowl of sunlight on the saltmarsh, clearly
    alone.
A slight hollow brings shelter on this husky threshing floor,
Stamped out flat by heavy, working weather.

The marshes are etched by veins of water so salt
It rustles faintly as it flows; sequin platelets buffed bright by
    acid –
So salt it iceburns, with the stick and pull of skin on frosted
    metal.

The water is carding its knotty white strings slowly
Through the blue brown fish-flesh of the mud.
Slowly laces and unlaces the filaments in the corridor of gills.

The marsh is a scribble of tough whip-grass and matted
    vetch;
Cross-hatched collage of God's leftovers;
Odd peelings from the plughole, pilled tweed
And steel wool, glued on in tufts by a nervous understudy.

Dry brown curves of grass, bowing down in pools of white
 light;
A crumbling-rusk-in-skimmed-milk landscape.
The man squints upwards into larksong and closes his eyes.

As he tilts, he inhales the song all the warm way up the light.
The eyelids thinly filter, impressing into hot blood-orange,
Then melting crabshell, embossed in pink and greening
 bronze;

Strange bunching and wellings, expansive dissolution;
The matt black stamen of the skylark's turning tongue,
The brain-stem's softly-bound bouquet of pulses.

near Blakeney, Norfolk

Sea and Coast

MATTHEW ARNOLD

Dover Beach

The sea is calm to-night,
The tide is full, the moon lies fair
Upon the Straits; – on the French coast, the light
Gleams, and is gone; the cliffs of England stand,
Glimmering and vast, out in the tranquil bay.
Come to the window, sweet is the night air!
Only, from the long line of spray
Where the ebb meets the moon-blanch'd sand,
Listen! you hear the grating roar
Of pebbles which the waves suck back, and fling,
At their return, up the high strand,
Begin, and cease, and then again begin,
With tremulous cadence slow, and bring
The eternal note of sadness in.

   Sophocles long ago
Heard it on the Aegaean, and it brought
Into his mind the turbid ebb and flow
Of human misery; we
Find also in the sound a thought,
Hearing it by this distant northern sea.

The sea of faith
Was once, too, at the full, and round earth's shore
Lay like the folds of a bright girdle furl'd;
But now I only hear
Its melancholy, long, withdrawing roar,
Retreating to the breath

Of the night-wind down the vast edges drear
And naked shingles of the world.

Ah, love, let us be true
To one another! for the world, which seems
To lie before us like a land of dreams,
So various, so beautiful, so new,
Hath really neither joy, nor love, nor light,
Nor certitude, nor peace, nor help for pain;
And we are here as on a darkling plain
Swept with confused alarms of struggle and flight,
Where ignorant armies clash by night.

    Kent

JOHN BETJEMAN

Winter Seascape

The sea runs back against itself
   With scarcely time for breaking wave
To cannonade a slatey shelf
   And thunder under in a cave

Before the next can fully burst,
   The headwind, blowing harder still,
Smooths it to what it was at first –
   A slowly rolling water hill.

Against the breeze the breakers haste,
   Against the tide their ridges run
And all the sea's a dappled waste
   Criss-crossing underneath the sun.

Far down the beach the ripples drag
   Blown backward, rearing from the shore,
And wailing gull and shrieking shag
   Alone can pierce the ocean roar.

Unheard, a mongrel hound gives tongue,
   Unheard are shouts of little boys:
What chance has any inland lung
   Against this multi-water noise?

Here where the cliffs alone prevail
   I stand exultant, neutral, free,
And from the cushion of the gale
   Behold a huge consoling sea.

   Cornwall

WILLIAM SHAKESPEARE

from King Lear, Act IV, Scene vi

Edgar:
Come on, sir; here's the place. Stand still. How fearful
And dizzy 'tis to cast one's eyes so low!
The crows and choughs that wing the midway air
Show scarce so gross as beetles. Halfway down
Hangs one that gathers sampire: dreadful trade;
Methinks he seems no bigger than his head.
The fishermen that walk upon the beach
Appear like mice; and yond tall anchoring bark,
Diminished to her cock; her cock, a buoy
Almost too small for sight. The murmuring surge
That on th' unnumb'red idle pebble chafes
Cannot be heard so high. I'll look no more,
Lest my brain turn, and the deficient sight
Topple down headlong. [...]

   Kent (Edgar's imagined evocation)

SYLVIA PLATH

Blackberrying

Nobody in the lane, and nothing, nothing but blackberries,
Blackberries on either side, though on the right mainly,
A blackberry alley, going down in hooks, and a sea
Somewhere at the end of it, heaving. Blackberries
Big as the ball of my thumb, and dumb as eyes
Ebon in the hedges, fat
With blue-red juices. These they squander on my fingers.
I had not asked for such a blood sisterhood; they must love
    me.
They accommodate themselves to my milkbottle, flattening
    their sides.

Overhead go the choughs in black, cacophonous flocks –
Bits of burnt paper wheeling in a blown sky.
Theirs is the only voice, protesting, protesting.
I do not think the sea will appear at all.
The high, green meadows are glowing, as if lit from within.
I come to one bush of berries so ripe it is a bush of flies,
Hanging their bluegreen bellies and their wing panes in a
    Chinese screen.
The honey-feast of the berries has stunned them; they believe
    in heaven.
One more hook, and the berries and bushes end.

The only thing to come now is the sea.
From between two hills a sudden wind funnels at me,
Slapping its phantom laundry in my face.
These hills are too green and sweet to have tasted salt.
I follow the sheep path between them. A last hook brings me
To the hills' northern face, and the face is orange rock

That looks out on nothing, nothing but a great space
Of white and pewter lights, and a din like silversmiths
Beating and beating at an intractable metal.

North Devon

DEREK MAHON

North Wind: Portrush

I shall never forget the wind
On this benighted coast.
It works itself into the mind
Like the high keen of a lost
Lear-spirit in agony
Condemned for eternity

To wander cliff and cove
Without comfort, without love.
It whistles off the stars
And the existential, black
Face of the cosmic dark:
We crouch to roaring fires.

Yet there are mornings when,
Even in midwinter, sunlight
Flares, and a rare stillness
Lies upon roof and garden,
Each object eldritch-bright,
The sea scarred but at peace.

Then, from the ship we say
Is the lit town where we live
(Our whiskey-and-forecast world),
A smaller ship that sheltered
All night in the restless bay
Will weigh anchor and leave.

What did they think of us
During their brief sojourn?
A string of lights on the prom
Dancing mad in the storm –
Who lives in such a place?
And will they ever return?

But the shops open at nine
As they have always done,
The wrapped-up bourgeoisie
Hardened by wind and sea.
The newspapers are late
But the milk shines in its crate.

Everything swept so clean
By tempest, wind and rain!
Elated, you might believe
That this was the first day –
A false sense of reprieve,
For the climate is here to stay.

So best prepare for the worst
That chaos and old night
Can do to us. Were we not
Raised on such expectations,
Our hearts starred with frost
Through countless generations?

Elsewhere the olive grove,
Le déjeuner sur l'herbe,
Poppies and parasols,
Blue skies and mythic love.
Here only the stricken souls
No spring can unperturb.

Prospero and his people never
Came to these stormy parts:
Few do who have the choice.

Yet, blasting the subtler arts,
That weird, plaintive voice
Choirs now and for ever.

County Antrim, Northern Ireland

SEAMUS HEANEY

The Peninsula

When you have nothing more to say, just drive
For a day all round the peninsula.
The sky is tall as over a runway,
The land without marks, so you will not arrive

But pass through, though always skirting landfall.
At dusk, horizons drink down sea and hill,
The ploughed field swallows the whitewashed gable
And you're in the dark again. Now recall

The glazed foreshore and silhouetted log,
That rock where breakers shredded into rags,
The leggy birds stilted on their own legs,
Islands riding themselves out into the fog,

And drive back home, still with nothing to say
Except that now you will uncode all landscapes
By this: things founded clean on their own shapes,
Water and ground in their extremity.

County Down

ANONYMOUS (12TH CENTURY)

St Columba's Island Hermitage

[translated from the Irish by K. H. Jackson]

Delightful I think it to be in the bosom of an isle, on the peak of a rock, that I might often see there the calm of the sea.

That I might see its heavy waves over the glittering ocean, as they chant a melody to their Father on their eternal course.

That I might see its smooth strand of clear headlands, no gloomy thing; that I might hear the voice of the wondrous birds, a joyful tune.

That I might hear the sound of the shallow waves against the rocks; that I might hear the cry by the graveyard, the noise of the sea.

That I might see its splendid flocks of birds over the full-watered ocean; that I might see its mighty whales, greatest of wonders.

That I might see its ebb and its flood-tide in their flow; that this might be my name, a secret I tell, 'He who turned his back on Ireland.'

That contrition of heart should come upon me as I watch it; that I might bewail my many sins, difficult to declare.

That I might bless the Lord who has power over all, Heaven with its pure host of angels, earth, ebb, flood-tide.

That I might pore on one of my books, good for my soul; a while kneeling for beloved Heaven, a while at psalms.

A while gathering dulse from the rock, a while fishing, a while giving food to the poor, a while in my cell.

A while meditating upon the Kingdom of Heaven, holy is the redemption; a while at labour not too heavy; it would be delightful!

Iona, West Coast of Scotland

Moors, Heaths and Barren Places

THE 'PEARL' POET

from Sir Gawain and the Green Knight

[translated from the Middle English by Ted Hughes]

Then he spurred Gringolet, and took up the trail.
Trees overhung him, the steep slope close to his shoulder.
He pushed on down through the rough, to the gorge-
  bottom.
Wherever he turned his eyes, it looked wilder.
Nothing anywhere near that could be a shelter.
Only cliffy brinks, beetling above him,
Knuckled and broken outcrops, with horned crags.
Clouds dragging low, torn by the scouts.
There he reined in his horse and puzzled awhile.
Turning his doubts over, he searched for the Chapel.
Still he could see nothing. He thought it strange.
Only a little mound, a tump, in a clearing,
Between the slope and the edge of the river, a knoll,
Over the river's edge, at a crossing place,
The burn bubbling under as if it boiled.
The Knight urged his horse and came closer.
He dismounted there, light as a dancer,
And tethered his costly beast to a rough branch.
Then he turned to the tump. He walked all round it,
Debating in himself what it might be.
Shaggy and overgrown with clumps of grass,
It had a hole in the end, and on each side.
Hollow within, nothing but an old cave
Or old gappy rock-heap, it could be either
    Or neither.
  'Ah God!' sighed Gawain,

'Is the Green Chapel here?
Here, about midnight,
Satan could say a prayer.'

'Surely,' he muttered, 'This is desolation.
This oratory is ugly, under its weeds.
The right crypt for that ogre, in his greenery,
To deal with his devotions devil-fashion.
My five wits warn me, this is the evil one,
Who bound me on oath to be here, to destroy me.
The chapel of Mischance – God see it demolished!
It is the worst-cursed Church I ever attended.'
With his helmet on his head, and his lance in his hand,
He clambered up on top of the bushy cell
And heard coming off the hill, from a face of rock,
The far side of the stream, a ferocious din.
What! It screeched in the crag, as if it would split it!
It sounded like a scythe a-shriek on a grind-stone!
What! It grumbled and scoured, like water in a mill!
What! It rushed and it rang, painful to hear!
'By God!' thought Gawain, 'I think that scummer
Is done in your honour, Knight, to welcome you
      As you deserve.
  Let God have his way! Ah well,
  It helps me not one bit.
  What if I lose my life?
  No noise is going to scare me.'

The Chapel has been persuasively identified with the chasm known as
Lud's Church in the Blackbrook Valley, North Staffordshire

EMILY BRONTË

'Loud without the wind was roaring'

Loud without the wind was roaring
   Through the waned autumnal sky;
Drenching wet, the cold rain pouring
   Spoke of stormy winters nigh.
     All too like that dreary eve
     Sighed within repining grief;

Sighed at first, but sighed not long –
   Sweet – how softly sweet it came!
Wild words of an ancient song,
   Undefined, without a name.

'It was spring, for the skylark was singing.'
   Those words, they awakened a spell –
They unlocked a deep fountain whose springing
   Nor absence nor distance can quell.

In the gloom of a cloudy November,
   They uttered the music of May;
They kindled the perishing ember
   In fervour that could not decay.

Awaken on all my dear moorlands
   The wind in its glory and pride!
O call me from valleys and highlands
   To walk by the hill-river's side!

It is swelled with the first snowy weather;
   The rocks they are icy and hoar
And darker waves round the long heather
   And the fern-leaves are sunny no more.

There are no yellow-stars on the mountain,
　The blue-bells have long died away
From the brink of the moss-bedded fountain,
　From the side of the wintery brae –

But lovelier than corn-fields all waving
　In emerald and scarlet and gold
Are the slopes where the north-wind is raving,
　And the glens where I wandered of old.

'It was morning; the bright sun was beaming.'
　How sweetly that brought back to me
The time when nor labour nor dreaming
　Broke the sleep of the happy and free.

But blithely we rose as the dusk heaven
　Was melting to amber and blue;
And swift were the wings to our feet given
　While we traversed the meadows of dew,

For the moors, for the moors where the short grass
　Like velvet beneath us should lie!
For the moors, for the moors where each high pass
　Rose sunny against the clear sky!

For the moors where the linnet was trilling
　Its song on the old granite stone;
Where the lark – the wild skylark was filling
　Every breast with delight like its own.

What language can utter the feeling
　That rose when, in exile afar,
On the brow of a lonely hill kneeling
　I saw the brown heath growing there.

It was scattered and stunted, and told me
　That soon even that would be gone;
It whispered, 'The grim walls enfold me;
　I have bloomed in my last summer's sun.'

But not the loved music whose waking
  Makes the soul of the Swiss die away
Has a spell more adored and heart-breaking
  Than in its half-blighted bells lay.

The spirit that bent 'neath its power,
  How it longed, how it burned to be free!
If I could have wept in that hour
  Those tears had been heaven to me.

Well, well, the sad minutes are moving
  Though loaded with trouble and pain;
And sometime the loved and the loving
  Shall meet on the mountains again.

  Haworth, West Yorkshire

ROBERT LOUIS STEVENSON

To S. R. Crockett

Blows the wind to-day, and the sun and the rain are flying,
  Blows the wind on the moors to-day and now,
Where about the graves of the martyrs the whaups are
    crying,
  My heart remembers how!

Grey recumbent tombs of the dead in desert places,
  Standing stones on the vacant wine-red moor,
Hills of sheep, and the howes of the silent vanished races,
  And winds, austere and pure:

Be it granted me to behold you again in dying,
  Hills of home! and to hear again the call;
Hear about the graves of the martyrs the peewees crying,
  And hear no more at all.

  ? The Pentlands

T. S. ELIOT

Rannoch, by Glencoe

Here the crow starves, here the patient stag
Breeds for the rifle. Between the soft moor
And the soft sky, scarcely room
To leap or soar. Substance crumbles, in the thin air
Moon cold or moon hot. The road winds in
Listlessness of ancient war,
Languor of broken steel,
Clamour of confused wrong, apt
In silence. Memory is strong
Beyond the bone. Pride snapped,
Shadow of pride is long, in the long pass
No concurrence of bone.

   Rannoch Moor, Scottish Highlands

SEAMUS HEANEY

Whinlands

All year round the whin
Can show a blossom or two
But it's in full bloom now.
As if the small yolk stain

From all the birds' eggs in
All the nests of the spring
Were spiked and hung
Everywhere on bushes to ripen.

Hills oxidize gold.
Above the smoulder of green shoot
And dross of dead thorns underfoot
The blossoms scald.

Put a match under
Whins, they go up of a sudden.
They make no flame in the sun
But a fierce heat tremor

Yet incineration like that
Only takes the thorn.
The tough sticks don't burn,
Remain like bone, charred horn.

Gilt, jaggy, springy, frilled
This stunted, dry richness
Persists on hills, near stone ditches,
Over flintbed and battlefield.

JOHN CLARE

from The Mores

Moors loosing from the sight far smooth & blea
Where swopt the plover in its pleasure free
Are vanished now with commons wild & gay
As poets visions of lifes early day
Mulberry bushes where the boy would run
To fill his hands with fruit – are grubbed & done
& hedgrow briars – flower lovers overjoyed
Came & got flower pots – these are all destroyed
& sky bound mores in mangled garbs are left
Like mighty jiants of their limbs bereft
Fence now meets fence in owners little bounds
Of field & meadow large as garden grounds

In little parcels little minds to please
With men & flocks imprisoned ill at ease
Each little path that led its pleasant way
As sweet as morning leading night astray
Where little flowers bloomed round a varied host
That travel felt delighted to be lost
Nor grudged the steps that he had taen as vain
When right roads traced his journeys end again
Nay on a broken tree hed sit awhile
To see the mores & fields & meadows smile
Sometimes with cowslaps smothered – then all white
With daiseys – then the summers splendid sight
Of corn fields crimson oer with the 'head ach' bloomd
Like splendid armys for the battle plumed
He gazed upon them with wild fancys eye
As fallen landscapes from an evening sky
These paths are stopt – the rude philistines thrall
Is laid upon them & destroyed them all
Each little tyrant with his little sign
Shows where man claims earths glows no more divine
On paths to freedom & to childhood dear
A board sticks up to notice 'no road here'
& on the tree with ivy over hung
The hated sign by vulgar taste is hung
As tho the very birds should learn to know
When they go there they must no further go
Thus with the poor scared freedom bade good bye
& much the[y] feel it in the smothered sigh
& birds & trees & flowers without a name
All sighed when lawless laws enclosure came
& dreams of plunder in such rebel schemes
Have found too truly that they were but dreams [...]

Helpston

Wind and Rain

HARTLEY COLERIDGE

Summer Rain

Thick lay the dust, uncomfortably white,
In glaring mimicry of Arab sands.
The woods and mountains slept in hazy light;
The meadows look'd athirst and tawny tann'd;
The little rills had left their channels bare,
With scarce a pool to witness what they were;
And the shrunk river gleam'd 'mid oozy stones,
That stared like any famish'd giant's bones.

Sudden the hills grew black, and hot as stove
The air beneath; it was a toil to be.
There was a growling as of angry Jove
Provoked by Juno's prying jealousy –
A flash – a crash – the firmament was split,
And down it came in drops – the smallest fit
To drown a bee in fox-glove bell conceal'd;
Joy fill'd the brook, and comfort cheer'd the field.

TED HUGHES

Rain

Rain. Floods. Frost. And after frost, rain.
Dull roof-drumming. Wraith-rain pulsing across purple-bare
  woods
Like light across heaved water. Sleet in it.
And the poor fields, miserable tents of their hedges.

Mist-rain off-world. Hills wallowing
In and out of a grey or silvery dissolution. A farm gleaming,
Then all dull in the near drumming. At field-corners
Brown water backing and brimming in grass.
Toads hop across rain-hammered roads. Every mutilated
    leaf there
Looks like a frog or a rained-out mouse. Cattle
Wait under blackened backs. We drive post-holes.
They half fill with water before the post goes in.
Mud-water spurts as the iron bar slam-burns
The oak stake-head dry. Cows
Tamed on the waste mudded like a rugby field
Stand and watch, come very close for company
In the rain that goes on and on, and gets colder.
They sniff the wire, sniff the tractor, watch. The hedges
Are straggles of gap. A few haws. Every half-ton cow
Sinks to the fetlock at every sliding stride.
They are ruining their field and they know it.
They look out sideways from under their brows which are
Their only shelter. The sunk scrubby wood
Is a pulverized wreck, rain riddles its holes
To the drowned roots. A pheasant looking black
In his waterproofs, bends at his job in the stubble.
The mid-afternoon dusk soaks into
The soaked thickets. Nothing protects them.
The fox corpses lie beaten to their bare bones,
Skin beaten off, brains and bowels beaten out.
Nothing but their blueprint bones last in the rain,
Sodden soft. Round their hay racks, calves
Stand in a shine of mud. The gateways
Are deep obstacles of mud. The calves look up, through
    plastered forelocks,
Without moving. Nowhere they can go
Is less uncomfortable. The brimming world
And the pouring sky are the only places
For them to be. Fieldfares squeal over, sodden

Toward the sodden wood. A raven,
Cursing monotonously, goes over fast
And vanishes in rain-mist. Magpies
Shake themselves hopelessly, hop in the spatter. Misery.
Surviving green of ferns and brambles is tumbled
Like an abandoned scrapyard. The calves
Wait deep beneath their spines. Cows roar
Then hang their noses to the mud.
Snipe go over, invisible in the dusk,
With their squelching cries.

Devon

SEAMUS O'SULLIVAN

Rain

All day long
The gray rain beating,
On the bare hills
Where the scant grass cannot cover,
The gray rocks peeping
Through the salt herbage.
All day long
The young lambs bleating
Stand for covering
Where the scant grass is
Under the gray wall,
Or seeking softer shelter
Under tattered fleeces
Nuzzle the warm udders.
All day long
The little waves leaping
Round the gray rocks
By the brown tide borders,

Round the black headlands
Streaming with rain.

Donegal, Ireland

IDRIS DAVIES

'O rain of July pouring down from the heavens'

O rain of July pouring down from the heavens,
Pouring and pelting from the vaults of the sky,
Pelting and slashing and lashing the trees,
Lashing the gardens behind the streets,
Sweeping the dust from the cabbage leaves,
And bringing Mrs Hughes' pet geranium out to the garden
    wall,
Sweep away, thunder-rain, the dross from our valleys,
Carry the rubbish to the seas and the oceans,
Wash away the slag-heaps of our troubles and sorrows,
Sweep away, thunder-rain, the slime from our valleys,
And let our streets, our home, our visions
Be cleansed and be shining when the evening comes
With its rainbow arching the smiling uplands,
With its glittering trees and laughing flowers,
And its mountains bright with the setting sun.

South Wales

D. H. LAWRENCE

The Rainbow

Even the rainbow has a body
made of the drizzling rain
and is an architecture of glistening atoms

built up, built up
yet you can't lay your hand on it,
nay, nor even your mind.

DAFYDD AP GWILYM

from To the Wind

[translated from the Welsh by William Barnes]

Swift is the course thou runnest now,
Along the highsloped mountain's brow,
Stripping the bushes on thy track,
And answering none, by none sent back.
No leader's might, no sworded train,
No blue-steeled blade, no flood, no rain,
No fire's flame, no wily will,
No son of man can keep thee still,
No drowning depth, no warning tongue,
No hook whereon thou may'st be hung.
Thou needest no swift steed to ride,
Nor bridge nor boat where rivers glide.
No catchpole takes thee, and no clan
Repels thee, gather'd man by man.
O when thou goest forth in play
With timber'd woods along thy way,
None sees thee naked on the plain,
Though thousands hear thee, nest of rain,
Loud teazing breaker of the oak tree's bough,
A pow'r of God on earth art thou. [...]

TED HUGHES

Wind

This house has been far out at sea all night,
The woods crashing through darkness, the booming hills,
Winds stampeding the fields under the window
Floundering black astride and blinding wet

Till day rose; then under an orange sky
The hills had new places, and wind wielded
Blade-light, luminous black and emerald,
Flexing like the lens of a mad eye.

At noon I scaled along the house-side as far as
The coal-house door. Once I looked up –
Through the brunt wind that dented the balls of my eyes
The tent of the hills drummed and strained its guyrope,

The fields quivering, the skyline a grimace,
At any second to bang and vanish with a flap:
The wind flung a magpie away and a black-
Back gull bent like an iron bar slowly. The house

Rang like some fine green goblet in the note
That any second would shatter it. Now deep
In chairs, in front of the great fire, we grip
Our hearts and cannot entertain book, thought,

Or each other. We watch the fire blazing,
And feel the roots of the house move, but sit on,
Seeing the window tremble to come in,
Hearing the stones cry out under the horizons.

? Heptonstall, West Yorkshire

HENRY VAUGHAN

The Storm

I see the Usk, and know my blood
    Is not a sea,
But a shallow, bounded flood
    Though red as he;
Yet have I flows, as strong as his,
    And boiling streams that rave
With the same curling force, and hiss,
    As doth the mountained wave.

But when his waters billow thus,
    Dark storms, and wind
Incite them to that fierce discuss,
    Else not inclined,
Thus the enlarged, enraged air
    Uncalms these to a flood,
But still the weather that's most fair
    Breeds tempests in my blood;

Lord, then round me with weeping clouds,
    And let my mind
In quick blasts sigh beneath those shrouds
    A spirit-wind,
So shall that storm purge this *recluse*
    Which sinful ease made foul,
And *wind*, and *water* to thy use
    Both *wash*, and *wing* my soul.

Powys

JAMES HURDIS

from The Favourite Village, Book III

Yet Winter has its pleasures. 'Tis delight
To mark the symptom of his frequent storm.
Not seldom, previous to the morrow's shower,
A flaky vapour the pure æther streaks;
As if some painter of gigantic arm
Had dipp'd his brush into the foamy wave,
Charg'd it with colour from the cliff, and dash'd
With wanton levity a milky bow
Across the dome of heav'n. Nor sometimes seems
His saucy hand with single stroke content,
But daubs with quick return the azure arch,
Upon the blessed canopy sublime
Vagaries flourishing, unsteady freaks,
Such, with her besom, round the morning hearth,
As giddy bar-maid fashions, trailing brisk
Her childish fancies o'er the sanded floor. [...]

EMILY BRONTË

'High waving heather, 'neath stormy blasts bending'

High waving heather, 'neath stormy blasts bending,
Midnight and moonlight and bright shining stars;
Darkness and glory rejoicingly blending,
Earth rising to heaven and heaven descending,
Man's spirit away from its drear dongeon sending,
Bursting the fetters and breaking the bars.

All down the mountain sides, wild forests lending
One mighty voice to the life-giving wind;
Rivers their banks in the jubilee rending,
Fast through the valleys a reckless course wending,
Wider and deeper their waters extending,
Leaving a desolate desert behind.

Shining and lowering and swelling and dying,
Changing for ever from midnight to noon;
Roaring like thunder, like soft music sighing,
Shadows on shadows advancing and flying,
Lightning-bright flashes the deep gloom defying,
Coming as swiftly and fading as soon.

West Yorkshire

The Hours and the Seasons

BASIL BUNTING

'Weeping oaks grieve, chestnuts raise'

Weeping oaks grieve, chestnuts raise
mournful candles. Sad is spring
to perpetuate, sad to trace
immortalities never changing.

Weary on the sea
for sight of land
gazing past the coming wave we
see the same wave;

drift on merciless reiteration of years;
descry no death; but spring
is everlasting
resurrection.

GERARD MANLEY HOPKINS

Spring

Nothing is so beautiful as spring –
   When weeds, in wheels, shoot long and lovely and lush;
   Thrush's eggs look little low heavens, and thrush
Through the echoing timber does so rinse and wring
The ear, it strikes like lightnings to hear him sing;
   The glassy peartree leaves and blooms, they brush
   The descending blue; that blue is all in a rush
With richness; the racing lambs too have fair their fling.
What is all this juice and all this joy?

    A strain of the earth's sweet being in the beginning
In Eden Garden. – Have, get, before it cloy,
    Before it cloud, Christ, lord, and sour with sinning,
Innocent mind and Mayday in girl and boy,
    Most, O maid's child, thy choice and worthy the winning.

North Wales

JOHN CLARE

The Heat of Noon

There lies a sultry lusciousness around
The far-stretched pomp of summer which the eye
Views with a dazzled gaze – and gladly bounds
Its prospects to some pastoral spots that lie
Nestling among the hedge, confining grounds
Where in some nook the haystacks newly made
Scents the smooth level meadow-land around
While underneath the woodland's hazley hedge
The crowding oxen make their swaily beds
And in the dry dyke thronged with rush and sedge
The restless sheep rush in to hide their heads
From the unlost and ever haunting flie
And under every tree's projecting shade
Places as battered as the road is made

    Cambridgeshire

ANNE FINCH, COUNTESS OF WINCHILSEA

A Nocturnal Reverie

In such a *Night*, when every louder Wind
Is to its distant Cavern safe confin'd;

And only gentle *Zephyr* fans his Wings,
And lonely *Philomel*, still waking, sings;
Or from some Tree, fam'd for the *Owl's* delight,
She, hollowing clear, directs the Wand'rer right:
In such a *Night*, when passing Clouds give place,
Or thinly vail the Heav'ns mysterious Face;
When in some River, overhung with Green,
The waving Moon and trembling Leaves are seen;
When freshen'd Grass now bears it self upright,
And makes cool Banks to pleasing Rest invite,
Whence springs the *Woodbind*, and the *Bramble*-Rose,
And where the sleepy *Cowslip* shelter'd grows;
Whilst now a paler Hue the *Foxglove* takes,
Yet checquers still with Red the dusky brakes
When scatter'd *Glow-worms*, but in Twilight fine,
Shew trivial Beauties watch their Hour to shine;
Whilst *Salisb'ry* stands the Test of every Light,
In perfect Charms, and perfect Virtue bright:
When Odours, which declin'd repelling Day,
Thro' temp'rate Air uninterrupted stray;
When darken'd Groves their softest Shadows wear,
And falling Waters we distinctly hear;
When thro' the Gloom more venerable shows
Some ancient Fabrick, awful in Repose,
While Sunburnt Hills their swarthy Looks conceal,
And swelling Haycocks thicken up the Vale:
When the loos'd *Horse* now, as his Pasture leads,
Comes slowly grazing thro' th' adjoining Meads,
Whose stealing Pace, and lengthen'd Shade we fear,
Till torn up Forage in his Teeth we hear:
When nibbling *Sheep* at large pursue their Food,
And unmolested Kine rechew the Cud;
When *Curlews* cry beneath the Village-walls,
And to her straggling Brood the *Partridge* calls;
Their shortliv'd Jubilee the Creatures keep,
Which but endures, whilst Tyrant-*Man* do's sleep;

When a sedate Content the Spirit feels,
And no fierce Light disturb, whilst it reveals;
But silent Musings urge the Mind to seek
Something, too high for Syllables to speak;
Till the free Soul to a compos'dness charm'd,
Finding the Elements of Rage disarm'd,
O'er all below a solemn Quiet grown,
Joys in th' inferiour World, and thinks it like her Own:
In such a *Night* let Me abroad remain,
Till Morning breaks, and All's confus'd again;
Our Cares, our Toils, our Clamours are renew'd,
Or Pleasures, seldom reach'd, again pursu'd.

   Wiltshire

ANDREW YOUNG

In Teesdale

No, not tonight,
Not by this fading light,
Not by those high fells where the forces
Fall from the mist like the white tails of horses.

From that dark slack
Where peat-hags gape too black
I turn to where the lighted farm
Holds out through the open door a golden arm.

No, not tonight,
Tomorrow by daylight;
Tonight I fear the fabulous horses
Whose white tails flash down the steep watercourses.

   North Yorkshire

EDWARD THOMAS

Digging

To-day I think
Only with scents, – scents dead leaves yield,
And bracken, and wild carrot's seed,
And the square mustard field;

Odours that rise
When the spade wounds the root of tree,
Rose, currant, raspberry, or goutweed,
Rhubarb or celery;

The smoke's smell, too,
Flowing from where a bonfire burns
The dead, the waste, the dangerous,
And all to sweetness turns.

It is enough
To smell, to crumble the dark earth,
While the robin sings over again
Sad songs of Autumn mirth.

JON STALLWORTHY

Burning the Stubble

Another harvest gathered in
worse than the last; only a bin
of rotten grain for all our trouble.
But there is a time for the plough,
a time for harvesting, and now
a time for burning the stubble.

Flames snap at the wind, and it
etches the eye with a bitter
mirage of summer. Returning
I looked for the dip in the ground,
the nest, the unfurled poppy; found
nothing but stubble burning

and charred ground hardening towards frost.
Fire before ice; and the ground must
be ploughed after burning the stubble,
the ground must be broken again.
There can be no new grain
without, first, burning the stubble.

ALFRED, LORD TENNYSON

Song

I

A spirit haunts the year's last hours
Dwelling amid these yellowing bowers:
        To himself he talks;
For at eventide, listening earnestly,
At his work you may hear him sob and sigh
        In the walks;
        Earthward he boweth the heavy stalks
Of the mouldering flowers:
    Heavily hangs the broad sunflower
        Over its grave i' the earth so chilly;
    Heavily hangs the hollyhock,
        Heavily hangs the tiger-lily.

II

The air is damp, and hush'd, and close,
As a sick man's room when he taketh repose
        An hour before death;
My very heart faints and my whole soul grieves
At the moist rich smell of the rotting leaves,
        And the breath
        Of the fading edges of box beneath,
And the year's last rose.
    Heavily hangs the broad sunflower
        Over its grave i' the earth so chilly;
    Heavily hangs the hollyhock,
        Heavily hangs the tiger-lily.

LAURENCE BINYON

The Burning of the Leaves

Now is the time for the burning of the leaves.
They go to the fire; the nostril pricks with smoke
Wandering slowly into the weeping mist.
Brittle and blotched, ragged and rotten sheaves!
A flame seizes the smouldering ruin, and bites
On stubborn stalks that crackle as they resist.

The last hollyhock's fallen tower is dust:
All the spices of June are a bitter reek,
All the extravagant riches spent and mean.
All burns! the reddest rose is a ghost.
Sparks whirl up, to expire in the mist: the wild
Fingers of fire are making corruption clean.

Now is the time for stripping the spirit bare,
Time for the burning of days ended and done,
Idle solace of things that have gone before,

Rootless hope and fruitless desire are there:
Let them go to the fire with never a look behind.
That world that was ours is a world that is ours no more.

They will come again, the leaf and the flower, to arise
From squalor of rottenness into the old splendour,
And magical scents to a wondering memory bring;
The same glory, to shine upon different eyes.
Earth cares for her own ruins, naught for ours.
Nothing is certain, only the certain spring.

ANONYMOUS

A Snowy Day

[translated from the Welsh by H. Idris Bell]

I cannot sleep or take the air –
Of a truth this load is hard to bear!
Ford or slope is none to be found,
Nor open space, nor bare ground.
No girl's word shall tempt me now
Out of my house into the snow.
The plaguey feathers drifting down
Like dragon's scales cling to the gown,
And all I wear would soon be
White as miller's coat to see.
True 'tis, the Winter Calends gone,
Ermine's the wear for everyone;
In January's month, first of the year,
God makes hermits everywhere.
Everywhere, the country round,
He has whitewashed the black ground,
Clothed in white each woodland glade,
On every copse a white sheet spread.
To every stump clings heavenly meal,

Like the white blossoms of April.
A cold veil on the forest lies,
A load of chalk crushes the trees.
Like wheaten flour the drifts appear,
A coat of mail that the plains wear,
A cold grit on field and fallow,
On earth's whole skin a thick tallow,
Foam-flakes flying thick and fast,
Fleeces big as a man's fist,
White bees of heaven on the wing,
Through all Gwynedd wandering.
Will God's plenty never cease –
So many feathers of holy geese,
Like winnowed chaff, heaped together,
A robe of ermine above the heather?
There in deep drifts the fine dust stays,
Where song was and the winding ways.
Who can tell me what folk they are
On the wintry earth spit from afar?
Heaven's white angels they must be
Busy about their carpentry.
The plank is lifted from the flour bin,
And down floats the flour within;
Silver cloaks of ice that pass,
Quicksilver, the coldest ever was,
A hampering chimer, white and chill,
Cement on hollow, ditch, and hill,
Earth's mail corslet, cold and hard,
A pavement vast as the sea's graveyard.
On all my land what monstrous fall,
From sea to sea a grey wall!
Who dare affront its rude domain?
A cloak of lead! – where is the rain?

HAROLD MASSINGHAM

Winter in Wensleydale

Winter starts – with viking-skirmishes,
Rapid scoutings of squally north-east rain,

Marauds through Middle Wensleydale
With sleet like Arctic acids

Scarring mat-grass and becks from Masham to Askrigg,
Pittering Semmerwater till it simmers;

Or fourteenth-century north-easterlies
Jostle wet shrubbery, whine through Jervaulx Abbey's
    bones,

Pelting its frosty-silver masonry
With hail.
            Then snow, sheep-grey, a graceful

Fluff at first, falls on fells
Till cairn is snowman, moor-mound's

Moby Dick, and tussock-moss
Is thin dale-tundra. Then, thickening,

Like Christmas-crystals in a shaken glass,
A white sahara-storm, a lunar system

On the move, its smithereens gusting westward,
Winter rages to Upper Wensleydale,

Where sheep tinkle or perish
In bleak freezings, blizzardous drifts, and farms

Are like iced-up, isolated Arctic tents –
Secured by logics,

The dale-brain of generations
Bequeathed like heirlooms,

A stone stronghold-ing build,
An enduring commonsense of tiny windows.

North Yorkshire

Order and Wilderness

ANDREW MARVELL

The Garden

How vainly men themselves amaze,
To win the palm, the oak, or bays;
And their incessant labours see
Crowned from some single herb, or tree,
Whose short and narrow-vergèd shade
Does prudently their toils upbraid;
While all the flowers and trees do close,
To weave the garlands of repose!

Fair Quiet, have I found thee here,
And Innocence, thy sister dear?
Mistaken long, I sought you then
In busy companies of men.
Your sacred plants, if here below,
Only among the plants will grow;
Society is all but rude
To this delicious solitude.

No white nor red was ever seen
So amorous as this lovely green.
Fond lovers, cruel as their flame,
Cut in these trees their mistress' name:
Little, alas! they know or heed,
How far these beauties her's exceed!
Fair trees! wheres'e'er your bark I wound,
No name shall but your own be found.

When we have run our passion's heat,
Love hither makes his best retreat.
The gods, that mortal beauty chase,

Still in a tree did end their race;
Apollo hunted Daphne so,
Only that she might laurel grow;
And Pan did after Syrinx speed,
Not as a nymph, but for a reed.

What wondrous life is this I lead!
Ripe apples drop about my head;
The luscious clusters of the vine
Upon my mouth do crush their wine;
The nectarine, and curious peach,
Into my hands themselves do reach;
Stumbling on melons, as I pass,
Insnared with flowers, I fall on grass.

Meanwhile the mind, from pleasure less,
Withdraws into its happiness;
The mind, that ocean where each kind
Does straight its own resemblance find;
Yet it creates, transcending these,
Far other worlds, and other seas,
Annihilating all that's made
To a green thought in a green shade.

Here at the fountain's sliding foot,
Or at some fruit-tree's mossy root,
Casting the body's vest aside,
My soul into the boughs does glide:
There, like a bird, it sits and sings,
Then whets and combs its silver wings,
And, till prepared for longer flight,
Waves in its plumes the various light.

Such was that happy garden-state,
While man there walked without a mate:
After a place so pure and sweet,
What other help could yet be meet!
But 'twas beyond a mortal's share

To wander solitary there:
Two paradises 'twere in one.
To live in paradise alone.

How well the skilful gardener drew
Of flowers, and herbs, this dial new;
Where, from above, the milder sun
Does through a fragrant zodiac run,
And, as it works, the industrious bee
Computes its time as well as we!
How could such sweet and wholesome hours
Be reckoned but with herbs and flowers?

    Nun-Appleton House, North Yorkshire

WILLIAM COWPER

from The Task, Book III

          Mansions once
Knew their own masters; and laborious hinds
Who had surviv'd the father, serv'd the son.
Now the legitimate and rightful lord
Is but a transient guest, newly arriv'd,
And soon to be supplanted. He that saw
His patrimonial timber cast its leaf,
Sells the last scantling, and transfers the price
To some shrewd sharper, ere it buds again.
Estates are landscapes, gaz'd upon a while,
Then advertis'd, and auctioneer'd away.
The country starves, and they that feed th' o'ercharg'd
And surfeited lewd town with her fair dues,
By a just judgment strip and starve themselves.
The wings that waft our riches out of sight
Grow on the gamester's elbows; and th' alert
And nimble motion of those restless joints,

That never tire, soon fans them all away.
Improvement too, the idol of the age,
Is fed with many a victim. Lo, he comes!
Th' omnipotent magician, Brown, appears!
Down falls the venerable pile, th' abode
Of our forefathers – a grave whisker'd race,
But tasteless. Springs a palace in its stead,
But in a distant spot; where, more expos'd,
It may enjoy th' advantage of the north,
And aguish east, till time shall have transform'd
Those naked acres to a shelt'ring grove.
He speaks. The lake in front becomes a lawn;
Woods vanish, hills subside, and vallies rise:
And streams, as if created for his use,
Pursue the track of his directing wand,
Sinuous or straight, now rapid and now slow,
Now murm'ring soft, now roaring in cascades –
Ev'n as he bids! Th' enraptur'd owner smiles.
'Tis finish'd, and yet, finish'd as it seems,
Still wants a grace, the loveliest it could show,
A mine to satisfy th' enormous cost.
Drain'd to the last poor item of his wealth,
He sighs, departs, and leaves th' accomplish'd plan
That he has touch'd, retouch'd, many a long day
Labour'd, and many a night pursu'd in dreams,
Just when it meets his hopes, and proves the heav'n
He wanted, for a wealthier to enjoy!

WILLIAM WHITEHEAD

On the Late Improvements at Nuneham

'The prospect, wherever beheld, must be good,
But has ten times its charms, when you burst from this wood,
A wood of my planting.' – The goddess cried, 'Hold!

'Tis grown very hot, and 'tis grown very cold':
She fann'd and she shudder'd, she cough'd and she sneez'd,
Inclin'd to be angry, inclin'd to be pleas'd,
Half smil'd, and half poured – then turn'd from the view,
And dropp'd him a courtesy, and blushing withdrew.
    Yet soon recollecting her thoughts, as she pass'd,
'I may have my revenge on this fellow at last:
For a lucky conjecture comes into my head,
That, whate'er he has done, and whate'er he has said,
The world's little malice will balk his design:
Each fault they call his, and each excellence mine.'

    Nuneham Courtenay, Oxfordshire

DOUGLAS DUNN

Gardeners

England, Loamshire, 1789
A gardener speaks, in the grounds of a great house, to his Lordship

Gardens, gardens, and we are gardeners...
Razored hedgerow, flowers, those planted trees
Whose avenues conduct a greater ease
Of shadow to your own and ladies' skins
And tilt this Nature to magnificence
And natural delight. But pardon us,
My Lord, if we reluctantly admit
Our horticulture not the whole of it,
Forgetting, that for you, this elegance
Is not our work, but your far tidier Sense.

Out of humiliation comes that sweet
Humility that does no good. We know
Our coarser artistries will make things grow.
Others design the craftsmanship we fashion
To please your topographical possession.

A small humiliation – Yes, we eat,
Our crops and passions tucked out of the view
Across a shire, the name of which is you,
Where every native creature runs upon
Hills, moors and meadows which your named eyes own.

Our eyes are nameless, generally turned
Towards the earth our fingers sift all day –
Your day, your earth, your eyes, wearing away
Not earth, eyes, days, but scouring, forcing down
What lives in us and which you cannot own.
One of us heard the earth cry out. It spurned
His hands. It threw stones in his face. We found
That man, my Lord, and he was mad. We bound
His hands together and we heard him say –
'Not me! Not me who cries!' We took away

That man – remember, Lord? – and then we turned,
Hearing your steward order us return,
His oaths, and how you treated us with scorn.
They call this grudge. Let me hear you admit
That in the country that's but half of it.
Townsmen will wonder, when your house was burned,
We did not burn your gardens and undo
What likes of us did for the likes of you;
We did not raze this garden that we made,
Although we hanged you somewhere in its shade.

ROBERT SOUTHEY

from The Old Mansion-House

STRANGER
Old friend! why you seem bent on parish duty,
Breaking the highway stones, ... and 'tis a task
Somewhat too hard methinks for age like yours!

OLD MAN
Why yes! for one with such a weight of years
Upon his back! ... I've lived here, man and boy,
In this same parish, well nigh the full age
Of man, being hard upon threescore and ten.
I can remember sixty years ago
The beautifying of this mansion here,
When my late Lady's father, the old Squire,
Came to the estate.

STRANGER
                    Why then you have outlasted
All his improvements, for you see they're making
Great alterations here.

OLD MAN
                         Ay ... great indeed!
And if my poor old Lady could rise up ...
God rest her soul! 'twould grieve her to behold
What wicked work is here.

STRANGER
                         They've set about it
In right good earnest. All the front is gone;
Here's to be turf, they tell me, and a road
Round to the door. There were some yew trees too
Stood in the court ...

OLD MAN
             Ay, Master! fine old trees!
Lord bless us! I have heard my father say
His grandfather could just remember back
When they were planted there. It was my task
To keep them trimm'd, and 'twas a pleasure to me;
All straight and smooth, and like a great green wall!
My poor old lady many a time would come
And tell me where to clip, for she had play'd
In childhood under them, and 'twas her pride

To keep them in their beauty. Plague, I say,
On their new-fangled whimsies! we shall have
A modern shrubbery here stuck full of firs
And your pert poplar trees; ... I could as soon
Have plough'd my father's grave as cut them down!

STRANGER
But 'twill be lighter and more cheerful now;
A fine smooth turf, and with a carriage road
That sweeps conveniently from gate to gate.
I like a shrubbery too, for it looks fresh;
And then there's some variety about it.
In spring the lilac and the snow-ball flower,
And the laburnum with its golden strings
Waving in the wind: And when the autumn comes
The bright red berries of the mountain-ash,
With pines enough in winter to look green,
And show that something lives. Sure this is better
Than a great hedge of yew, making it look
All the year round like winter, and for ever
Dropping its poisonous leaves from the under boughs
Wither'd and bare.

OLD MAN
            Ay! so the new Squire thinks;
And pretty work he makes of it! What 'tis
To have a stranger come to an old house!

   Cumberland

ALGERNON CHARLES SWINBURNE

from A Forsaken Garden

In a coign of the cliff between lowland and highland,
   At the sea-down's edge between windward and lee,

Walled round with rocks as an inland island,
   The ghost of a garden fronts the sea.
A girdle of brushwood and thorn encloses
   The steep square slope of the blossomless bed
Where the weeds that grew green from the graves of its roses
      Now lie dead.

The fields fall southward, abrupt and broken,
   To the low last edge of the long lone land.
If a step should sound or a word be spoken,
   Would a ghost not rise at the strange guest's hand?
So long have the grey bare walks lain guestless,
   Through branches and briars if a man make way,
He shall find no life but the sea-wind's, restless
      Night and day.

The dense hard passage is blind and stifled
   That crawls by a track none turn to climb
To the strait waste place that the years have rifled
   Of all but the thorns that are touched not of time.
The thorns he spares when the rose is taken;
   The rocks are left when he wastes the plain.
The wind that wanders, the weeds wind-shaken,
      These remain. [...]

Here death may deal not again for ever;
   Here change may come not till all change end.
From the graves they have made they shall rise up never,
   Who have left nought living to ravage and rend.
Earth, stones, and thorns of the wild ground growing,
   While the sun and the rain live, these shall be;
Till a last wind's breath upon all these blowing
      Roll the sea.

Till the slow sea rise and the sheer cliff crumble,
   Till terrace and meadow the deep gulfs drink,
Till the strength of the waves of the high tides humble
   The fields that lessen, the rocks that shrink,

Here now in his triumph where all things falter,
   Stretched out on the spoils that his own hand spread,
As a god self-slain on his own strange altar,
     Death lies dead.

   near Bonchurch, Isle of Wight

EDWARD THOMAS

Tall Nettles

Tall nettles cover up, as they have done
These many springs, the rusty harrow, the plough
Long worn out, and the roller made of stone:
Only the elm butt tops the nettles now.

This corner of the farmyard I like most:
As well as any bloom upon a flower
I like the dust on the nettles, never lost
Except to prove the sweetness of a shower.

JON STALLWORTHY

Thistles

Half grown before half seen,
like urchins in armour
double their size they stand
their ground boldly, their keen
swords out. But the farmer
ignores them. Not a hand

will he lift to cut them down:
they are not worth his switch
he says. Uncertain whom
they challenge, having grown

into their armour, each
breaks out a purple plume.

Under this image
of their warrior blood
they make a good death,
meeting the farmer's blade
squarely in their old age.
White then as winter breath

from every white head
a soul springs up. The wind
is charged with spirits: no –
not spirits of the dead
for these are living, will land
at our backs and go

to ground. Farmer and scythe
sing to each other. He
cannot see how roots writhe
underfoot, how the sons
of this fallen infantry
will separate our bones.

GERARD MANLEY HOPKINS

Inversnaid

This darksome burn, horseback brown,
His rollrock highroad roaring down,
In coop and in comb the fleece of his foam
Flutes and low to the lake falls home.

A windpuff-bonnet of fáwn-fróth
Turns and twindles over the broth
Of a pool so pitchblack, féll fró wning,
It rounds and rounds Despair to drowning.

Degged with dew, dappled with dew
Are the groins of the braes that the brook treads through,
Wiry heathpacks, flitches of fern,
And the beadbonny ash that sits over the burn.

What would the world be, once bereft
Of wet and of wildness? Let them be left,
O let them be left, wildness and wet;
Long live the weeds and the wilderness yet.

Stirlingshire/Central Scotland

SIR JONAS MOORE

from A True and Natural Description of the Great Level of the Fenns

I sing Floods muzled, and the Ocean tam'd,
Luxurious Rivers govern'd, and reclaim'd,
Waters with Banks confin'd, as in a Gaol,
Till kinder Sluces let them go on Bail;
Streams curb'd with Dammes like Bridles, taught t'obey,
And run as strait, as if they saw their way.

The Fens

Trees and the Deaths of Trees

U. A. FANTHORPE

King Edward's Flora

Your mind commandeers an island.
It seems simple. The neighbours
Are fish, not Christian fretful kings.

But in my halflight rear hulking trees,
Sulky, inidigenous. Their names crack
Like an enemy's laugh. Short words, long trees.

It is not simple, cousin. I am the heir.
In me shines the clear claim of Wessex.
But the trees were before. Their roots run back

Below Grendel's forest. Ash was earliest.
Odin carved man from him; then alder,
The spirit tree, whose blood breaks red

Like ours. Alder is old. And guilty aspen,
Our Saviour's hangman, that chronicles Calvary
By a fine tremor in sweet summer air.

Then the holy ones: oak, many-fingered;
Holly, that fights for us against darkness,
And never fades; holy thorn that is quick

In the dead of the year, at birth-time; yew,
Slow and sacred, that nothing grows under;
Red-berried rowan, that warns off witches.

Cut-and-come-again bushes, hazel and willow;
And walnut the wanderer, tramping north
In the legions' brown fists.

All the bright welter of things
That maim, detain, deceive: bramble and briar,
Furze, moss, reed, rush, sedge; thistle the spearman.

These are my shieldwall. Take them, cousin,
You or Harold. Settle it between you,
For I choose ending: Edward the heirless,

My children the stone forest
At the West Minster. These are the trees
That I make holy. You, I can see,

Will be William of the Wastes.
My woods will not content you.

But take care, cousin. Trees are unchancy.
I say more than I know, being the last –
Son of Bad Counsel, Edward the healer –

You will plant your dynasty, if Harold lets you,
But the trees will not endure it. Your saplings totter
Under my trees. A red man sprawls, a white ship founders.

The boy from the gorse-bush will snaffle the lot.

   England at the time of Edward the Confessor

AEMILIA LANYER

from The Description of Cooke-ham

Now let me come unto that stately tree,
Wherein such goodly prospects you did see,
That oak that did in height his fellows pass,
As much as lofty trees, low-growing grass,
Much like a comely cedar, straight and tall,
Whose beauteous stature far exceeded all;
How often did you visit this fair tree,

Which seeming joyful in receiving thee,
Would like a palm tree spread his arms abroad,
Desirous that you there should make abode,
Whose fair green leaves much like a comely veil,
Defended Phoebus when he would assail,
Whose pleasing boughs did yield a cool fresh air,
Joying his happiness when you were there;
Where being seated you might plainly see
Hills, vales and woods, as if on bended knee
They had appeared, your honour to salute,
Or to prefer some strange, unlooked-for suit;
All interlaced with brooks and crystal springs,
A prospect fit to please the eyes of kings,
And thirteen shires appear all in your sight,
Europe could not afford much more delight.

WILLIAM COWPER

from Yardley Oak

Thou wast a bauble once; a cup and ball,
Which babes might play with; and the thievish jay
Seeking her food, with ease might have purloin'd
The auburn nut that held thee, swallowing down
Thy yet close-folded latitude of boughs
And all thine embryo vastness, at a gulp.
But Fate thy growth decreed: autumnal rains
Beneath thy parent tree mellow'd the soil
Design'd thy cradle, and a skipping deer,
With pointed hoof dibbling the glebe, prepar'd
The soft receptacle in which secure
Thy rudiments should sleep the winter through.
So Fancy dreams – Disprove it, if ye can,
Ye reas'ners broad awake, whose busy search
Of argument, employ'd too oft amiss,

Sifts half the pleasures of short life away.
    Thou fell'st mature, and in the loamy clod
Swelling, with vegetative force instinct
Didst burst thine egg, as theirs the fabled Twins
Now stars; two lobes, protruding, pair'd exact;
A leaf succeeded, and another leaf,
And all the elements thy puny growth
Fost'ring propitious, thou becam'st a twig. [...]

And Time hath made thee what thou art – a cave
For owls to roost in. Once thy spreading boughs
O'erhung the champain; and the numerous flock
That graz'd it stood beneath that ample cope
Uncrowded, yet safe-shelter'd from the storm.
No flock frequents thee now. Thou hast outliv'd
Thy popularity and art become
(Unless verse rescue thee awhile) a thing
Forgotten, as the foliage of thy youth.
    While thus through all the stages thou hast push'd
Of treeship, first a seedling hid in grass,
Then twig, then sapling, and, as century roll'd
Slow after century, a giant bulk
Of girth enormous, with moss-cushion'd root
Upheav'd above the soil, and sides imboss'd
With prominent wens globose, till at the last
The rottenness, which time is charg'd t' inflict
On other mighty ones, found also thee –
What exhibitions various hath the world
Witness'd of mutability in all
That we account most durable below!
Change is the diet, on which all subsist
Created changeable, and change at last
Destroys them. – Skies uncertain now the heat
Transmitting cloudless, and the solar beam
Now quenching in a boundless sea of clouds, –
Calm and alternate storm, moisture and drought,

Invigorate by turns the springs of life
In all that live, plant, animal, and man,
And in conclusion mar them. Nature's threads,
Fine passing thought, ev'n in her coarsest works,
Delight in agitation, yet sustain
The force, that agitates not unimpair'd,
But, worn by frequent impulse, to the cause
Of their best tone their dissolution owe. [...]

   Thine arms have left thee. Winds have rent them off
Long since, and rovers of the forest wild
With bow and shaft have burnt them. Some have left
A splinter'd stump bleach'd to a snowy white;
And some memorial none where once they grew.
Yet life still lingers in thee, and puts forth
Proof not contemptible of what she can,
Even where death predominates. The spring
Thee finds not less alive to her sweet force
Than yonder upstarts of the neighbour wood,
So much thy juniors, who their birth receiv'd
Half a millennium since the date of thine.
   But since, although well qualified by age
To teach, no spirit dwells in thee, nor voice
May be expected from thee, seated here
On thy distorted root, with hearers none
Or prompter, save the scene, I will perform
Myself the oracle, and will discourse
In my own ear such matter as I may.
Thou, like myself, hast stage by stage attain'd
Life's wintry bourn; thou, after many years,
I after few; but few or many prove
A span in retrospect; for I can touch
With my least finger's end my own decease
And with extended thumb my natal hour,
And hadst thou also skill in measurement
As I, the past would seem as short to thee.

Evil and few – said Jacob – at an age
Thrice mine, and few and evil, I may think
The Prediluvian race, whose buxom youth
Endured two centuries, accounted theirs.
'Shortliv'd as foliage is the race of man.
The wind shakes down the leaves, the budding grove
Soon teems with others, and in spring they grow.
So pass mankind. One generation meets
Its destin'd period, and a new succeeds.'
Such was the tender but undue complaint
Of the Mæonian in old time; for who
Would drawl out centuries in tedious strife
Severe with mental and corporeal ill
And would not rather chuse a shorter race
To glory, a few decades here below?

Yardley Chase, Northamptonshire/Buckinghamshire border

DOUGLAS YOUNG

Last Laugh

The Minister said it wad dee,
the cypress bush I plantit.
But the bush grew til a tree,
naething dauntit.

Hit's growin, stark and heich,
derk and straucht and sinister,
kirkyairdie-like and dreich.
But whaur's the Minister?

EDWARD THOMAS

Aspens

All day and night, save winter, every weather,
Above the inn, the smithy, and the shop,
The aspens at the cross-roads talk together
Of rain, until their last leaves fall from the top.

Out of the blacksmith's cavern comes the ringing
Of hammer, shoe, and anvil; out of the inn
The clink, the hum, the roar, the random singing –
The sounds that for these fifty years have been.

The whisper of the aspens is not drowned,
And over lightless pane and footless road,
Empty as sky, with every other sound
Not ceasing, calls their ghosts from their abode,

A silent smithy, a silent inn, nor fails
In the bare moonlight or the thick-furred gloom,
In tempest or the night of nightingales,
To turn the cross-roads to a ghostly room.

And it would be the same were no house near.
Over all sorts of weather, men, and times,
Aspens must shake their leaves and men may hear
But need not listen, more than to my rhymes.

Whatever wind blows, while they and I have leaves
We cannot other than an aspen be
That ceaselessly, unreasonably grieves,
Or so men think who like a different tree.

GERARD MANLEY HOPKINS

Binsey Poplars

felled 1879

My aspens dear, whose airy cages quelled,
Quelled or quenched in leaves the leaping sun,
All felled, felled, are all felled;
   Of a fresh and following folded rank
         Not spared, not one
           That dandled a sandalled
      Shadow that swam or sank
On meadow and river and wind-wandering weed-winding
   bank.

O if we but knew what we do
      When we delve or hew –
   Hack and rack the growing green!
      Since country is so tender
   To touch, her being só slender,
   That, like this sleek and seeing ball
   But a prick will make no eye at all.

   Where we, even where we mean
      To mend her we end her,
     When we hew or delve:
After-comers cannot guess the beauty been.
   Ten or twelve, only ten or twelve
    Strokes of havoc únselve
     The sweet especial scene,
    Rural scene, a rural scene,
    Sweet especial rural scene.

(near) Oxford

IVOR GURNEY

Felling a Tree

The surge of spirit that goes with using an axe,
The first heat – and calming down till the stiff back's
Unease passed, and the hot moisture came on body.
There under banks of Dane and Roman with the golden
Imperial coloured flower, whose name is lost to me –
Hewing the trunk desperately with upward strokes;
Seeing the chips fly – (it was at shoulder height, the trunk)
The green go, and the white appear –
Who should have been making music, but this had to be
    done
To earn a cottage shelter, and milk, and a little bread:
To right a body, beautiful as water and honour could make
    one –
And like the soldier lithe of body in the foremost rank
I stood there, muscle stiff, free of arm, working out fear.
Glad it was the ash tree's hardness not of the oaks', of the
    iron oak.
Sweat dripped from me – but there was no stay and the
    echoing bank
Sent back sharp sounds of hacking and of true straight
    woodcraft.
Some Roman from the pinewood caught memory and
    laughed.
Hit, crack and false aim, echoed from the amphitheatre
Of what was Rome before Romulus drew shoulder of
    Remus
Nearer his own – or Fabius won his salvation of victories.
In resting I thought of the hidden farm and Rome's hidden
    mild yoke
Still on the Gloucester heart strong after love's fill of centuries,
For all the happy, or the quiet, Severn or Leadon streams.

Pondered on music's deep truth, poetry's form or metre,
Rested – and took a thought and struck onward again,
Who had frozen by Chaulnes out of all caring of pain –
Learnt Roman fortitude at Laventie or Ypres,
Saw bright edge bury dull in the beautiful wood,
Touched splinters so wonderful – half through and soon to
    come down
From that ledge of rock under harebell, the yellow flower –
    the pinewood's crown.
Four inches more – and I should hear the crash and great
    thunder
Of an ash Crickley had loved for a century, and kept her
    own.
Thoughts of soldier and musician gathered to me
The desire of conquest ran in my blood, went through me –
There was a battle in my spirit and my blood shared it,
Maisemore – and Gloucester – bred me, and Cotswold
    reared it,
This great tree standing nobly in the July's day full light
Nearly to fall – my courage broke – and gathered – my
    breath feared it.
My heart – and again I struck, again the splinters and steel
    glinters
Dazzled my eyes – and the pain and the desperation and near
    victory
Carried me onwards – there were exultations and mockings
    sunward
Sheer courage, as of boat sailings in equinoctial unsafe
    squalls,
Stiffened my virtue, and the thing was done. No. Dropped
    my body,
The axe dropped – for a minute, taking breath, and
    gathering the greedy
Courage – looking for rest to the farm and grey loose-piled
    walls,
Rising like Troilus to the first word of 'Ready',

The last desperate onslaught – took the two inches of too
     steady
Trunk – on the rock edge it lurched, threatening my
     labouring life
(Nearly on me). Like Trafalgar's own sails imperiously
     moving to defeat
Across the wide sky unexpected glided and the high bank's
     pines and fell straight
Lower and lower till the crashing of the fellow trees made
     strife.
The thud of earth, and the full tree lying low in state,
With all its glory of life and sap quick in the veins...
Such beauty, for the farm fires and heat against chilly rains,
Golden glows in the kitchen from what a century made
     great...

The axe fell from my hand, and I was proud of my hand,
Crickley forgave, for her nobleness, the common fate of trees
As noble or more noble, the oak, the elm that is treacherous,
But dear for her cherishing to this beloved and this rocky
     land.
Over above all the world there, in a tired glory swerved
     there,
To a fall, the tree that for long had watched Wales glow
     strong,
Seen Severn, and farm, and Brecon, Black Mountains times
     without reckon.
And tomorrow would be fuel for the bright kitchen – for
     brown tea, against cold night.

   Cotswolds

CHARLOTTE MEW

The Trees Are Down

– and he cried with a loud voice;
Hurt not the earth, neither the sea, nor the trees

They are cutting down the great plane-trees at the end of the
   gardens.
For days there has been the grate of the saw, the swish of the
   branches as they fall,
The crash of the trunks, the rustle of trodden leaves,
With the 'Whoops' and the 'Whoas', the loud common talk,
   the loud common laughs of the men, above it all.

I remember one evening of a long past Spring
Turning in at a gate, getting out of a cart, and finding a large
   dead rat in the mud of a drive.
I remember thinking: alive or dead, a rat was a god-forsaken
   thing,
But at least, in May, that even a rat should be alive.

The week's work here is as good as done. There is just one
   bough
On the roped bole, in the fine grey rain,
      Green and high
      And lonely against the sky.
         (Down now! –)
      And but for that,
      If an old dead rat
Did once, for a moment, unmake the Spring, I might never
   have thought of him again.

It is not for a moment the Spring is unmade today;
These were great trees, it was in them from root to stem:
When the men with the 'Whoops' and the 'Whoas' have
   carted the whole
      of the whispering loveliness away

Half the Spring, for me, will have gone with them.
It is going now, and my heart has been struck with the hearts
    of the planes;
Half my life it has beat with these, in the sun, in the rains,
        In the March wind, the May breeze,
In the great gales that came over to them across the roofs
                    from the great seas.
        There was only a quiet rain when they were dying;
        They must have heard the sparrows flying,
And the small creeping creatures in the earth where they
    were lying –
        But I, all day, I heard an angel crying:
            'Hurt not the trees.'

AMY CLAMPITT

The Hurricane and Charlotte Mew

The trees are down all over the south of England –
                    the green, tossed
tops of beeches and sycamores in the deer park at Knole,
the Sussex oaks, the clumped pine-tufts in what had been
                    left of Ashdown Forest,
upended by the winds of a hurricane hurled in,
improbably, all the way from the Caribbean, on the
                    heels of what began
                    as an ordinary rain

like the fine gray rain she remembered had been falling
                    the day the last
roped bole at the end of Euston Square Gardens, after
a week's work of sawing, dismembering, and carting off,
                    gave way and fell,
and what gave way within her, for what was gone, had

a finality that, for her, was apocalyptic, but was also
                    no more tangible
        a wisp than the handful

she'd seen the shade-catchers, sister and brother, snatch
                    as they ran past.
But that would have been while the great tossed tops at
                    the end of the garden
stood, as they were standing all over the south of England
until that night, surprised by some flaw in the flow of the
                    Gulf Stream, they fell
by the thousand, the tens of thousands. Ashdown Forest will
    not
                    be the same again.

What persists, what is not to be uprooted or dismembered,
                    I would discover,
sauntering there with a girl and a boy with a kite, last year,
                    is the vast,
skittish, shade-catching turmoil of more usual English
    weather –
                    the wet, head-high bracken,
the drippingly black-and-gold gorse we sheltered under.
Notwithstanding the great, stunned, fallen stems that lie there,
Charlotte Mew, had she been with us, would have been
                    part of the fun.

    South-east England

SIR PHILIP SIDNEY

from 'O sweete woods the delight of solitarines'

O sweete woods the delight of solitarines!
O how much I do like your solitarines!
Here no treason is hidd, vailed in innocence,
Nor envie's snaky ey, finds any harbor here,

Nor flatterers' venomous insinuations,
Nor conning humorists' puddled opinions,
Nor courteous ruin of proffered usury,
Nor time pratled away, cradle of ignorance,
Nor causelesse duty, nor comber of arrogance,
Nor trifling title of vanity dazleth us,
Nor golden manacles, stand for a paradise,
Here wrong's name is unheard: slander a monster is.
Keepe thy sprite from abuse, here no abuse doth haunte.
What man grafts in a tree dissimulation? [...]

O sweet woods the delight of solitarines!
O how much I do like your solitarines!
Where man's mind hath a freed consideration
Of goodnes to receive lovely direction.
Where senses do behold th'order of heav'nly hoste,
And wise thoughts do behold what the creator is:
Contemplation here holdeth his only seate:
Bownded with no limitts, borne with a wing of hope
Clymes even unto the starres, Nature is under it.
Nought disturbs thy quiet, all to thy service yeeld,
Each sight draws on a thought, thought mother of science,
Sweet birds kindly do graunt harmony unto thee,
Faire trees' shade is enough fortification,
Nor danger to thy selfe if be not in thy selfe.

   Penshurst, Kent

GENE KEMP

from The Mink War

What a wood. What a wonder.
The weirdest wood in the world.
Wistman's, the Whisht Wood.
It's in all the guide books.

Black boulders bulge over
A carpet of clitter,
Random rocks tumble
Helter-skelter,
Barely the width of a whisker between them.
Hurled by mad giants
With fury, with hatred,
In crazy, wild battles
Long, long ago.

The Whisht Wood's
Contorted, distorted,
Dwarfed and deformed,
Gnarled, crooked and stunted,
Striving and thrusting,
Heaving and stretching,
Struggling all over.
Reach for the light!
The scrub oak, the mosses,
The lichen, the grasses,
The ivy, the bracken,
The brambles, the flowers:
Give me room.
Let me breathe.
Give me room,
Or I die!
While the adders stir in the brown leaf mould of centuries.

The wood is a person,
Nature's old pensioner.
Crabby and crooked,
Wilful and wayward,
Watching the river,
Hugging the hill.
Wearing green garments –
Leafy cloaks and hats –
Changing her fashion in autumn

To something more dashing,
Gold, red and tawny,
Before she goes naked.
Decorating herself
With lichen and bracken,
Accommodating small animals
And birds in her hair.

This wood hates people.
Go away, people – nasty things, people.
You are too tall.
My trees are tiny,
My paths are small.
Back to your Nature Trail.
Don't come here again.

And don't look behind you,
Or your own shadow
Will gobble you up!

    Dartmoor, Devon

THOMAS HARDY

In a Wood

See *The Woodlanders*

Pale beech and pine-tree blue,
    Set in one clay,
Bough to bough cannot you
    Bide out your day?
When the rains skim and skip,
Why mar sweet comradeship,
Blighting with poison-drip
    Neighbourly spray?

Heart-halt and spirit-lame,
    City-opprest,
Unto this wood I came
    As to a nest;
Dreaming that sylvan peace
Offered the harrowed ease –
Nature a soft release
    From men's unrest.

But, having entered in,
    Great growths and small
Show them to men akin –
    Combatants all!
Sycamore shoulders oak,
Bines the slim sapling yoke,
Ivy-spun halters choke
    Elms stout and tall.

Touches from ash, O wych,
    Sting you like scorn!
You, too, brave hollies, twitch
    Sidelong from thorn.
Even the rank poplars bear
Lothly a rival's air,
Cankering in black despair
    If overborne.

Since, then, no grace I find
    Taught me of trees,
Turn I back to my kind,
    Worthy as these.
There at least smiles abound,
There discourse trills around,
There, now and then, are found
    Life-loyalties.

    Dorset

Rocks and Stones

NORMAN NICHOLSON

Rock Face

In the quarry
I found the face – brow and nose and eyes
Cleft in a stare of ten-year-old surprise,
With slate lids slid backwards, grass and plantain
Tufted in ear and nostril, and an ooze
Like drip from marble mouth that spews
Into the carved trough of a city fountain.
Now the rock is blasted, and the dub
Chock-full of soil and rubble, and the shale
Carried away in cart and lorry,
Yet still like cracked reflections in a pool,
Or image broken in a smithereen of mirrors,
Or picture jigged and sawn with paste and scissors,
The rock face, temple, mouth and all,
Peers bleakly at me from this dry-stone wall.

    Cumbria

KATHLEEN RAINE

Stone on High Crag

Still stone
In heart of hill
Here alone
Hoodie and buzzard
By ways of air

Circling come.
From far shine
On wind-worn pinnacle
Star and moon
And sun, sun,
Wings bright in sun
Turn and return.

Centre of wing-spanned
Wheeling ways
Older than menhir
Lichen-roughened
Granite-grained
Rock-red
Rain-pocketed
Wind-buffeted
Heat-holding
Bird-whitened
Beak-worn
Insect-labyrinthine
Turf-embedded
Night-during
Race-remembered
Stand the known.

Canna, Inner Hebrides

JOHN FULLER

Cairn

Stairs leading nowhere, roof
To no accommodation, monument
To itself, half-scattered.

An old badge of belonging
To the available heights,
A shrug and a smile, as though

Having climbed two thousand feet
You could climb a few feet more
And the view might be different.

   Lleyn Peninsula, North Wales

W. H. AUDEN

In Praise of Limestone

If it form the one landscape that we, the inconstant ones,
    Are consistently homesick for, this is chiefly
Because it dissolves in water. Mark these rounded slopes
    With their surface fragrance of thyme and, beneath,
A secret system of caves and conduits; hear the springs
    That spurt out everywhere with a chuckle,
Each filling a private pool for its fish and carving
    Its own little ravine whose cliffs entertain
The butterfly and the lizard; examine this region
    Of short distances and definite places:
What could be more like Mother or a fitter background
    For her son, the flirtatious male who lounges
Against a rock in the sunlight, never doubting
    That for all his faults he is loved; whose works are but
Extensions of his power to charm? From weathered outcrop
    To hill-top temple, from appearing waters to
Conspicuous fountains, from a wild to a formal vineyard,
    Are ingenious but short steps that a child's wish
To receive more attention than his brothers, whether
    By pleasing or teasing, can easily take.
Watch, then, the band of rivals as they climb up and down
    Their steep stone gennels in twos and threes, at times

Arm in arm, but never, thank God, in step; or engaged
　　On the shady side of a square at midday in
Voluble discourse, knowing each other too well to think
　　There are any important secrets, unable
To conceive a god whose temper-tantrums are moral
　　And not to be pacified by a clever line
Or a good lay: for, accustomed to a stone that responds,
　　They have never had to veil their faces in awe
Of a crater whose blazing fury could not be fixed;
　　Adjusted to the local needs of valleys
Where everything can be touched or reached by walking,
　　Their eyes have never looked into infinite space
Through the lattice-work of a nomad's comb; born lucky,
　　Their legs have never encountered the fungi
And insects of the jungle, the monstrous forms and lives
　　With which we have nothing, we like to hope, in common.
So, when one of them goes to the bad, the way his mind
　　　works
　　Remains comprehensible: to become a pimp
Or deal in fake jewellery or ruin a fine tenor voice
　　For effects that bring down the house, could happen to all
But the best and the worst of us...

　　　　　　　　　　　　　　　　That is why, I suppose,
　　The best and worst never stayed here long but sought
Immoderate soils where the beauty was not so external,
　　The light less public and the meaning of life
Something more than a mad camp. 'Come!' cried the granite
　　　wastes,
　　'How evasive is your humor, how accidental
Your kindest kiss, how permanent is death.' (Saints-to-be
　　Slipped away sighing.) 'Come!' purred the clays and
　　　gravels,
　　'On our plains there is room for armies to drill; rivers
Wait to be tamed and slaves to construct you a tomb
　　In the grand manner: soft as the earth is mankind and both
　　Need to be altered.' (Intendant Caesars rose and

Left, slamming the door.) But the really reckless were
    fetched
  By an older colder voice, the oceanic whisper:
'I am the solitude that asks and promises nothing;
  That is how I shall set you free. There is no love;
There are only the various envies, all of them sad.'

  They were right, my dear, all those voices were right
And still are; this land is not the sweet home that it looks,
  Nor its peace the historical calm of a site
Where something was settled once and for all: A backward
  And dilapidated province, connected
To the big busy world by a tunnel, with a certain
  Seedy appeal, is that all it is now? Not quite:
It has a worldly duty which in spite of itself
  It does not neglect, but calls into question
All the Great Powers assume; it disturbs our rights. The
    poet,
  Admired for his earnest habit of calling
The sun the sun, his mind Puzzle, is made uneasy
  By these marble statues which so obviously doubt
His antimythological myth; and these gamins,
  Pursuing the scientist down the tiled colonnade
With such lively offers, rebuke his concern for Nature's
  Remotest aspects: I, too, am reproached, for what
And how much you know. Not to lose time, not to get
    caught,
  Not to be left behind, not, please! to resemble
The beasts who repeat themselves, or a thing like water
  Or stone whose conduct can be predicted, these
Are our Common Prayer, whose greatest comfort is music
  Which can be made anywhere, is invisible,
And does not smell. In so far as we have to look forward
  To death as a fact, no doubt we are right: But if
Sins can be forgiven, if bodies rise from the dead,
  These modifications of matter into

Innocent athletes and gesticulating fountains,
  Made solely for pleasure, make a further point:
The blessed will not care what angle they are regarded from,
  Having nothing to hide. Dear, I know nothing of
Either, but when I try to imagine a faultless love
  Or the life to come, what I hear is the murmur
Of underground streams, what I see is a limestone
  landscape.

HUGH MACDIARMID

from On a Raised Beach

I must get into this stone world now.
Ratchel, striae, relationships of tesserae,
  Innumerable shades of grey,
  Innumerable shapes,
And beneath them all a stupendous unity,
Infinite movement visibly defending itself
Against all the assaults of weather and water,
Simultaneously mobilised at full strength
At every point of the universal front,
  Always at the pitch of its powers,
  The foundation and end of all life.
I try them with the old Norn words – hraun
Duss, rønis, queedaruns, kollyarum:
They hvarf from me in all directions
Over the hurdifell – klett, millya, hellya, hellyina bretta,
Hellyina wheeda, hellyina grø, bakka, ayre, –
  and lay my world in kolgref.

This is no heap of broken images.
Let men find the faith that builds mountains
Before they seek the faith that moves them. Men cannot
  hope

To survive the fall of the mountains
Which they will no more see than they saw their rise
Unless they are more concentrated and determined,
Truer to themselves and with more to be true to,
Than these stones, and as inerrable as they are.
Their sole concern is that what can be shaken
Shall be shaken and disappear
And only the unshakable be left.
What hardihood in any man has part or parcel in the latter?
It is necessary to make a stand and maintain it forever.
These stones go through Man, straight to God, if there is
     one.
What have they not gone through already?
Empires, civilisations, aeons. Only in them
If in anything, can His creation confront Him.
They came so far out of the water and halted forever.
That larking dallier, the sun, has only been able to play
With superficial by-products since;
The moon moves the waters backwards and forwards,
But the stones cannot be lured an inch farther
Either on this side of eternity or the other.
Who thinks God is easier to know than they are?
Trying to reach men any more, any otherwise, than they are?
These stones will reach us long before we reach them.
Cold, undistracted, eternal and sublime.

Ruins and Great Houses

ANONYMOUS (12TH CENTURY)

The Ruin

[translated from the Old English by Richard Hamer]

Splendid this rampart is, though fate destroyed it,
The city buildings fell apart, the works
Of giants crumble. Tumbled are the towers,
Ruined the roofs, and broken the barred gate,
Frost in the plaster, all the ceilings gape,
Torn and collapsed and eaten up by age.
And grit holds in its grip, the hard embrace
Of earth, the dead departed master-builders,
Until a hundred generations now
Of people have passed by. Often this wall
Stained red and grey with lichen has stood by
Surviving storms while kingdoms rose and fell.
And now the high curved wall itself has fallen.

The heart inspired, incited to swift action.
Resolute masons, skilled in rounded building
Wondrously linked the framework with iron bonds.
The public halls were bright, with lofty gables,
Bath-houses many; great the cheerful noise,
And many mead-halls filled with human pleasures.
Till mighty fate brought change upon it all.
Slaughter was widespread, pestilence was rife,
And death took all those valiant men away.
The martial halls became deserted places,
The city crumbled, its repairers fell,
Its armies to the earth. And so these halls
Are empty, and this red curved roof now sheds

Its tiles, decay has brought it to the ground,
Smashed it to piles of rubble, where long since
A host of heroes, glorious, gold-adorned,
Gleaming in splendour, proud and flushed with wine,
Shone in their armour, gazed on gems and treasure,
On silver, riches, wealth and jewellery,
On this bright city with its wide domains.
Stone buildings stood, and the hot stream cast forth
Wide sprays of water, which a wall enclosed
In its bright compass, where convenient
Stood hot baths ready for them at the centre.
Hot streams poured forth over the clear grey stone,
To the round pool and down into the baths.

   probably Bath

ANDREW MARVELL

from Upon Appleton House

To The Lord Fairfax

Within this sober frame expect
Work of no foreign architect,
That unto caves the quarries drew,
And forests did to pastures hew;
Who, of his great design in pain,
Did for a model vault his brain;
Whose columns should so high be rais'd,
To arch the brows which on them gaz'd.
Why should, of all things, man, unrul'd,
Such unproportion'd dwellings build?
The beasts are by their dens express'd,
And birds contrive an equal nest;
The low-roof'd tortoises do dwell
In cases fit of tortoise-shell;

No creature loves an empty space;
Their bodies measure out their place.
But he, superfluously spread,
Demands more room alive than dead;
And in his hollow palace goes,
Where winds, as he, themselves may lose.
What need of all this marble crust,
To impark the wanton mole of dust,
That thinks by breadth the world to unite,
Though the first builders fail'd in height?
But all things are composed here,
Like nature, orderly, and near;
In which we the dimensions find
Of that more sober age and mind,
When larger-sized men did stoop
To enter at a narrow loop,
As practising in doors so strait,
To strain themselves through heaven's gate.

   Yorkshire

JAMES CLARENCE MANGAN

Lament over the Ruins of the Abbey of Teach Molaga

[from the Irish]

  I wandered forth at night alone
Along the dreary, shingly, billow-beaten shore;
Sadness that night was in my bosom's core,
   My soul and strength lay prone.

  The thin wan moon, half overveiled
By clouds, shed her funereal beams upon the scene;
While in low tones, with many a pause between,
   The mournful night-wind wailed.

Musing of Life, and Death, and Fate,
I slowly paced along, heedless of aught around,
Till on the hill, now, alas! ruin-crowned,
   Lo! the old Abbey-gate!

Dim in the pallid moonlight stood,
Crumbling to slow decay, the remnant of that pile
Within which dwelt so many saints erewhile
   In loving brotherhood!

The memory of the men who slept
Under those desolate walls – the solitude – the hour –
Mine own lorn mood of mind – all joined to o'erpower
   My spirit – and I wept!

In yonder Goshen once – I thought –
Reigned Piety and Peace: Virtue and Truth were there;
With Charity and the blessed spirit of Prayer
   Was each fleet moment fraught!

There, unity of Work and Will
Blent hundreds into one: no jealousies or jars
Troubled their placid lives: their fortunate stars
   Had triumphed o'er all Ill!

There, kneeled each morn and even
The Bell for Matin – Vesper: Mass was said or sung –
From the bright silver censer as it swung
   Rose balsamy clouds to Heaven.

Through the round cloistered corridors
A many a midnight hour, bareheaded and unshod,
Walked the Grey Friars, beseeching from their God
   Peace for these western shores.

The weary pilgrim bowed by Age
Oft found asylum there – found welcome, and found wine.
Oft rested in its halls the Paladine,
   The Poet and the Sage!

Alas! alas! how dark the change!
Now round its mouldering walls, over its pillars low,
The grass grows rank, the yellow gowans blow,
     Looking so sad and strange!

Unsightly stones choke up its wells;
The owl hoots all night long under the altar-stairs;
The fox and badger make their darksome lairs
     In its deserted cells!

Tempest and Time – the drifting sands –
The lightning and the rains – the seas that sweep around
These hills in winter-nights, have awfully crowned
     The work of impious hands!

The sheltering, smooth-stoned massive wall –
The noble figured roof – the glossy marble piers –
The monumental shapes of elder years –
     Where are they? Vanished all!

Rite, incense, chant, prayer, mass, have ceased –
All, all have ceased! Only the whitening bones half sunk
In the earth now tell that ever here dwelt monk,
     Friar, acolyte, or priest.

Oh! woe, that Wrong should triumph thus!
Woe that the olden right, the rule and the renown
Of the Pure-souled and Meek should thus go down
     Before the Tyrannous!

Where wert thou, Justice, in that hour?
Where was thy smiting sword? What had those good men done,
That thou shouldst tamely see them trampled on
     By brutal England's Power?

Alas! I rave! ... If Change is here,
Is it not o'er the land? Is it not too in me?
Yes! I am changed even more than what I see.
     Now is my last goal near!

My worn limbs fail – my blood moves cold –
Dimness is on mine eyes – I have seen my children die;
They lie where I too in brief space shall lie –
   Under the grassy mould!

I turned away, as toward my grave,
And, all my dark way homeward by the Atlantic's verge,
Resounded in mine ears like to a dirge
   The roaring of the wave.

   Co. Cork, Ireland

WILLIAM WORDSWORTH

from The Ruined Cottage

            It was a plot
Of garden ground now wild, its matted weeds
Marked with the steps of those whom as they passed,
The gooseberry trees that shot in long lank slips,
Or currants hanging from their leafless stems
In scanty strings, had tempted to o'erleap
The broken wall. Within that cheerless spot,
Where two tall hedgerows of thick alder boughs
Joined in a damp cold nook, I found a well
Half covered up with willow flowers and grass.
I slaked my thirst and to the shady bench
Returned, and while I stood unbonneted
To catch the motion of the cooler air
The old man said, 'I see around me here
Things which you cannot see. We die, my Friend,
Nor we alone, but that which each man loved
And prized in his pecular nook of earth
Dies with him, or is changed, and very soon
Even of the good is no memorial left.
The poets, in their elegies and songs

Lamenting the departed, call the groves,
They call upon the hills and streams to mourn,
And senseless rocks – nor idly, for they speak
In these their invocations with a voice
Obedient to the strong creative power
Of human passion. Sympathies there are
More tranquil, yet perhaps of kindred birth,
That steal upon the meditative mind
And grow with thought. Beside yon spring I stood,
And eyed its waters till we seemed to feel
One sadness, they and I. For them a bond
Of brotherhood is broken: time has been
When every day the touch of human hand
Disturbed their stillness, and they ministered
To human comfort. When I stopped to drink
A spider's web hung to the water's edge,
And on the wet and slimy footstone lay
The useless fragment of a wooden bowl.
It moved my very heart. [...]'

SIR WALTER SCOTT

from Rokeby, Canto V

III

Now through the wood's dark mazes past,
The opening lawn he reached at last,
Where, silvered by the moonlight ray,
The ancient Hall before him lay.
Those martial terrors long were fled,
That frowned of old around its head:
The battlements, the turrets grey,
Seemed half abandoned to decay;
On barbican and keep of stone

Stern Time the foeman's work had done;
Where banners the invader braved,
The hare-bell now and wall-flower waved;
In the rude guard-room, where of yore
Their weary hours the warders wore,
Now, while the cheerful faggots blaze,
On the paved floor the spindle plays;
The flanking guns dismounted lie,
The moat is ruinous and dry,
The grim portcullis gone – and all
The fortress turned to peaceful hall.

BEN JONSON

from To Penshurst

Thou art not, PENSHURST, built to envious show,
   Of touch, or marble; nor canst boast a row
Of polish'd pillars, or a roofe of gold:
   Thou hast no lantherne, whereof tales are told;
Or stayre, or courts; but stand'st an ancient pile,
   And these grudg'd at, art reverenc'd the while.
Thou joy'st in better markes, of soyle, of ayre,
   Of wood, of water: therein thou art faire.
Thou hast thy walkes for health, as well as sport:
   Thy *Mount*, to which the *Dryads* doe resort,
Where PAN, and BACCHUS their high feasts have made,
   Beneath the broad beech, and the chest-nut shade;
That taller tree, which of a nut was set,
   At his great birth, where all the Muses met.
There, in the writhed barke, are cut the names
   Of many a SYLVANE, taken with his flames.
And thence, the ruddy *Satyres* often provoke
   The lighter *Faunes*, to reach thy *Ladies oke*.
Thy copp's, too, nam'd of GAMAGE, thou hast there,

That never failes to serve thee season'd deere,
When thou would'st feast, or exercise thy friends.
   The lower land, that to the river bends,
Thy sheepe, thy bullocks, kine, and calves doe feed:
   The middle grounds thy mares, and horses breed.
Each banke doth yeeld thee coneyes; and the topps
   Fertile of Wood, ASHORE, and SYDNEY's copp's
To crowne thy open table, doth provide
   The purpled pheasant, with the speckled side:
The painted patrich lyes in every field,
   And, for thy messe, is willing to be kill'd.
And if the high-swolne *Medway* faile thy dish,
   Thou hast thy ponds, that pay thee tribute fish,
Fat, aged carps, that runne into thy net.
   And pikes, now weary their owne kinde to eat,
As loth, the second draught, or cast to stay,
   Officiously, at first, themselves betray.
Bright eeles, that emulate them, and leape on land,
   Before the fisher, or into his hand.
Then hath thy orchard fruit, thy garden flowers,
   Fresh as the ayre, and new as are the houres.
The earely cherry, with the later plum,
   Fig, grape, and quince, each in his time doth come:
The blushing apricot, and woolly peach
   Hang on thy walls, that every child may reach.
And though thy walls be of the countrey stone,
   They'are rear'd with no mans ruine, no mans grone,
There's none, that dwell about them, wish them downe;
   But all come in, the farmer, and the clowne:
And no one empty-handed, to salute
   Thy lord, and lady, though they have no sute.

ALEXANDER POPE

Blenheim Palace

See, sir, here's the grand approach,
This way is for his Grace's coach;
There lies the bridge, and here's the clock,
Observe the lion and the cock,
The spacious court, the colonnade,
And mark how wide the hall is made!
The chimneys are so well designed,
They never smoke in any wind.
This gallery's contrived for walking,
The windows to retire and talk in;
The council-chamber for debate,
And all the rest are rooms of state.

   'Thanks, sir,' cried I, ''tis very fine,
But where d'ye sleep, or where d'ye dine?
I find by all you have been telling,
That 'tis a house, but not a dwelling.'

V. SACKVILLE-WEST

Sissinghurst

A tired swimmer in the waves of time
I throw my hands up: let the surface close:
Sink down through centuries to another clime,
And buried find the castle and the rose.
      Buried in time and sleep,
      So drowsy, so overgrown,
That here the moss is green upon the stone,
      And lichen stains the keep.

I've sunk into an image, water-drowned,
Where stirs no wind and penetrates no sound,
Illusive, fragile to a touch, remote,
Foundered within the well of years as deep
As in the waters of a stagnant moat.
Yet in and out of these decaying halls
I move, and not a ripple, not a quiver,
Shakes the reflection though the waters shiver, –
My tread is to the same illusion bound.
Here, tall and damask as a summer flower,
Rise the brick gables and the spring tower;
     Invading Nature crawls
With ivied fingers over rosy walls,
     Searching the crevices,
Clasping the mullion, riveting the crack,
Binding the fabric crumbling to attack,
And questing feelers of the wandering fronds
     Grope for interstices,
Holding this myth together under-seas,
     Anachronistic vagabonds!

And here, by birthright far from present fashion,
As no disturber of the mirrored trance
I move, and to the world above the waters
     Wave my incognisance.

For here, where days and years have lost their number,
I let a plummet down in lieu of date,
And lose myself within a slumber
     Submerged, elate.

Churches and Churchyards

R. S. THOMAS

The Belfry

I have seen it standing up grey,
Gaunt, as though no sunlight
Could ever thaw out the music
Of its great bell; terrible
In its own way, for religion
Is like that. There are times
When a black frost is upon
One's whole being, and the heart
In its bone belfry hangs and is dumb.

But who is to know? Always,
Even in winter in the cold
Of a stone church, on his knees
Someone is praying, whose prayers fall
Steadily through the hard spell
Of weather that is between God
And himself. Perhaps they are warm rain
That brings the sun and afterwards flowers
On the raw graves and throbbing of bells.

THOMAS GRAY

Elegy Written in a Country Churchyard

The curfew tolls the knell of parting day,
The lowing herd wind slowly o'er the lea,
The ploughman homeward plods his weary way,
And leaves the world to darkness and to me.

Now fades the glimmering landscape on the sight,
And all the air a solemn stillness holds,
Save where the beetle wheels his droning flight,
And drowsy tinklings lull the distant folds;

Save that from yonder ivy-mantled tower
The moping owl does to the moon complain
Of such as, wandering near her secret bower,
Molest her ancient solitary reign.

Beneath those rugged elms, that yew-tree's shade,
Where heaves the turf in many a mouldering heap,
Each in his narrow cell for ever laid,
The rude forefathers of the hamlet sleep.

The breezy call of incense-breathing morn,
The swallow twittering from the straw-built shed,
The cock's shrill clarion or the echoing horn,
No more shall rouse them from their lowly bed.

For them no more the blazing hearth shall burn,
Or busy housewife ply her evening care:
No children run to lisp their sire's return,
Or climb his knees the envied kiss to share.

Oft did the harvest to their sickle yield,
Their furrow oft the stubborn glebe has broke;
How jocund did they drive their team afield!
How bowed the woods beneath their sturdy stroke!

Let not Ambition mock their useful toil,
Their homely joys and destiny obscure;
Nor Grandeur hear, with a disdainful smile,
The short and simple annals of the poor.

The boast of heraldry, the pomp of power,
And all that beauty, all that wealth e'er gave,
Awaits alike the inevitable hour.
The paths of glory lead but to the grave.

Nor you, ye Proud, impute to these the fault,
If Memory o'er their tomb no trophies raise,
Where through the long-drawn aisle and fretted vault
The pealing anthem swells the note of praise.

Can storied urn or animated bust
Back to its mansion call the fleeting breath?
Can Honour's voice provoke the silent dust,
Or Flattery soothe the dull cold ear of Death?

Perhaps in this neglected spot is laid
Some heart once pregnant with celestial fire;
Hands that the rod of empire might have swayed,
Or waked to ecstasy the living lyre.

But Knowledge to their eyes her ample page
Rich with the spoils of time did ne'er unroll;
Chill Penury repressed their noble rage,
And froze the genial current of the soul.

Full many a gem of purest ray serene
The dark unfathomed caves of ocean bear:
Full many a flower is born to blush unseen,
And waste its sweetness on the desert air.

Some village-Hampden that with dauntless breast
The little tyrant of his fields withstood;
Some mute inglorious Milton here may rest,
Some Cromwell guiltless of his country's blood.

The applause of listening senates to command,
The threats of pain and ruin to despise,
To scatter plenty o'er a smiling land,
And read their history in a nation's eyes,

Their lot forbade: nor circumscribed alone
Their growing virtues, but their crimes confined;
Forbade to wade through slaughter to a throne,
And shut the gates of mercy on mankind,

The struggling pangs of conscious truth to hide,
To quench the blushes of ingenuous shame,
Or heap the shrine of Luxury and Pride
With incense kindled at the Muse's flame.

Far from the madding crowd's ignoble strife
Their sober wishes never learned to stray;
Along the cool sequestered vale of life
They kept the noiseless tenor of their way.

Yet even these bones from insult to protect
Some frail memorial still erected nigh,
With uncouth rhymes and shapeless sculpture decked,
Implores the passing tribute of a sigh.

Their name, their years, spelt by the unlettered muse,
The place of fame and elegy supply:
And many a holy text around she strews,
That teach the rustic moralist to die.

For who to dumb Forgetfulness a prey,
This pleasing anxious being e'er resigned,
Left the warm precincts of the cheerful day,
Nor cast one longing lingering look behind?

On some fond breast the parting soul relies,
Some pious drops the closing eye requires;
Even from the tomb the voice of Nature cries,
Even in our ashes live their wonted fires.

For thee who, mindful of the unhonoured dead,
Dost in these lines their artless tale relate;
If chance, by lonely Contemplation led,
Some kindred spirit shall inquire thy fate,

Haply some hoary-headed swain may say,
'Oft have we seen him at the peep of dawn
Brushing with hasty steps the dews away
To meet the sun upon the upland lawn.

'There at the foot of yonder nodding beech
That wreathes its old fantastic roots so high,
His listless length at noontide would he stretch,
And pore upon the brook that babbles by.

'Hard by yon wood, now smiling as in scorn,
Muttering his wayward fancies he would rove,
Now drooping, woeful wan, like one forlorn,
Or crazed with care, or crossed in hopeless love.

'One morn I missed him on the customed hill,
Along the heath and near his favourite tree;
Another came; nor yet beside the rill,
Nor up the lawn, nor at the wood was he;

'The next with dirges due in sad array
Slow through the church-way path we saw him borne.
Approach and read (for thou canst read) the lay,
Graved on the stone beneath yon aged thorn.'

Stoke Poges, Buckinghamshire

A. E. HOUSMAN

Hughley Steeple

The vane on Hughley steeple
  Veers bright, a far-known sign,
And there lie Hughley people,
  And there lie friends of mine.
Tall in their midst the tower
  Divides the shade and sun,
And the clock strikes the hour
  And tells the time to none.

To south the headstones cluster,
  The sunny mounds lie thick;

The dead are more in muster
  At Hughley than the quick.
North, for a soon-told number,
  Chill graves the sexton delves,
And steeple-shadowed slumber
  The slayers of themselves.

To north, to south, lie parted,
  With Hughley tower above,
The kind, the single-hearted,
  The lads I used to love.
And, south or north, 'tis only
  A choice of friends one knows,
And I shall ne'er be lonely
  Asleep with these or those.

  Shropshire

EDWARD THOMAS

The Mountain Chapel

Chapel and gravestones, old and few,
Are shrouded by a mountain fold
From sound and view
Of life. The loss of the brook's voice
Falls like a shadow. All they hear is
The eternal noise
Of wind whistling in grass more shrill
Than aught as human as a sword,
And saying still:
"'Tis but a moment since man's birth
And in another moment more
Man lies in earth
For ever; but I am the same
Now, and shall be, even as I was

Before he came;
Till there is nothing I shall be.'
Yet there the sun shines after noon
So cheerfully
The place almost seems peopled, nor
Lacks cottage chimney, cottage hearth:
It is not more
In size than is a cottage, less
Than any other empty home
In homeliness.
It has a garden of wild flowers
And finest grass and gravestones warm
In sunshine hours
The year through. Men behind the glass
Stand once a week, singing, and drown
The whistling grass
Their ponies munch. And yet somewhere,
Near or far off, there's a man could
Live happy here,
Or one of the gods perhaps, were they
Not of inhuman stature dire,
As poets say
Who have not seen them clearly, if
At sound of any wind of the world
In grass-blades stiff
They would not startle and shudder cold
Under the sun. When gods were young
This wind was old.

KATHLEEN RAINE

Highland Graveyard

Today a fine old face has gone under the soil;
For generations past women hereabouts have borne
Her same name and stamp of feature.
Her brief identity was not her own
But theirs who formed and sent her out
To wear the proud bones of her clan, and live its story,
Who now receive back into the ground
Worn features of ancestral mould.

A dry-stone wall bounds off the dislimned clay
Of many an old face forgotten and young face gone
From boundless nature, sea and sky.
A wind-withered escalonia like a song
Of ancient tenderness lives on
Some woman's living fingers set as shelter for the dead, to tell
In evergreen unwritten leaves,
In scent of leaves in western rain
That one remembered who is herself forgotten.

Many songs they knew who now are silent.
Into their memories the dead are gone
Who haunt the living in an ancient tongue
Sung by old voices to the young,
Telling of sea and isles, of boat and byre and glen;
And from their music the living are reborn
Into a remembered land,
To call ancestral memories home
And all that ancient grief and love our own.

Canna, Inner Hebrides

BASIL BUNTING

At Briggflatts Meetinghouse

Boasts time mocks cumber Rome. Wren
set up his own monument.
Others watch fells dwindle, think
the sun's fires sink.

Stones indeed sift to sand, oak
blends with saints' bones.
Yet for a little longer here
stone and oak shelter

silence while we ask nothing
but silence. Look how clouds dance
under the wind's wing, and leaves
delight in transience.

   Cumbria

TONY HARRISON

The Earthen Lot

for Alistair Elliot
'From Isphahan to Northumberland, there is no building that does not
show the influence of that oppressed and neglected herd of men.'
William Morris, *The Art of the People*

Sand, caravans, and teetering sea-edge graves.

The seaward side's for those of lowly status.
Not only gales gnaw at their names, the waves
jostle the skulls and bones from their quietus.

The Church is a solid bulwark for their betters
against the scouring sea-salt that erodes
these chiselled sandstone formal Roman letters
to flowing calligraphic Persian odes,
singing of sherbet, sex in Samarkand,
with Hafiz at the hammams and harems,
O anywhere but bleak Northumberland
with responsibilities for others' dreams!

Not for the Northern bard the tamarinds
where wine is always cool, and *kusi* hot –

his line from Omar scrivened by this wind 's:

Some could articulate, while others not.

   Newbiggin-by-the-Sea, Northumberland

Death in the Countryside

ALEXANDER POPE

from Windsor-forest

See! from the brake the whirring pheasant springs,
And mounts exulting on triumphant wings:
Short is his joy; he feels the fiery wound,
Flutters in blood, and panting beats the ground.
Ah! what avail his glossy, varying dyes,
His purple crest, and scarlet-circled eyes,
The vivid green his shining plumes unfold,
His painted wings, and breast that flames with gold?
Nor yet, when moist *Arcturus* clouds the sky,
The woods and fields their pleasing toils deny.
To plains with well-breath'd beagles we repair,
And trace the mazes of the circling hare:
(Beasts, urg'd by us, their fellow beasts pursue,
And learn of man each other to undo.)
With slaught'ring guns th'unweary fowler roves,
When frosts have whiten'd all the naked groves;
Where doves in flocks the leafless trees o'ershade,
And lonely woodcocks haunt the wat'ry glade.
He lifts the tube, and levels with his eye;
Strait a short thunder breaks the frozen sky:
Oft', as in airy rings they skim the heath,
The clam'rous plovers feel the leaden death:
Oft', as the mounting larks their notes prepare,
They fall, and leave their little lives in air.

Berkshire

EDWARD THOMAS

The Gallows

There was a weasel lived in the sun
With all his family,
Till a keeper shot him with his gun
And hung him up on a tree,
Where he swings in the wind and rain,
In the sun and in the snow,
Without pleasure, without pain,
On the dead oak tree bough.

There was a crow who was no sleeper,
But a thief and a murderer
Till a very late hour: and this keeper
Made him one of the things that were,
To hang and flap in rain and wind,
In the sun and in the snow.
There are no more sins to be sinned
On the dead oak tree bough.

There was a magpie, too,
Had a long tongue and a long tail;
He could both talk and do –
But what did that avail?
He, too, flaps in the wind and rain
Alongside weasel and crow,
Without pleasure, without pain,
On the dead oak tree bough.

And many other beasts
And birds, skin, bone and feather,
Have been taken from their feasts
And hung up there together,
To swing and have endless leisure

In the sun and in the snow,
Without pain, without pleasure,
On the dead oak tree bough.

MARGARET CAVENDISH,
DUCHESS OF NEWCASTLE

The Hunting of the Hare

Betwixt two Ridges of Plowd-land, lay Wat,
Whose Body press'd to th'Earth lay close, and squat.
His Nose upon his two Fore-feet close lies,
Glaring obliquely with his great gray Eyes.
His Head he alwaies sets against the Wind;
If turne his Taile, his Haires blow up behind:
Which he too cold will grow, but he is wise,
And keeps his Coat still downe, so warm he lies.
Thus rests he all the day, still th'Sun doth set,
Then up he riseth his Reliefe to get,
And walks about until the Sun doth rise,
Then back returnes, downe in his Forme he lyes.
At last, Poore Wat was found, as he there lay,
By Hunts-men, with their Dogs which came that way
Whom seeing, he got up, and fast did run,
Hoping some waies the Cruell Dogs to shun.
But they by Nature have so quick a Sent,
That by their Nose they trace what way he went.
And with their deep, wide Mouths set forth a Cry,
Which answer'd was by Ecchoes in the Skie.
Then Wat was struck with Terrour, and with Feare,
Thinkes every Shadow still the Dogs they were.
And running out some distance from the noise,
To hide himselfe, his Thoughts he new imploies.
Under a Clod of Earth in Sand-pit wide,
Poore Wat sat close, hoping himselfe to hide.

There long he had not been, but strait his Eares
The Winding Hornes, and crying Dogs he heares:
Then starting up with Feare, he leap'd, and such
Swift speed he made, the Ground he scarce did touch;
Into a great thick Wood he strait way gets,
Where underneath a broken Bough he sits.
At every Leafe that with the wind did shake,
Did bring such Terrour, made his Heart to ake.
That Place he left, to Champion Plaines he went,
Winding about, for to deceive their Sent.
And while they snuffling were, to find his Track,
Poore Wat, being weary, his swift pace did slack.
On his two hinder legs for ease did sit,
His Fore-feet rub'd his Face from Dust, and Sweat.
Licking his Feet, he wip'd his Eares so cleane,
That none could tell that Wat had hunted been.
But casting round about his faire great Eyes,
The Hounds in full Careere he neere him 'spies:
To Wat it was so terrible a Sight,
Feare gave him Wings, and made his Body light.
Though weary was before, by running long,
Yet now his Breath he never felt more strong.
Like those that dying are, think Health returnes,
When tis but a faint Blast, which Life out burnes.
For Spirits seek to guard the Heart about,
Striving with Death, but Death doth quench them out.
The Hounds so fast came on, and with such cry,
That he no hopes hath left, nor help could 'spy.
With that the Winds did pity poore Wats case,
And with their Breath the Sent blew from the Place.
Then every Nose is busily imployed,
And every Nostrill is set open, wide:
And every Head doth seek a severall way,
To find the Grasse, or Track where the Sent lay.
For witty industry is never slack,
'Tis like to Witchery and brings lost things back.

For though the Wind had tied the Sent up close,
A Busie Dog thrust in his Snuffling Nose:
And drew that out, with it did foremost run,
Then Hornes blew loud, for th' rest to follow on.
The great slow-Hounds, their throats did set a Base,
The Fleet Swift Hounds, as Tenours next in place;
The little Beagles did a Trebble sing,
And through the Aire their Voices round did ring,
Which made such Consort, as they ran along;
That, had they spoken Words, 't had been a Song
The Hornes kept time, the Hunters shout for Joy,
And seem'd most Valiant, poor Wat to destroy:
Spurring their Horses to a full Careere,
Swim Rivers deep, leap Ditches without feare;
Indanger Life, and Limbes, so fast will ride,
Onely to see how patiently Wat died.
For why, the Dogs so neere his Heeles did get,
That their sharp Teeth they in his Breech did set.
Then tumbling downe, did fall with weeping Eyes,
Gives up his Ghost, and thus poore Wat he dies.
Men hooping loud, such Acclamations make,
As if the Devill they did Prisoner take.
When they do but a shiftlesse Creature kill;
To hunt, there needs no Valiant Souldiers skill.
But Man doth think that Exercise, and Toile,
To keep their Health, is best, which makes most spoile.
Thinking that Food, and Nourishment so good,
And Appetite, that feeds on Flesh, and Blood.
When they do Lions, Wolves, Beares, Tigers see,
To kill poore Sheep, strait say, they cruell be.
But for themselves all Creatures think too few,
For Luxury, wish God would make more new.
As if God did make Creatures for Mans meat,
To give them Life, and Sense, for Man to eat;
Or else for Sport, or Recreations sake,
Destroy those Lifes that God saw good to make:

Making their Stomacks, Graves, which full they fill
With Murther'd Bodies, that in sport they kill.
Yet Man doth think himselfe so gentle, mild,
When of all Creatures he's most cruell wild.
And is so Proud, thinks onely he shall live,
That God a God-like Nature him did give.
And that all Creatures for his sake alone,
Was made for him, to Tyrannize upon.

JAMES THOMSON

from The Seasons ('Autumn')

The stag, too, singled from the herd, where long
He ranged the branching monarch of the shades,
Before the tempest drives. At first, in speed
He sprightly puts his faith, and, roused by fear,
Gives all his swift aerial soul to flight.
Against the breeze he darts, that way the more
To leave the lessening murderous cry behind.
Deception short! though, fleeter than the winds
Blown o'er the keen-aired mountain by the North,
He bursts the thickets, glances through the glades,
And plunges deep into the wildest wood.
If slow, yet sure, adhesive to the track
Hot-steaming, up behind him come again
The inhuman rout, and from the shady depth
Expel him, circling through his every shift.
He sweeps the forest oft; and sobbing sees
The glades, mild opening to the golden day,
Where in kind contest with his butting friends
He wont to struggle, or his loves enjoy.
Oft in the full-descending flood he tries
To lose the scent, and lave his burning sides —
Oft seeks the herd; the watchful herd, alarmed,

With selfish care avoid a brother's woe.
What shall he do? His once so vivid nerves,
So full of buoyant spirit, now no more
Inspire the course; but fainting, breathless toil
Sick seizes on his heart: he stands at bay,
And puts his last weak refuge in despair.
The big round tears run down his dappled face;
He groans in anguish; while the growling pack,
Blood-happy, hang at his fair jutting chest,
And mark his beauteous chequered sides with gore.

JOHN MASEFIELD

from Reynard the Fox

The fox was strong, he was full of running,
He could run for an hour and then be cunning,
But the cry behind him made him chill,
They were nearer now and they meant to kill.
They meant to run him until his blood
Clogged on his heart as his brush with mud,
Till his back bent up and his tongue hung flagging,
And his belly and brush were filthed from dragging.
Till he crouched stone-still, dead-beat and dirty,
With nothing but teeth against the thirty.
And all the way to that blinding end
He would meet with men and have none his friend:
Men to holloa and men to run him,
With stones to stagger and yells to stun him;
Men to head him, with whips to beat him,
Teeth to mangle and mouths to eat him.
And all the way, that wild high crying,
To cold his blood with the thought of dying,
The horn and the cheer, and the drum-like thunder
Of the horsehooves stamping the meadow under.

He upped his brush and went with a will
For the Sarsen Stones on Wan Dyke Hill.

? Somerset

EBENEZER ELLIOT

from The Year of Seeds: Section XL

What Gods are these? Bright red, or white and green,
Some of them jockey-capp'd and some in hats,
The gods of vermin have their runs, like rats.
Each has six legs, four moving, pendent two,
Like bottled tails, the tilting four between.
Behold Land-Interest's compound Man-and-Horse,
Which so enchants his outraged helot-crew,
Hedge-gapping, with his horn, and view-halloo,
O'er hunter's clover – glorious broom and gorse!
The only crop his godship ever grew:
Except his crop of hate, and smouldering ire,
And cloak'd contempt, of coward insult born,
And hard-faced labour, paid with straw for corn,
And fain to reap it with a scythe of fire.

TED HUGHES

Coming Down through Somerset

I flash-glimpsed in the headlights – the high moment
Of driving through England – a killed badger
Sprawled with helpless legs. Yet again
Manoeuvred lane-ends, retracked, waited
Out of decency for headlights to die,
Lifted by one warm hind leg in the world-night

A slain badger. August dust-heat. Beautiful,
Beautiful, warm, secret beast. Bedded him
Passenger, bleeding from the nose. Brought him close
Into my life. Now he lies on the beam
Torn from a great building. Beam waiting two years
To be built into new building. Summer coat
Not worth skinning off him. His skeleton – for the future.
Fangs, handsome concealed. Flies, drumming,
Bejewel his transit. Heatwave ushers him hourly
Towards his underworlds. A grim day of flies
And sunbathing. Get rid of that badger.
A night of shrunk rivers, glowing pastures,
Sea-trout shouldering up through trickles. Then the sun again
Waking like a torn-out eye. How strangely
He stays on into the dawn – how quiet
The dark bear-claws, the long frost-tipped guard hairs!
Get rid of that badger today.
And already the flies
More passionate, bringing their friends. I don't want
To bury and waste him. Or skin him (it is too late).
Or hack off his head and boil it
To liberate his masterpiece skull. I want him
To stay as he is. Sooty gloss-throated,
With his perfect face. Paws so tired,
Power-body relegated. I want him
To stop time. His strength staying, bulky,
Blocking time. His rankness, his bristling wildness,
His thrillingly painted face.
A badger on my moment of life.
Not years ago, like the others, but now.
I stand
Watching his stillness, like an iron nail
Driven, flush to the head,
Into a yew post. Something has to stay.

    Somerset

Pastoral and Realism

EDMUND SPENSER

from The Faerie Queene, Book VI, Canto IX

From thence into the open fields he fled,
Whereas the Heardes were keeping of their neat,
And shepherds singing to their flockes (that fed)
Layes of sweete love and youthes delightfull heat:
Him thether eke, for all his fearefull threat.
He followed fast, and chaced him so nie,
That to the folds, where sheepe at night doe seat,
And to the litle cots, where shepherds lie
In winters wrathfull time, he forced him to flie.

There on a day, as he pursew'd the chace,
He chaunst to spy a sort of shepheard groomes,
Playing on pipes and caroling apace,
The whyles their beasts there in the budded broomes
Beside them fed, and nipt the tender bloomes;
For other worldly wealth they cared nought.
To whom Sir *Calidore* yet sweating comes,
And them to tell him courteously besought,
If such a beast they saw, which he had thether brought.

They answer'd him that no such beast they saw,
Nor any wicked feend that mote offend
Their happie flockes, nor daunger to them draw;
But if that such there were (as none they kend)
They prayd high God them farre from them to send.
Then one of them, him seeing so to sweat,
After his rusticke wise, that well he weend,
Offred him drinke to quench his thirstie heat,
And, if he hungry were, him offred eke to eat.

The knight was nothing nice, where was no need,
And tooke their gentle offer: so adowne
They prayd him sit, and gave him for to feed
Such homely what as serves the simple clowne,
That doth despise the dainties of the towne.
Tho, having fed his fill, he there besyde
Saw a faire damzell, which did weare a crowne
Of sundry flowres with silken ribbands tyde,
Yclad in home-made greene that her owne hands had dyde.

Upon a litle hillocke she was placed
Higher then all the rest, and round about
Environ'd with a girland, goodly graced,
Of lovely lasses; and them all without
The lustic shepheard swaynes sate in a rout,
The which did pipe and sing her prayses dew,
And oft rejoyce, and oft for wonder shout,
As if some miracle of heavenly hew
Were downe to them descended in that earthly vew.

WILLIAM SHAKESPEARE

from Henry VI, Part III, Act II, Scene v

King Henry:
O God! methinks it were a happy life
To be no better than a homely swain:
To sit upon a hill, as I do now,
To carve out dials quaintly point by point,
Thereby to see the minutes, how they run:
How many make the hour full complete,
How many hours bring about the day,
How many days will finish up the year,
How many years a mortal man may live.
When this is known, then to divide the times:

So many hours must I tend my flock;
So many hours must I take my rest;
So many hours must I contemplate;
So many hours must I sport myself;
So many days my ewes have been with young;
So many weeks ere the poor fools will yean;
So many years ere I shall shear the fleece:
So minutes, hours, days, months and years,
Pass'd over to the end they were created,
Would bring white hairs unto a quiet grave.
Ah, what a life were this, how sweet, how lovely!
Gives not the hawthorn bush a sweeter shade
To shepherds, looking on their silly sheep,
Than doth a rich embroider'd canopy
To kings, that fear their subjects' treachery?
O yes it doth; a thousand-fold it doth.
And to conclude; the shepherd's homely curds,
His cool thin drink out of his leather bottle,
His wonted sleep under a fresh tree's shade,
All which secure and sweetly he enjoys,
Is far beyhond a prince's delicates,
His viands sparkling in a golden cup,
His body couched in a curious bed,
When care, mistrust, and treason wait on him.

THOMAS DEKKER

from The Sun's Darling

Haymakers, rakers, reapers, and mowers,
   Wait on your Summer-Queen!
Dress up with musk-rose her eglantine bowers,
   Daffodils strew the green!
        Sing, dance, and play,
        'Tis holiday!

The sun does bravely shine
On our ears of corn.
    Rich as a pearl
    Comes every girl.
This is mine, this is mine, this is mine.
Let us die ere away they be borne.

Bow to our Sun, to our Queen, and that fair one
    Come to behold our sports:
Each bonny lass here is counted a rare one,
    As those in princes' courts.
        These and we
        With country glee,
Will teach the woods to resound,
And the hills with echoes hollow.
        Skipping lambs
        Their bleating dams
'Mongst kids shall trip it round;
For joy thus our wenches we follow.

Wind jolly huntsmen, your neat bugles shrilly,
    Hounds make a lusty cry;
Spring up, you falconers, partridges freely,
    Then let your brave hawks fly!
        Horses amain,
        Over ridge, over plain,
The dogs have the stag in chase:
'Tis a sport to content a king.
        So ho! ho! through the skies
        How the proud bird flies,
And sousing, kills with a grace!
Now the deer falls; hark! how they ring.

WILLIAM COWPER

from The Task, Book I

[...] When Winter soaks the fields, and female feet,
Too weak to struggle with tenacious clay,
Or ford the rivulets, are best at home,
The task of new discov'ries falls on me.
At such a season, and with such a charge,
Once went I forth; and found, till then unknown,
A cottage, whither oft we since repair.
'Tis perch'd upon the green-hill top, but close
Environ'd with a ring of branching elms
That overhang the thatch, itself unseen
Peeps at the vale below; so thick beset
With foliage of such dark redundant growth,
I call'd the low-roof'd lodge the *peasant's nest*.
And, hidden as it is, and far remote
From such unpleasing sounds as haunt the ear
In village or in town, the bay of curs
Incessant, clinking hammers, grinding wheels,
And infants clam'rous whether pleas'd or pain'd,
Oft have I wish'd the peaceful covert mine.
Here, I have said, at least I should possess
The poet's treasure, silence, and indulge
The dreams of fancy, tranquil and secure.
Vain thought! the dweller in that still retreat
Dearly obtains the refuge it affords.
Its elevated scite forbids the wretch
To drink sweet waters of the crystal well;
He dips his bowl into the weedy ditch,
And, heavy-laden, brings his bev'rage home,
Far-fetch'd and little worth, nor seldom waits,
Dependant on the baker's punctual call,
To hear his creaking panniers at the door,

Angry and sad, and his last crust consum'd.
So farewell envy of the *peasant's nest!*
If solitude make scant the means of life,
Society for me! – thou seeming sweet,
Be still a pleasing object in my view;
My visit still, but never mine abode. [...]

   Olney

GEORGE CRABBE

from The Village, Book I

Yes, thus the Muses sing of happy swains,
Because the Muses never knew their pains:
They boast their peasants' pipes, but peasants now
Resign their pipes and plod behind the plough;
And few amid the rural tribe have time
To number syllables and play with rhyme;
Save honest DUCK, what son of verse could share
The poet's rapture and the peasant's care?
Or the great labours of the field degrade
With the new peril of a poorer trade?

From this chief cause these idle praises spring,
That, themes so easy, few forbear to sing;
For no deep thought, the trifling subjects ask,
To sing of shepherds is an easy task;
The happy youth assumes the common strain,
A nymph his mistress and himself a swain;
With no sad scenes he clouds his tuneful prayer,
But all, to look like her, is painted fair.
I grant indeed that fields and flocks have charms,
For him that gazes or for him that farms;
But when amid such pleasing scenes I trace
The poor laborious natives of the place,

And see the mid-day sun, with fervid ray,
On their bare heads and dewy temples play;
While some, with feebler hands and fainter hearts
Deplore their fortune, yet sustain their parts,
Then shall I dare these real ills to hide,
In tinsel trappings of poetic pride?

No, cast by Fortune on a frowning coast,
Which neither groves nor happy vallies boast;
Where other cares than those the Muse relates,
And other shepherds dwell with other mates;
By such examples taught, I paint the cot,
As truth will paint it, and as bards will not:
Nor you, ye poor, of letter'd scorn complain,
To you the smoothest song is smooth in vain;
O'ercome by labour and bow'd down by time,
Feel you the barren flattery of a rhyme?
Can poets sooth you, when you pine for bread,
By winding myrtles round your ruin'd shed?
Can their light tales your weighty griefs o'erpower,
Or glad with airy mirth the toilsome hour?

Lo! where the heath, with withering brake grown o'er,
Lends the light turf that warms the neighbouring poor;
From thence a length of burning sand appears,
Where the thin harvest waves its wither'd ears;
Rank weeds, that every art and care defy,
Reign o'er the land and rob the blighted rye:
There thistles stretch their prickly arms afar,
And to the ragged infant threaten war;
There poppies nodding, mock the hope of toil,
There the blue bugloss paints the sterile soil;
Hardy and high, above the slender sheaf,
The slimy mallow waves her silky leaf;
O'er the young shoot the charlock throws a shade,
And clasping tares cling round the sickly blade;

With mingled tints the rocky coasts abound,
And a sad splendor vainly shines around.

So looks the nymph whom wretched arts adorn,
Betray'd by man, then left for man to scorn;
Whose cheek in vain assumes the mimic rose,
While her sad eyes the troubled breast disclose;
Whose outward splendor is but Folly's dress,
Exposing most, when most it gilds distress.

Here joyless roam a wild amphibious race,
With sullen woe display'd in every face;
Who, far from civil arts and social fly,
And scowl at strangers with suspicious eye.

   Aldeburgh, Suffolk coast

JAMES HEDDERWICK

from The Villa by the Sea

Mine is that delightful villa,
   Sweetly nesting by the sea;
Yet I sigh for a scintilla
   Of the bliss it promised me.

Though a pleasant cottage *orné*,
   Rich in trellis-work and flowers,
Here to sit and end my journey,
   How could I beguile the hours?

Love of Nature is a duty,
   And I fain would love it more.
But I weary of the beauty
   I have seen for weeks before.

Lofty are the hills and regal,
   Still they are the hills of old;

And like any other sea-gull
  Is the sea-gull I behold.

Tiresome 'tis to be a dreamer.
  When will it be time to dine?
Oh, that almost stand-still steamer,
  How it crawls across the brine!

  ? near Glasgow

WILLIAM SHAKESPEARE

from As You Like It, Act II, Scene v

Amiens sings:
  Under the greenwood tree,
  Who loves to lie with me,
  And turn his merry note
  Unto the sweet bird's throat,
Come hither, come hither, come hither:
    Here shall he see
    No enemy
But winter and rough weather. [...]

Amiens and his retinue sing:
  Who doth ambition shun,
  And loves to live i' the sun,
  Seeking the food he eats,
  And pleased with what he gets,
Come hither, come hither, come hither:
    Here shall he see
    No enemy
But winter and rough weather. [...]

Jaques replies:
  If it do come to pass
  That any man turn ass,

Leaving his wealth and ease
A stubborn will to please,
Ducdamè, ducdamè, ducdamè:
    Here shall he see
    Gross fools as he,
An if he will come to me.

Forest of Arden

Working the Land

JOHN CLARE

The Foddering Boy

The foddering boy along the crumping snows
With strawband-belted legs and folded arm
Hastens and on the blast that keenly blows
Oft turns for breath and beats his fingers warm
And shakes the lodging snows from off his cloaths
Buttoning his doublet closer from the storm
And slouching his brown beaver o'er his nose
Then faces it agen – and seeks the stack
Within its circling fence – where hungry lows
Expecting cattle making many a track
About the snows – impatient for the sound
When in hugh forkfulls trailing at his back
He litters the sweet hay about the ground
And brawls to call the staring cattle round

Northamptonshire/Cambridgeshire

PATRICK KAVANAGH

from The Great Hunger: Section XIII

The world looks on
And talks of the peasant:
The peasant has no worries;
In his little lyrical fields
He ploughs and sows;
He eats fresh food,

He loves fresh women,
He is his own master
As it was in the Beginning
The simpleness of peasant life.
The birds that sing for him are eternal choirs,
Everywhere he walks there are flowers.
His heart is pure,
His mind is clear,
He can talk to God as Moses and Isaiah talked –
The peasant who is only one remove from the beasts he
    drives.
The travellers stop their cars to gape over the green bank
    into his fields:–

There is the source from which all cultures rise,
And all religions,
There is the pool in which the poet dips
And the musician.
Without the peasant base civilisation must die,
Unless the clay is in the mouth the singer's singing is useless.
The travellers touch the roots of the grass and feel renewed
When they grasp the steering wheels again.

The peasant is the unspoiled child of Prophecy,
The peasant is all virtues – let us salute him without irony
The peasant ploughman who is half a vegetable –
Who can react to sun and rain and sometimes even
Regret that the Maker of Light had not touched him more
    intensely.
Brought him up from the sub-soil to an existence
Of conscious joy. He was not born blind.
He is not always blind: sometimes the cataract yields
To sudden stone-falling or the desire to breed.

The girls pass along the roads
And he can remember what man is,
But there is nothing he can do.

Is there nothing he can do?
Is there no escape?
No escape, no escape.

The cows and horses breed,
And the potato-seed
Gives a bud and a root and rots
In the good mother's way with her sons;
The fledged bird is thrown
From the nest – on its own.
But the peasant in his little acres is tied
To a mother's womb by the wind-toughened navel-cord
Like a goat tethered to the stump of a tree –
He circles around and around wondering why it should be.
No crash,
No drama.
That was how his life happened.
No mad hooves galloping in the sky,
But the weak, washy way of true tragedy –
A sick horse nosing around the meadow for a clean place to
    die.

Co. Monaghan, Ireland

R. S. THOMAS

A Peasant

Iago Prytherch his name, though, be it allowed,
Just an ordinary man of the bald Welsh hills,
Who pens a few sheep in a gap of cloud.
Docking mangels, chipping the green skin
From the yellow bones with a half-witted grin
Of satisfaction, or churning the crude earth
To a stiff sea of clods that glint in the wind –
So are his days spent, his spittled mirth

Rarer than the sun that cracks the cheeks
Of the gaunt sky perhaps once in a week.
And then at night see him fixed in his chair
Motionless, except when he leans to gob in the fire.
There is something frightening in the vacancy of his mind.
His clothes, sour with years of sweat
And animal contact, shock the refined,
But affected, sense with their stark naturalness.
Yet this is your prototype, who, season by season
Against siege of rain and the wind's attrition,
Preserves his stock, an impregnable fortress
Not to be stormed even in death's confusion.
Remember him, then, for he, too, is a winner of wars,
Enduring like a tree under the curious stars.

Wales

DOUGLAS DUNN

Washing the Coins

You'd start at seven, and then you'd bend your back
Until they let you stand up straight, your hands
Pressed on your kidneys as you groaned for lunch,
Thick sandwiches in grease-proofed bundles, piled
Beside the jackets by the hawthorn hedges.
And then you'd bend your little back again
Until they let you stand up straight. Your hands,
On which the earth had dried in layers, itched, itched,
Though worse still was that ache along the tips
Of every picking finger, each broken nail
That scraped the ground for sprawled potatoes
The turning digger churned out of the drills.
Muttering strong Irish men and women worked
Quicker than local boys. You had to watch them.

They had the trick of sideways-bolted spuds
Fast to your ear, and the upset wire basket
That broke your heart but made the Irish laugh.
You moaned, complained, and learned the rules of work.
Your boots, enlarging as the day wore on,
Were weighted by the magnets of the earth,
And rain in the face was also to have
Something in common with bedraggled Irish.
You held your hands into the rain, then watched
Brown water drip along your chilling fingers
Until you saw the colour of your skin
Through rips disfiguring your gloves of mud.
It was the same for everyone. All day
That bead of sweat tickled your smeared nose
And a glance upwards would show you trees and clouds
In turbulent collusions of the sky
With ground and ground with sky, and you portrayed
Among the wretched of the native earth,.
Towards the end you felt you understood
The happy rancour of the Irish howkers.
When dusk came down, you stood beside the byre
For the farmer's wife to pay the labour off.
And this is what I remember by the dark
Whitewash of the byre wall among shuffling boots.
She knew me, but she couldn't tell my face
From an Irish boy's, and she apologized
And roughed my hair as into my cupped hands
She poured a dozen pennies of the realm
And placed two florins there, then cupped her hands
Around my hands, like praying together.
It is not good to feel you have no future.
My clotted hands turned coins to muddy copper.
I tumbled all my coins upon our table.
My mother ran a basin of hot water.
We bathed my wages and we scrubbed them clean.
Once all that sediment was washed away,

That residue of field caked on my money,
I filled the basin to its brim with cold;
And when the water settled I could see
Two English kings among their drowned Britannias.

  Renfrewshire

V. SACKVILLE-WEST

from The Land ('Winter')

The common saying goes, that on the hill
A man may lie in bed to work his farm,
Propping his elbows on his window-sill
To watch his harvest growing like a charm.
But the man who works the wet and weeping soil
Down in the Weald, must marl and delve and till
His three-horse land, fearing nor sweat nor droil.
For through the winter he must fight the flood,
The clay, that yellow enemy, that rots
His land, sucks at his horses' hooves
So that his waggon plunges in the mud,
And horses strain, but waggon never moves;
Delays his plough, and holds his spud
With yeavy spite in trenching garden-plots,
The catchy clay, that does its utmost harm,
And comes into his house, to spoil
Even his dwelling creeps into his bones
Before their time, and makes them ache,
Leaving its token in his husky tones;
And all through summer he must see the clay
Harden as brick, and bake,
And open cracks to swallow up his arm,
Where neither harrow, hoe, nor rake
Can rasp a tilth, but young and eager shoots

Pierce into blank, and wither at the roots.
Yet with his stupid loyalty he will say,
Being a wealden man of wealden land,
Holding his wealden honour as a pledge,
'In times of drought those farms up on the ridge,
Light soil, half sand,
With the first summer gale blow half away',
And lifts his eye towards the hill with scorn.
But only a bold man ploughs the Weald for corn,
Most are content with fruit or pasture, knowing
Too well both drought and winter's heavy going;
So the lush Weald to-day
Lies green in distance, and the horizon's sweep
Deepens to blue in woods, with pointed spire
Pricking the foreground by the village tiles,
And the hop-kiln's whitened chimney stares between
Paler and darker green of Kentish miles,
And rarely a patch of corn in metal fire
Burnished by sunset ruffles in the green;
But meadow, shaw, and orchard keep
The glaucous country like a hilly sea
Pure in its monotone.

Kent

JAMES HURDIS

from The Favourite Village, Book IV

Now moves again, but with a sluggard's pace,
Not well awake, the plough. The harness'd team
Moves slowly forward, and not seldom stays,
Impeded sore by congregated clods.
The rooky tribe attend, and, perch'd at hand,
Watch the moist furrow with superior eye,

And brisk alight, upon the worm to prey,
Or sweeter grub unhous'd. Frequently there
Loiters, a grey-coat pensioner, the mew,
(His treasury the main left far behind,)
And shares the spoil terrene, with outstretch'd wing
The ploughman's clodded heel pursuing close,
And settling timorous. At length arrives
The hour of rest long look'd for, and the team
Of wearied steers, from the bright share releas'd,
Leave in the midst of the fresh field upturn'd
The plough recumbent, and with hurried pace
March cheerful homeward. Expedition clanks
The heavy chain which knits them pair to pair,
And oft the forward ox, impatient, drags
The lingerer behind, his brawny neck
Straining with pressure of the cumbrous yoke.
    Forth goes the weeding dame, her daily task
To travel the green wheat-field, ancle-deep
In the fresh blade of harvest yet remote.
Now with exerted implement she checks
The growth of noisome weeds, to toil averse,
An animal gregarious, fond of talk.
Lo! where the gossipping banditti stand
Amid field idle all, and all alike
With shrill voice prating, fluent as the pye.
Far off let me the noisy group behold,
Nothing molested by their loud harangue,
And think it well to see the fertile field
By their red tunics peopled, and the frock
Of the white husbandman that ploughs hard by,
Or guides the harrow team, or flings the grain
At ev'ry footstep with exerted arm
Over the yawning furrow. Never more
Pleases the rural landscape, than when man,
Drawn by the vernal sunbeam from his cell,
The needful culture of the field renews.

TED HUGHES

Crow Hill

The farms are oozing craters in
Sheer sides under the sodden moors:
When it is not wind it is rain,
Neither of which will stop at doors:
One will damp beds and the other shake
Dreams beneath sleep it cannot break.

Between the weather and the rock
Farmers make a little heat;
Cows that sway a bony back,
Pigs upon delicate feet
Hold off the sky, trample the strength
That shall level these hills at length.

Buttoned from the blowing mist
Walk the ridges of ruined stone.
What humbles these hills has raised
The arrogance of blood and bone,
And thrown the hawk upon the wind,
And lit the fox in the dripping ground.

West Yorkshire

THOMAS HARDY

In Time of 'The Breaking of Nations'

I

Only a man harrowing clods
   In a slow silent walk
With an old horse that stumbles and nods
   Half asleep as they stalk.

II

Only thin smoke without flame
   From the heaps of couch-grass;
Yet this will go onward the same
   Though Dynasties pass.

III

Yonder a maid and her wight
   Come whispering by:
War's annals will cloud into night
   Ere their story die.

   Dorset

Ownership and Dispossession

RUDYARD KIPLING

The Land

When Julius Fabricius, Sub-Prefect of the Weald,
In the days of Diocletian owned our Lower River-field,
He called to him Hobdenius – a Briton of the Clay,
Saying: 'What about that River-piece for layin' in to hay?'

And the aged Hobden answered: 'I remember as a lad
My father told your father that she wanted dreenin' bad.
An' the more that you neeglect her the less you'll get her
    clean.
Have it jest *as* you've a mind to, but, if I was you, I'd dreen.'

So they drained it long and crossways in the lavish Roman
    style –
Still we find among the river-drift their flakes of ancient tile,
And in drouthy middle August, when the bones of meadows
    show,
We can trace the lines they followed sixteen hundred years
    ago.

Then Julius Fabricius died as even Prefects do,
And after certain centuries, Imperial Rome died too.
Then did robbers enter Britain from across the Northern main
And our Lower River-field was won by Ogier the Dane.

Well could Ogier work his war-boat – well could Ogier
    wield his brand –
Much he knew of foaming waters – not so much of farming
    land.
So he called to him a Hobden of the old unaltered blood,
Saying: 'What about the River-piece; she doesn't look no good?'

And that aged Hobden answered: "Tain't for *me* to
    interfere,
But I've known that bit o' meadow now for five and fifty year.
Have it *jest* as you've a mind to, but I've proved it time on
    time,
If you want to change her nature you have *got* to give her
    lime!'

Ogier sent his wains to Lewes, twenty hours' solemn walk,
And drew back great abundance of the cool, grey, healing
    chalk.
And old Hobden spread it broadcast, never heeding what
    was in 't –
Which is why in cleaning ditches, now and then we find a
    flint.

Ogier died. His sons grew English – Anglo-Saxon was their
    name –
Till out of blossomed Normandy another pirate came;
For Duke William conquered England and divided with his
    men,
And our Lower River-field he gave to William of Warenne.

But the Brook (you know her habit) rose one rainy autumn
    night
And tore down sodden flitches of the bank to left and right.
So, said William to his Bailiff as they rode their dripping
    rounds:
'Hob, what about that River-bit – the Brook's got up no
    bounds?'

And that aged Hobden answered: "Tain't my business to
    advise,
But ye might ha' known 'twould happen from the way the
    valley lies.
Where ye can't hold back the water you must try and save
    the sile.
Hev it jest as you've a *mind* to, but, if I was you, I'd spile!'

They spiled along the water-course with trunks of willow-
    trees,
And planks of elms behind 'em and immortal oaken knees.
And when the spates of Autumn whirl the gravel-beds away
You can see their faithful fragments, iron-hard in iron clay.

Georgii Quinti Anno Sexto, I, who own the River-field,
Am fortified with title-deeds, attested, signed and sealed,
Guaranteeing me, my assigns, my executors and heirs
All sorts of powers and profits which – are neither mine nor
    theirs.

I have rights of chase and warren, as my dignity requires.
I can fish – but Hobden tickles. I can shoot – but Hobden
    wires.
I repair, but he reopens, certain gaps which, men allege,
Have been used by every Hobden since a Hobden swapped a
    hedge.

Shall I dog his morning progress o'er the track-betraying dew?
Demand his dinner-basket into which my pheasant flew?
Confiscate his evening faggot under which the conies ran,
And summons him to judgment? I would sooner summons
    Pan.

His dead are in the churchyard – thirty generations laid.
Their names were old in history when Domesday Book was
    made;
And the passion and the piety and prowess of his line
Have seeded, rooted, fruited in some land the Law calls
    mine.

Not for any beast that burrows, not for any bird that flies,
Would I lose his large sound council, miss his keen amending
    eyes.
He is bailiff, woodman, wheelwright, field-surveyor,
    engineer,
And if flagrantly a poacher – 'tain't for me to interfere.

'Hob, what about that River-bit?' I turn to him again,
With Fabricius and Ogier and William of Warenne.
'Hev it jest as you've a mind to, *but*' – and here he takes
   command.
For whoever pays the taxes old Mus' Hobden owns the land.

  ? Sussex

U. A. FANTHORPE

On Buying OS sheet 163

I own all this. Not loutish acres
That tax the spirit, but the hawking
Eye's freehold, paper country.

Thirtytwo inches of aqueduct,
Windmill (disused), club house, embankment,
Public conveniences

In rural areas. This is my
Landlocked landscape that lives in cipher,
And is truer than walking.

Red and imperial, the Romans
Stride eastward. Mysterious, yellow,
The Salt Way halts and is gone.

Here, bigger than the hamlets they are,
Wild wayside syllables stand blooming:
Filkins, Lechlade, Broughton Poggs.

Here only I discard the umber
Reticulations of sad cities,
The pull and drag of mud.

  Cheltenham and Cirencester (Gloucestershire)

OLIVER GOLDSMITH

from The Deserted Village

Sweet smiling village, loveliest of the lawn,
Thy sports are fled, and all thy charms withdrawn;
Amidst thy bowers the tyrant's hand is seen,
And desolation saddens all thy green:
One only master grasps the whole domain,
And half a tillage stints thy smiling plain;
No more thy glassy brook reflects the day,
But choked with sedges, works its weedy way;
Along thy glades, a solitary guest,
The hollow-sounding bittern guards its nest;
Amidst thy desert walks the lapwing flies,
And tires their echoes with unvaried cries.
Sunk are thy bowers, in shapeless ruin all,
And the long grass o'ertops the mouldering wall;
And, trembling, shrinking from the spoiler's hand,
Far, far away, thy children leave the land.

Ill fares the land, to hastening ills a prey,
Where wealth accumulates, and men decay:
Princes and lords may flourish, or may fade;
A breath can make them, as a breath has made;
But a bold peasantry, their country's pride,
When once destroyed, can never be supplied.

A time there was, ere England's griefs began,
When every rood of ground maintained its man;
For him light labour spread her wholesome store,
Just gave what life required, but gave no more:
His best companions, innocence and health;
And his best riches, ignorance of wealth.

But times are altered; trade's unfeeling train
Usurp the land and dispossess the swain;
Along the lawn, where scattered hamlets rose,

Unwieldly wealth, and cumbrous pomp repose;
And every want to opulence allied,
And every pang that folly pays to pride.
Those gentle hours that plenty bade to bloom,
Those calm desires that asked but little room,
Those healthful sports that graced the peaceful scene,
Lived in each look, and brightened all the green;
These, far departing seek a kinder shore,
And rural mirth and manners are no more.
    Sweet Auburn! parent of the blissful hour,
Thy glades forlorn confess the tyrant's power.
Here as I take my solitary rounds,
Amidst thy tangling walks, and ruined grounds,
And, many a year elapsed, return to view
Where once the cottage stood, the hawthorn grew,
Remembrance wakes with all her busy train,
Swells at my breast, and turns the past to pain.

    possibly Wiltshire

JOHN CLARE

Remembrances

Summer pleasures they are gone like to visions every one
& the cloudy days of autumn & of winter cometh on
I tried to call them back but unbidden they are gone
Far away from heart & eye & for ever far away
Dear heart & can it be that such raptures meet decay
I thought them all eternal when by Langley bush I lay
I thought them joys eternal when I used to shout & play
On its bank at 'clink & bandy' 'chock' & 'taw' & ducking
    stone
Where silence sitteth now on the wild heath as her own
Like a ruin of the past all alone

When I used to lie & sing by old east wells boiling spring
When I used to tie the willow boughs together for a 'swing'
& fish with crooked pins & thread & never catch a thing
With heart just like a feather – now as heavy as a stone
When beneath old lea close oak I the bottom branches broke
To make our harvest cart like so many working folk
& then to cut a straw at the brook to have a soak
O I never dreamed of parting or that trouble had a sting
Or that pleasures like a flock of birds would ever take to
    wing
Leaving nothing but a little naked spring

When jumping time away on old cross berry way
& eating awes like sugar plumbs ere they had lost the may
& skipping like a leveret before the peep of day
On the rolly polly up & downs of pleasant swordy well
When in round oaks narrow lane as the south got black
    again
We sought the hollow ash that was shelter from the rain
With our pockets full of peas we had stolen from the grain
How delicious was the dinner time on such a showry day
O words are poor receipts for what time hath stole away
The ancient pulpit trees & the play

When for school oer 'little field' with its brook & wooden
    brig
Where I swaggered like a man though I was not half so big
While I held my little plough though twas but a willow twig
& drove my team along made of nothing but a name
'Gee hep' & 'hoit' & 'woi' – O I never call to mind
These pleasant names of places but I leave a sigh behind
While I see the little mouldywharps hang sweeing to the
    wind
On the only aged willow that in all the field remains
& nature hides her face where theyre sweeing in their chains
& in a silent murmuring complains

Here was commons for their hills where they seek for
    freedom still
Though every commons gone & though traps are set to kill
The little homeless miners – O it turns my bosom chill
When I think of old 'sneap green' puddocks nook & hilly
    snow
Where bramble bushes grew & the daisy gemmed in dew
& the hills of silken grass like to cushions to the view
Where we threw the pissmire crumbs when we'd nothing
    else to do
All leveled like a desert by the never weary plough
All vanished like the sun where that cloud is passing now
& settled here for ever on its brow

O I never thought that joys would run away from boys
Or that boys would change their minds & forsake such
    summer joys
But alack I never dreamed that the world had other toys
To petrify first feelings like the fable into stone
Till I found the pleasure past & a winter come at last
Then the fields were sudden bare & the sky got over cast
& boyhoods pleasing haunts like a blossom in the blast
Was shrivelled to a withered weed & trampled down & done
Till vanished was the morning spring & set that summer sun
& winter fought her battle strife & won

By Langley bush I roam but the bush hath left its hill
On cowper green I stray tis a desert strange & chill
& spreading lea close oak ere decay had penned its will
To the axe of the spoiler & self interest fell a prey
& cross berry way & old round oaks narrow lane
With its hollow trees like pulpits I shall never see again
Inclosure like a Buonaparte let not a thing remain
It levelled every bush & tree & levelled every hill
& hung the moles for traitors – though the brook is running
    still
It runs a naker brook cold & chill

O had I known as then joy had left the paths of men
I had watched her night & day besure & never slept agen
& when she turned to [go] O I'd caught her mantle then
& wooed her like a lover by my lonely side to stay
Aye knelt & worshiped on as love in beautys bower
& clung upon her smiles as a bee upon a flower
& gave her heart my poesys all cropt in a sunny hour
As keepsakes & pledges all to never fade away
But love never heeded to treasure up the may
So it went the common road with decay

Helpston

WILLIAM BARNES

The Common a-Took In

Oh! no, Poll, no! Since they've a-took
The common in, our lew wold nook
Don't seem a-bit as used to look
    When we had runnèn room;
Girt banks do shut up ev'ry drong,
An' stratch wi' thorny backs along
Where we did use to run among
    The vuzzen an' the broom.

Ees; while the ragged colts did crop
The nibbled grass, I used to hop
The emmetbuts, vrom top to top,
    So proud o' my spry jumps:
Wi' thee behind or at my zide,
A-skippèn on so light an' wide
'S thy little frock would let thee stride,
    Among the vuzzy humps.

An' while the lark up auver head
Did twitter, I did sarch the red
Thick bunch o' broom, or yoller bed
   O' vuzzen vor a nest;
An' thou di'st hunt about, to meet
Wi' strawberries so red an' sweet,
Or clogs or shoes off hosses veet,
   Or wild thyme vor thy breast;

Or when the cows did run about
A-stung, in zummer, by the stout,
Or when they plaÿ'd, or when they foüght,
   Di'st stand a-lookèn on:
An' where white geese, wi' long red bills,
Did veed among the emmet-hills,
There we did goo to vind their quills
   Alongzide o' the pon'.

What fun there wer among us, when
The haÿward come, wi' all his men,
To drève the common, an' to pen
   Strange cattle in the pound;
The cows did bleäre, the men did shout
An' toss their eärms an' sticks about,
An' vo'ks, to own their stock, come out
   Vrom all the housen round.

   Bagber Common, Dorset

IAIN CRICHTON SMITH

The Clearances

The thistles climb the thatch. Forever
this sharp scale in our poems,
as also the waste music of the sea.

The stars shine over Sutherland
in a cold ceilidh of their own,
as, in the morning, the silver cane

cropped among corn. We will remember this.
Though hate is evil we cannot
but hope your courtier's heels in hell

are burning: that to hear
the thatch sizzling in tanged smoke
your hot ears slowly learn.

   Sutherland

NORMAN MACCAIG

A man in Assynt

Glaciers, grinding West, gouged out
these valleys, rasping the brown sandstone,
and left, on the hard rock below – the
ruffled foreland –
this frieze of mountains, filed
on the blue air – Stac Polly,
Cul Beag, Cul Mor, Suilven,
Canisp – a frieze and
a litany.

Who owns this landscape?
Has owning anything to do with love?
For it and I have a love-affair, so nearly human
we even have quarrels. –
When I intrude too confidently
it rebuffs me with a wind like a hand
or puts in my way
a quaking bog or a loch
where no loch should be. Or I turn stonily

away, refusing to notice
the rouged rocks, the mascara
under a dripping ledge, even
the tossed, the stony limbs waiting.

I can't pretend
it gets sick for me in my absence,
though I get
sick for it. Yet I love it
with special gratitude, since
it sends me no letters, is never
jealous and, expecting nothing
from me, gets nothing but
cigarette packets and footprints.

Who owns this landscape? –
The millionaire who bought it or
the poacher staggering downhill in the early morning
with a deer on his back?

Who possesses this landscape? –
The man who bought it or
I who am possessed by it?

False questions, for
this landscape is
masterless
and intractable in any terms
that are human.
It is docile only to the weather
and its indefatigable lieutenants –
wind, water and frost.
The wind whets the high ridges
and stunts silver birches and alders.
Rain falling down meets
springs gushing up –
they gather and carry down to the Minch
tons of sour soil, making bald

the bony scalp of Cul Mor. And frost
thrusts his hand in cracks and, clenching his fist,
bursts open the sandstone plates,
the armour of Suilven:
he bleeds stones down chutes and screes,
smelling of gunpowder.

Or has it come to this,
that this dying landscape belongs
to the dead, the crofters and fighters
and fishermen whose larochs
sink into the bracken
by Loch Assynt and Loch Crocach? –
to men trampled under the hoofs of sheep
and driven by deer to
the ends of the earth – to men whose loyalty
was so great it accepted their own betrayal
by their own chiefs and whose descendants now
are kept in their place
by English businessmen and the indifference
of a remote and ignorant government.

Where have they gone, the people
who lived between here and
Quinag, that tall
huddle of anvils that puffs out
two ravens into the blue and
looks down on the lochs of Stoer
where trout idle among reeds and
waterlilies – take one of them home

and smell, in a flower
the sepulchral smell of water.

   Sutherland

GEORGE MACKAY BROWN

Dead Fires

At Burnmouth the door hangs from a broken hinge
And the fire is out.

The windows of Shore empty sockets
And the hearth coldness.

At Bunertoon the small drains are choked.
Thrushes sing in the chimney.

Stars shine through the roofbeams of Scar.
No flame is needed
To warm ghost and nettle and rat.

Greenhill is sunk in a new bog.
No kneeling woman
Blows red wind through squares of ancient turf.

The Moss is a tumble of stones.
That one black stone
Is the stone where the hearth fire was rooted.

In Crawnest the sunken hearth
Was an altar for priests of legend,
Old seamen from the clippers with silken beards.

The three-toed pot at the wall of Park
Is lost to woman's cunning.
A slow fire of rust eats the cold iron.

The sheep drift through Reumin all winter.
Sheep and snow
Blanch fleetingly the black stone.

From that sacred stone the children of the valley
Drifted lovewards
And out of labour to the lettered kirkyard stone.

The fire beat like a heart in each house
From the first cornerstone
Till they led through a sagging lintel the last old one.

The poor and the good fires are all quenched.
Now, cold angel, keep the valley
From the bedlam and cinders of A Black Pentecost.

Orkney

BASIL BUNTING

Gin the Goodwife Stint

The ploughland has gone to bent
and the pasture to heather;
gin the goodwife stint,
she'll keep the house together.

Gin the goodwife stint
and the bairns hunger
the Duke can get his rent
one year longer.

The Duke can get his rent
and we can get our ticket
twa pund emigrant
on a C.P.R. packet.

Northumbria

Industrialization

PATRICK HANNAY

Croydon of the Charcoal Burners

In midst of these stands Croydon cloth'd in black,
In a low bottom sink of all these hills:
And is receipt of all the dirty wrack
Which from their tops still in abundance trills.
The unpav'd lanes with muddy mire it fills.
      If one shower fall, or if that blessing stay,
      You may well smell, but never see your way.

Surrey

JOHN DYER

from The Fleece

  Take we now our eastward course
To the rich fields of Burstal. Wide around
Hillock and valley, farm and village, smile;
And ruddy roofs and chimney-tops appear
Of busy Leeds, upwafting to the clouds
The incense of thanksgiving; all is joy,
And trade and business guide the living scene,
Roll the full cars, adown the winding Aire
Load the slow-sailing barges, pile the pack
On the low-tinkling train of slow-pac'd steeds.
As when a sunny day invites abroad
The sedulous ants, they issue from their cells
In bands unnumber'd, eager for their work;

O'er high, o'er low, they lift, they draw, they haste
With warm affection to each other's aid;
Repeat their virtuous efforts and succeed.
Thus all is here in motion, all is life;
The creaking wain brings copious store of corn;
The grazier's sleeky kine obstruct the roads;
The neat-dress'd housewives, for the festal board
Crown'd with full baskets, in the field-way paths
Come tripping on; the echoing hills repeat
The stroke of axe and hammer; scaffolds rise
And growing edifices; heaps of stone
Beneath the chisel beauteous shapes assume
Of frieze and column. Some with even line
New streets are marking in the neighbouring fields,
And sacred domes of worship. Industry,
Which dignifies the artist, lifts the swain,
And the straw cottage to a palace turns,
Over the work presides. Such was the scene
Of hurrying Carthage, when the Trojan chief
First view'd her growing turrets. So appear
Th' increasing walls of busy Manchester,
Sheffield and Birmingham, whose reddening fields
Rise and enlarge their suburbs. Lo, in throngs
For every realm the careful factors meet
Whispering each other. In long ranks the bales,
Like war's bright files, beyond the sight extend.
Straight ere the sounding bell the signal strikes,
Which ends the hour of traffic, they conclude
The speedy compact; and well-pleas'd transfer
With mutual benefit superior wealth
To many a kingdom's rent or tyrant's hoard.

Industrial towns of the North

JAMES BISSET

from Ramble of the Gods through Birmingham

Next day they rambled round the town, and swore,
'That such a place they never saw before':
They visited our Wharfs, and, wond'ring, found
Some thousand tons of coal piled on the ground,
And scores of boats, in length full sixty feet,
With loads of mineral fuel quite replete;
Whilst carts and country waggons filled each space,
And loaded teams stood ranged around the place.
    The Gods beheld the whole with great surprise,
And asked, 'from whence we gained such large supplies?'
For, though well versed in all empyreal scenes,
They here were posed, to find our 'Ways and Means.' –
    When satisfied – then told some hundred ton
Would be consumed that day, ere setting sun,
In Birmingham alone, – amazed they stood,
And ev'ry pile with admiration viewed.
    They next, attracted by the vivid gleams,
Saw marcasites dissolve in liquid streams,
And stubborn ores expand, and, smelting, flow
By strength of calefaction from below.
    To see the Pin-works then the Gods repair,
Nor wondered less at what they met with there,
To find it was in any mortal's pow'r
To point and cut twelve thousand pins an hour;
And fifty thousand heads their shapes acquire
In half that time, spun round elastic wire.
    The different Button-works they next review,
And seemed well pleased with sights so rare and new:
The various ores they saw rich hues impart,
Assuming different shapes, by skilful art;
And beauteous metals polished charms display,

In radiant colours ranged in fair array;
The process of the gilding looked well o'er,
Yet scarce could tell rich-gilt from semilore;
Each stamp, each lathe and press they careful scanned,
Then went to see the paper trays japanned;
Examined nicely ev'ry curious part,
And much admired th' improvements of the art...
Next, at the Gun-works, they surprised beheld
The lusty Cyclops musket-barrels weld;
Whilst peals like rattling thunder shook the roof,
When nit'rous powers proclaimed them Standard Proof.
The dread explosions, winged by echoes round,
Made Gods themselves to startle at the sound.
      To see the Buckle-works they next repaired;
'Twas ere that fancy trade was so impaired,
When all the makers had a full employ,
Which made some thousand hearts to dance for joy;
For buckles then by high and low were wore,
Nor were by Sprigs of Fashion deemed 'a Bore.'
A fatal epithet, however glossed,
For thousands by that word their bread have lost.
Ingenious engines proved mechanic pow'rs,
And happy passed the months, weeks, days and hours;
'The Toy-Shop of the World' then reared its crest,
Whilst hope and joy alternate filled each breast.
      Inventions curious, various kinds of toys,
Then occupied the time of men and boys,
And blooming girls at work were often seen,
That twice their ages joined was scarce fifteen,
Sent by their parents out their bread to seek,
Who'd earn, perhaps, some shillings in a week;
And many women, too, you then might see,
With children on the lap, or round the knee,
An honest livelihood intent to gain,
And their sweet infant race help to maintain.
Charmed with the sight, the Gods the whole reviewed,

And seemed with admiration quite subdued.
   To see each warlike weapon they resort,
And viewed the polished blade of various sort,
The scimitar, the sword, the faulchion bright,
Formed for the dreadful horrors of the fight;
Sharp pointed poniards and the sabre keen,
Spikes, spears and lances were in thousands seen.
   From thence they went well satisfied away,
To see the whip ingenious engines play;
Then Lloyd's famed mill for slitting iron rods,
Was honoured by the presence of the Gods.
   To Whitmore's then, intent on earth to scan
The wond'rous works of still more wond'rous man,
They next resorted; and hydraulics new,
Machines and rolling-mills with pleasure view;
Whilst sturdy Cyclops, anvils ranged around,
With thund'ring hammers made the air resound.

D. H. LAWRENCE

North Country

In another country, black poplars shake themselves over a
   pond,
And rooks and the rising smoke-waves scatter and wheel
   from the works beyond:
The air is dark with north and with sulphur, the grass is a
   darker green,
And people darkly invested with purple move palpable
   through the scene.

Soundlessly down across the counties, out of the resonant
   gloom
That wraps the north in stupor and purple travels the deep,
   slow boom

Of the man-life north imprisoned, shut in the hum of the
 purpled steel
As it spins to sleep on its motion, drugged dense in the sleep
 of the wheel.

Out of the sleep, from the gloom of motion, soundlessly,
 somnambule
Moans and booms the soul of a people imprisoned, asleep in
 the rule
Of the strong machine that runs mesmeric, booming the
 spell of its word
Upon them and moving them helpless, mechanic, their will
 to its will deferred.

Yet all the while comes the droning inaudible, out of the
 violet air,
The moaning of sleep-bound beings in travail that toil and
 are will-less there.
In the spellbound north, convulsive now with a dream near
 morning, strong
With violent achings heaving to burst the sleep that is now
 not long.

North of England

JOHN DALTON

from A Descriptive Poem, Addressed to Two
Ladies, at their Return from Viewing the Mines,
near Whitehaven

Agape the sooty collier stands,
His axe suspended in his hands,
His Ethiopian teeth the while
'Grin horrible a ghastly smile,'
To see two goddesses so fair

Descend to him from fields of air.
Not greater wonder seized th' abode
Of gloomy Dis, infernal god,
With pity when th' Orphean lyre
Did ev'ry iron heart inspire,
Soothed tortured ghosts with heavenly strains,
And respited eternal pains.
    But on you move through ways less steep
To loftier chambers of the deep,
Whose jetty pillars seem to groan
Beneath a ponderous roof of stone.
Then with increasing wonder gaze
The dark inextricable maze,
Where cavern crossing cavern meets
(City of subterraneous streets!),
Where in a triple storey end
Mines that o'er mines by flights ascend.
    But who in order can relate
What terrors still your steps await?
How issuing from the sulphurous coal
Thick Acherontic rivers roll?
How in close centre of these mines,
Where orient morning never shines,
Nor the winged zephyrs e'er resort,
Infernal Darkness holds her court?
How, breathless, with faint pace and slow,
Through her grim sultry realm you go,
Till purer rising gales dispense
Their cordials to the sick'ning sense?
    Your progress next the wondering muse
Through narrow galleries pursues;
Where earth, the miner's way to close,
Did once the massy rock oppose.
In vain: his daring axe he heaves,
Towards the black vein a passage cleaves:
Dissevered by the nitrous blast,

The stubborn barrier bursts at last.
Thus, urged by Hunger's clamorous call,
Incessant Labour conquers all.

Cumbria

C. DAY LEWIS

From Feathers to Iron: Poem 12

As one who wanders into old workings
Dazed by the noonday, desiring coolness,
Has found retreat barred by fall of rockface;
Gropes through galleries where granite bruises
Taut palm and panic patters close at heel;
Must move forward as tide to the moon's nod,
As mouth to breast in blindness is beckoned.
Nightmare nags at his elbow and narrows
Horizon to pinpoint, hope to hand's breadth.
Slow drip the seconds, time is stalactite,
For nothing intrudes here to tell the time,
Sun marches not, nor moon with muffled step.
He wants an opening, – only to break out,
To see the dark glass cut by day's diamond,
To relax again in the lap of light.

But we seek a new world through old workings,
Whose hope lies like seed in the loins of earth,
Whose dawn draws gold from the roots of darkness.
Not shy of light nor shrinking from shadow
Like Jesuits in jungle we journey
Deliberately bearing to brutish tribes
Christ's assurance, arts of agriculture.
As a train that travels underground track
Feels current flashed from far-off dynamos,
Our wheels whirling with impetus elsewhere

Generated we run, are ruled by rails.
Train shall spring from tunnel to terminus,
Out on to plain shall the pioneer plunge,
Earth reveal what veins fed, what hill covered.
Lovely the leap, explosion into light.

TONY HARRISON

National Trust

Bottomless pits. There's one in Castleton,
and stout upholders of our law and order
one day thought its depth worth wagering on
and borrowed a convict hush-hush from his warder
and winched him down; and back, flayed, grey, mad, dumb.

Not even a good flogging made him holler.

O gentlemen, a better way to plumb
the depths of Britain 's dangling a scholar,
say, here at the booming shaft at Towanroath,
now National Trust, a place where they got tin,
those gentlemen who silenced the men's oath
and killed the language that they swore it in.

The dumb go down in history and disappear
and not one gentleman's been brought to book:

Mes den hep tavas a-gollas y dyr

(Cornish) – 'the tongueless man gets his land took.'

North Yorkshire

GILLIAN CLARKE

East Moors

At the end of a bitter April
the cherries flower at last in Penylan.
We notice the white trees and the flash
of sea with two blue islands beyond
the city, where the steelworks used to smoke.

I live in the house I was born in,
am accustomed to the sudden glow
of flame in the night sky, the dark sound
of something heavy dropped, miles off,
the smell of sulphur almost natural.

In Roath and Rumney now, washing strung
down the narrow gardens will stay clean.
Lethargy settles in front rooms and wives
have lined up little jobs for men to do.

A few men stay to see it through. Theirs
the bitterest time as rolling mills
make rubble. Demolition gangs
erase skylines whose hieroglyphs
recorded all our stories.

I am reminded of that Sunday
years ago when we brought the children
to watch two water cooling towers
blown up, recall the appalling void
in the sunlight, like a death.

On this first day of May an icy
rain is blowing through this town,
quieter, cleaner, poorer from today.
The cherries are in flower in Penylan.
Already over East Moors the sky whitens, blind.

South Glamorgan

Violation of Nature and
the Landscape

OLIVER GOLDSMITH

from The Deserted Village

   Ye friends to truth, ye statesmen, who survey
The rich man's joys encrease, the poor's decay,
'Tis yours to judge, how wide the limits stand
Between a splendid and a happy land.
Proud swells the tide with loads of freighted ore,
And shouting Folly hails them from her shore;
Hoards even beyond the miser's wish abound,
And rich men flock from all the world around.
Yet count our gains. This wealth is but a name
That leaves our useful products still the same.
Not so the loss. The man of wealth and pride
Takes up a space that many poor supplied;
Space for his lake, his park's extended bounds,
Space for his horses, equipage, and hounds;
The robe that wraps his limbs in silken sloth,
Has robbed the neighbouring fields of half their growth;
His seat, where solitary sports are seen,
Indignant spurns the cottage from the green;
Around the world each needful product flies,
For all the luxuries the world supplies.
While thus the land, adorned for pleasure, all
In barren splendour feebly waits the fall.
   As some fair female unadorned and plain,
Secure to please while youth confirms her reign,
Slights every borrowed charm that dress supplies,
Nor shares with art the triumph of her eyes.

But when those charms are past, for charms are frail,
When time advances, and when lovers fail,
She then shines forth, solicitous to bless,
In all the glaring impotence of dress.
Thus fares the land, by luxury betrayed;
In nature's simplest charms at first arrayed;
But verging to decline, its splendours rise,
Its vistas strike, its palaces surprise;
While, scourged by famine from the smiling land,
The mournful peasant leads his humble band;
And while he sinks, without one arm to save,
The country blooms – a garden, and a grave.

    Possibly Wiltshire

WILLIAM WORDSWORTH

Nutting

          It seems a day
(I speak of one from many singled out)
One of those heavenly days that cannot die;
When, in the eagerness of boyish hope,
I left our cottage-threshold, sallying forth
With a huge wallet o'er my shoulders slung,
A nutting-crook in hand; and turned my steps
Tow'rd some far-distant wood, a Figure quaint,
Tricked out in proud disguise of cast-off weeds
Which for that service had been husbanded,
By exhortation of my frugal Dame –
Motley accoutrement, of power to smile
At thorns, and brakes, and brambles, – and in truth
More ragged than need was! O'er pathless rocks,
Through beds of matted fern, and tangled thickets,
Forcing my way, I came to one dear nook

Unvisited, where not a broken bough
Drooped with its withered leaves, ungracious sign
Of devastation; but the hazels rose
Tall and erect, with tempting clusters hung,
A virgin scene! – A little while, I stood,
Breathing with such suppression of the heart
As joy delights in; and with wise restraint
Voluptuous, fearless of a rival, eyed
The banquet; – or beneath the trees I sate
Among the flowers, and with the flowers I played;
A temper known to those who, after long
And weary expectation, have been blest
With sudden happiness beyond all hope.
Perhaps it was a bower beneath whose leaves
The violets of five seasons re-appear
And fade, unseen by any human eye;
Where fairy water-breaks do murmur on
For ever; and I saw the sparkling foam,
And – with my cheek on one of those green stones
That, fleeced with moss, under the shady trees,
Lay round me, scattered like a flock of sheep –
I heard the murmur and the murmuring sound,
In that sweet mood when pleasure loves to pay
Tribute to ease; and, of its joy secure,
The heart luxuriates with indifferent things,
Wasting its kindliness on stocks and stones,
And on the vacant air. Then up I rose,
And dragged to earth both branch and bough, with crash
And merciless ravage: and the shady nook
Of hazels, and the green and mossy bower,
Deformed and sullied, patiently gave up
Their quiet being: and unless I now
Confound my present feelings with the past,
Ere from the mutilated bower I turned
Exulting, rich beyond the wealth of kings,
I felt a sense of pain when I beheld

The silent trees, and saw the intruding sky. –
Then, dearest Maiden, move along these shades
In gentleness of heart; with gentle hand
Touch – for there is a spirit in the woods.

  Lake District

STEPHEN SPENDER

The Pylons

The secret of these hills was stone, and cottages
Of that stone made,
And crumbling roads
That turned on sudden hidden villages.

Now over these small hills, they have built the concrete
That trails black wire;
Pylons, those pillars
Bare like nude, giant girls that have no secret.

The valley with its gilt and evening look
And the green chestnut
Of customary root,
Are mocked dry like the parched bed of a brook.

But far above and far as sight endures
Like whips of anger
With lightning's danger
There runs the quick perspective of the future.

This dwarfs our emerald country by its trek
So tall with prophecy:
Dreaming of cities
Where often clouds shall lean their swan-white neck.

W. H. AUDEN

from 'The summer holds: upon its glittering lake'

Hiker with sunburn blisters on your office pallor,
Cross-country champion with corks in your hands,
When you have eaten your sandwich, your salt and your
    apple,
When you have begged your glass of milk from the ill-kept
    farm,
What is it you see?

I see barns falling, fences broken,
Pasture not ploughland, weeds not wheat.
The great houses remain but only half are inhabited,
Dusty the gunrooms and the stable clocks stationary.
Some have been turned into prep-schools where the diet is in
    the hands of an experienced matron,
Others into club-houses for the golf-bore and the top-hole.
Those who sang in the inns at evening have departed; they
    saw their hope in another country,
Their children have entered the service of the suburban
    areas; they have become typists, mannequins and factory
    operatives; they desired a different rhythm of life.
But their places are taken by another population, with views
    about nature,
Brought in charabanc and saloon along arterial roads;
Tourists to whom the Tudor cafés
Offer Bovril and buns upon Breton ware
With leather-work as a sideline: Filling stations
Supplying petrol from rustic pumps.
Those who fancy themselves as foxes or desire a special
    setting for spooning
Erect their villas at the right places,
Airtight, lighted, elaborately warmed;

And nervous people who will never marry
Live upon dividends in the old-world cottages
With an animal for friend or a volume of memoirs.

JOHN BETJEMAN

The Planster's Vision

Cut down that timber! Bells, too many and strong,
    Pouring their music through the branches bare,
    From moon-white church-towers down the windy air
Have pealed the centuries out with Evensong.
Remove those cottages, a huddled throng!
    Too many babies have been born in there,
    Too many coffins, bumping down the stair,
Carried the old their garden paths along.

I have a Vision of The Future, chum,
    The workers' flats in fields of soya beans
        Tower up like silver pencils, score on score:
And Surging Millions hear the Challenge come
    From microphones in communal canteens
        'No Right! No Wrong! All's perfect, evermore.'

PHILIP LARKIN

Going, Going

I thought it would last my time –
The sense that, beyond the town,
There would always be fields and farms,
Where the village louts could climb
Such trees as were not cut down;
I knew there'd be false alarms

In the papers about old streets
And split-level shopping, but some
Have always been left so far;
And when the old part retreats
As the bleak high-risers come
We can always escape in the car.

Things are tougher than we are, just
As earth will always respond
However we mess it about;
Chuck filth in the sea, if you must:
The tides will be clean beyond.
– But what do I feel now? Doubt?

Or age, simply? The crowd
Is young in the M1 café;
Their kids are screaming for more –
More houses, more parking allowed,
More caravan sites, more pay.
On the Business Page, a score

Of spectacled grins approve
Some takeover bid that entails
Five per cent profit (and ten
Per cent more in the estuaries): move
Your works to the unspoilt dales
(Grey area grants)! And when

You try to get near the sea
In summer...
                    It seems, just now,
To be happening so very fast;
Despite all the land left free
For the first time I feel somehow
That it isn't going to last,

That before I snuff it, the whole
Boiling will be bricked in

Except for the tourist parts –
First slum of Europe: a role
It won't be so hard to win,
With a cast of crooks and tarts.

And that will be England gone,
The shadows, the meadows, the lanes,
The guildhalls, the carved choirs.
There'll be books; it will linger on
In galleries; but all that remains
For us will be concrete and tyres.

Most things are never meant.
This won't be, most likely: but greeds
And garbage are too thick-strewn
To be swept up now, or invent
Excuses that make them all needs.
I just think it will happen, soon.

JOHN HEATH-STUBBS

The Green Man's Last Will and Testament

An Eclogue
for Adrian Risdon

In a ragged spinney (scheduled
For prompt development as a bijou housing estate)
I saw the green daemon of England's wood
As he wrote his testament. The grey goose
Had given him one of her quills for a pen;
The robin's breast was a crimson seal;
The long yellow centipede held a candle.

He seemed like a hollow oak-trunk, smothered with ivy:
At his feet or roots clustered the witnesses,
Like hectic toadstools, or pallid as broom-rape:

Wood-elves – goodfellows, hobs and lobs,
Black Anis, the child-devouring hag,
From her cave in the Dane Hills, saucer-eyed
Phantom dogs, Black Shuck and Barghest, with the cruel
   nymphs
Of the northern streams, Peg Powler of the Tees
And Jenny Greenteeth of the Ribble,
Sisters of Bellisama, the very fair one.

'I am sick, I must die,' he said. 'Poisoned like Lord Randal
From hedges and ditches. My ditches run with pollution,
My hedgerows are gone, and the hedgerow singers.
The rooks, disconsolate, have lost their rookery:
The elms are all dead of the Dutch pox.
No longer the nightjar churns in the twilit glade,
Nor the owl, like a white phantom, silent-feathered
Glides to the barn. The red-beaked chough,
Enclosing Arthur's soul, is seen no more
Wheeling and calling over the Cornish cliffs.
Old Tod has vacated his deep-dug earth;
He has gone to rummage in the city dustbins.
Tiggy is squashed flat on the M1.

'My delicate deer are culled, and on offshore islands
My sleek silkies, where puffin and guillemot
Smother and drown in oil and tar.
The mechanical reaper has guillotined
Ortygometra, though she was no traitor,
Crouching over her cradle – no longer resounds
Crek-crek, *crek-crek*, among the wheatfields,
Where the scarlet cockle is missing and the blue cornflower.
My orchids and wild hyacinths are raped and torn,
My lenten lilies and my fritillaries.
Less frequent now the debate
Of cuckoo and nightingale – and where is the cuckoo's
   maid,
The snake-necked bird sacred to Venus,

Her mysteries and the amber twirling wheel?
In no brightness of air dance now the butterflies –
Their hairy mallyshags are slaughtered among the nettles.
The innocent bats are evicted from the belfries,
The death-watch remains, and masticates history.

'I leave to the people of England
All that remains:
Rags and patches – a few old tales
And bawdy yokes, snatches of song and galumphing dance-
    steps.
Above all my obstinacy – obstinacy of flintstones
That breed in the soil, and pertinacity
Of unlovely weeds – chickweed and groundsel,
Plantain, shepherd's purse and Jack-by-the-hedge.
Let them keep it as they wander in the inhuman towns.

'And the little children, imprisoned in ogrish towers,
    enchanted
By a one-eyed troll in front of a joyless fire –
I would have them remember the old games and the old
    dances:
Sir Roger is dead, Sir Roger is dead,
She raised him up under the apple tree;
Poor Mary is a-weeping, weeping like Ariadne,
Weeping for her husband on a bright summer's day.'

Villages and Small Towns

R. S. THOMAS

The Village

Scarcely a street, too few houses
To merit the title; just a way between
The one tavern and the one shop
That leads nowhere and fails at the top
Of the short hill, eaten away
By long erosion of the green tide
Of grass creeping perpetually nearer
This last outpost of time past.

So little happens; the black dog
Cracking his fleas in the hot sun
Is history. Yet the girl who crosses
From door to door moves to a scale
Beyond the bland day's two dimensions.

Stay, then, village, for round you spins
On slow axis a world as vast
And meaningful as any poised
By great Plato's solitary mind.

   Tregynon, Montgomery

THOMAS HOOD

Our Village – by a Villager

Our village, that's to say, not Miss Mitford's village, but our
  village of Bullock Smithy,
Is come into by an avenue of trees, three oak pollards, two
  elders, and a withy;
And in the middle there's a green of about not exceeding an
  acre and a half;
It's common to all, and fed off by nineteen cows, six ponies,
  three horses, five asses, two foals, seven pigs, and a calf!
Besides a pond in the middle, as is held by a similar sort of
  common-law lease,
And contains twenty ducks, six drakes, three ganders, two
  dead dogs, four drowned kittens, and twelve geese.
Of course the green's cropt very close, and does famous for
  bowling when the little village-boys play at cricket;
Only some horse, or pig, or cow, or great jackass, is sure to
  come and stand right before the wicket.
There's fifty-five private houses, let alone barns, and
  workshops, and pigsties, and poultry huts, and such-like
  sheds;
With plenty of public-houses – two Foxes, one Green Man,
  three Bunch of Grapes, one Crown, and six King's Heads.
The Green Man is reckoned the best, as the only one that for
  love or money can raise
A postilion, a blue-jacket, two deplorable lame white horses,
  and a ramshackled 'neat postchaise'.
There's one parish church for all the people, whatsoever
  may be their ranks in life or their degrees,
Except one very damp, small, dark, freezing-cold, little
  Methodist Chapel of Ease;
And close by the churchyard there's a stonemason's yard,
  that when the time is seasonable

Will furnish with afflictions sore and marble urns and
  cherubims very low and reasonable.
There's a cage, comfortable enough; I've been in it with Old
  Jack Jeffrey and Tom Pike;
For the Green Man next door will send you in ale, gin, or
  anything else you like.
I can't speak of the stocks, as nothing remains of them but
  the upright post;
But the pound is kept in repairs for the sake of Cob's horse,
  as is always there almost.
There's a smithy of course, where that queer sort of a chap
  in his way, Old Joe Bradley,
Perpetually hammers and stammers, for he stutters and
  shoes horses very badly.
There's a shop of all sorts, that sells everything, kept by the
  widow of Mr Task;
But when you go there, it's ten to one she's out of everything
  you ask.
You'll know her house by the swarm of boys, like flies,
  about the old sugary cask:
There are six empty houses, and not so well papered inside
  as out,
For bill-stickers wont beware, but sticks notices of sales and
  election placards all about.
That's the Doctor's with a green door, where the garden
  pots in the windows are seen –
A weakly monthly rose that don't blow, and a dead
  geranium, and a tea-plant with five black leaves and one
  green.
As for hollyoaks at the cottage doors, and honeysuckles and
  jasmines, you may go and whistle;
But the tailor's front garden grows two cabbages, a dock, a
  ha'porth of pennyroyal, two dandelions, and a thistle.
There are three small orchards – Mr Busby's the
  schoolmaster's is the chief –

With two pear-trees that don't bear; one plum and an apple,
that every year is stripped by a thief.
There's another small day-school too, kept by the
respectable Mrs Gaby,
A select establishment, for six little boys and one big, and
four little girls and a baby;
There's a rectory, with pointed gables and strange odd
chimneys that never smokes,
For the rector don't live on his living like other Christian
sort of folks;
There's a barber's, once a week well filled with rough black-
bearded, shock-headed churls,
And a window with two feminine men's heads, and two
masculine ladies in false curls;
There's a butcher's, and a carpenter's, and a plumber's, and
a small greengrocer's, and a baker,
But he wont bake on a Sunday; and there's a sexton that's a
coalmerchant besides, and an undertaker;
And a toyshop, but not a whole one, for a village can't
compare with the London shops;
One window sells drums, dolls, kites, carts, bats, Clout's
balls, and the other sells malt and hops.
And Mrs Brown, in domestic economy not to be a bit behind
her betters,
Lets her house to a milliner, a watchmaker, a rat-catcher, a
cobbler, lives in it herself, and it's the post-office for
letters:
Now I've gone through all the village – ay, from end to end,
save and except one more house,
But I haven't come to that – and I hope I never shall – and
that's the Village Poorhouse!

IDRIS DAVIES

'The village of Fochriw grunts among the higher hills'

The village of Fochriw grunts among the higher hills;
The dwellings of miners and pigeons and pigs
Cluster around the little grey war memorial.
The sun brings glitter to the long street roofs
And the crawling promontories of slag,
The sun makes the pitwheels to shine,
And praise be to the sun, the great unselfish sun,
The sun that shone on Plato's shoulders,
That dazzles with light the Taj Mahal.
The same sun shone on the first mineowner,
On the vigorous builder of this grim village,
And praise be to the impartial sun.
He had no hand in the bruising of valleys,
He had no line in the vigorous builder's plan,
He had no voice in the fixing of wages,
He was the blameless one.
And he smiles on the village this morning,
He smiles on the far-off grave of the vigorous builder,
On the ivied mansion of the first mineowner,
On the pigeon lofts and the Labour Exchange,
And he smiles as only the innocent can.

Mid-Glamorgan

JOHN BETJEMAN

The Small Towns of Ireland

The small towns of Ireland by bards are neglected,
  They stand there, all lonesome, on hilltop and plain.
The Protestant glebe house by beech trees protected
  Sits close to the gates of his Lordship's demesne.

But where is his Lordship, who once in a phaeton
  Drove out twixt his lodges and into the town?
Oh his tragic misfortunes I will not dilate on;
  His mansion's a ruin, his woods are cut down.

His impoverished descendant is dwelling in Ealing,
  His daughters must type for their bread and their board,
O'er the graves of his forebears the nettle is stealing
  And few will remember the sad Irish Lord.

Yet still stands the Mall where his agent resided,
  The doctor, attorney and such class of men.
The elegant fanlights and windows provided
  A Dublin-like look for the town's Upper Ten.

'Twas bravely they stood by the Protestant steeple
  As over the town rose their roof-trees afar.
Let us slowly descend to the part where the people
  Do mingle their ass-carts by Finnegan's bar.

I hear it once more, the soft sound of those voices,
  When fair day is filling with farmers the Square,
And the heart in my bosom delights and rejoices
  To think of the dealing and drinking done there.

I see thy grey granite, O grim House of Sessions!
  I think of the judges who sat there in state
And my mind travels back to our monster processions
  To honour the heroes of brave Ninety-Eight.

The barracks are burned where the Redcoats oppressed us,
   The gaol is broke open, our people are free.
Though Cromwell once cursed us, Saint Patrick has blessed
      us –
   The merciless English have fled o'er the sea.

Look out where yon cabins grow smaller to smallest,
   Straw-thatched and one-storey and soon to come down,
To the prominent steeple, the newest and tallest
   Of Saint Malachy's Catholic Church in our town:

The fine architécture, the wealth of mosaic,
   The various marbles on altars within –
To attempt a description were merely prosaic,
   So, asking your pardon, I will not begin.

O my small town of Ireland, the raindrops caress you,
   The sun sparkles bright on your field and your Square
As here on your bridge I salute you and bless you,
   Your murmuring waters and turf-scented air.

   Republic of Ireland

IVOR GURNEY

Tewkesbury

Some Dane looking out from the water-settlements,
If settlements there were, must have thought as I,
'Square stone should fill that bit of lower sky.
Were I a king and had my influence,
Farms should go up for this, flames make terror go high.
But I would set my name in high eminence.'
Forthampton walking, thinking and looking to Tewkesbury,
Where a cricketer was born and a battle raged desperate,
And mustard grew, and Stratford boys early or late

May have come, and rivers, green Avon, brown Severn,
  meet.
And Norman Milo set a seal on the plain –
'Here man rules; his works to be found here;
Acknowledges supremacy, his strengths to be in vain;
And gathers by a sign the broad meadows in round here.'

What is best of England, going quick from beauty,
Is manifest, the slow spirit going straight on,
The dark intention corrected by eyes that see,
The somehow getting there, the last conception
Bettered, and something of one's own spirit outshown;
Grown as oaks grow, done as hard things are done.

Of worthy towns worthy should be Messenger
Of News that's food to heart of Everyman,
The curious of his kind. And on this birthday,
This twice a hundred mark of age and honour,
Well do we salute 'Journal' of Land's fame;
That's gossip to our region villages,
And Record to the Merchant with his lad,
Art's Table and the Tale of Sport and Stage.
Those country folk that stare to see the queer
Rough-textured first-of-kind, have often taken
Their whole week's thought from 'Journal's' gathering-in,
Severn and Vale alike, and known our England,
Europe, the wider world, from that respected
Close-ordered print; and we in hacked-up Flanders
Read Sunday School, Fairs, football-scores alike.
(Raikes, that kind-thoughted, gay man, had laughed,
We sitting there in drips of rain to ponder
On small home businesses, so mired and chill.)
Well to the sober, beautiful city serves
This grave news-printing, old in praise as years,
Looked for at week-ends; worthy of that first
Director, whom in London surprised one sees
Smile from the dun wall on the curious.

But he, could return be, having heard the presses
And thunderous printing, seen and grasped so much,
By fumbling questions groping near the truth,
Would yet have asked what thought the townsfolk had,
This 'Journal', how it stood yet in their minds;
And, answered, should indeed be well content.

Towns are not often lucky in their print-sheets;
But this, the Roman City, has for servant
A Teller wise of grave news-currency.

Gloucestershire

W. R. RODGERS

Armagh

There is a through-otherness about Armagh
Of tower and steeple,
Up on the hill are the arguing graves of the kings,
And below are the people.

Through-other as the rooks that swoop and swop
Over the sober hill
Go the people gallivanting from shop to shop
Guffawing their fill.
And the little houses run through the market-town
Slap up against the great,
Like the farmers all clabber and muck walking arm by arm
With the men of estate.

Raised at a time when Reason was all the rage,
Of grey and equal stone,
This bland face of Armagh covers an age
Of clay and feather and bone.

Through-other is its history, of Celt and Dane,
Norman and Saxon,
Who ruled the place and sounded the gamut of fame
From cow-horn to klaxon.

There is a through-otherness about Armagh
Delightful to me,
Up on the hill are the graves of the garrulous kings
Who at last can agree.

Co. Armagh, Northern Ireland

Ambiguous Terrain

ROBERT LLOYD

The Cit's Country Box

The wealthy Cit, grown old in trade,
Now wishes for the rural shade,
And buckles to his one-horse chair
Old Dobbin or the foundered mare;
While, wedged in closely by his side,
Sits Madam, his unwieldy bride,
With Jacky on a stool before 'em,
And out they jog in due decorum.
Scarce past the turnpike half a mile,
How all the country seems to smile!
And as they slowly jog together,
The Cit commends the road and weather;
While Madam dotes upon the trees,
And longs for ev'ry house she sees,
Admires its views, its situation,
And thus she opens her oration:
    'What signify the loads of wealth,
Without that richest jewel, health?
Excuse the fondness of a wife,
Who dotes upon your precious life!
Such easeless toil, such constant care,
Is more than human strength can bear.
One may observe it in your face –
Indeed, my dear, you break apace:
And nothing can your health repair,
But exercise and country air.
Sir Traffic has a house, you know,
About a mile from Cheney Row:

He's a *good* man, indeed 'tis true,
But not so *warm*, my dear, as you:
And folks are always apt to sneer –
One would not be out-done, my dear!'
   Sir Traffic's name so well applied
Awaked his brother-merchant's pride;
And Thrifty, who had all his life
Paid utmost deference to his wife,
Confessed her arguments had reason,
And by th' approaching summer season,
Draws a few hundreds from the stocks,
And purchases his country box.
   Some three or four mile out of town
(An hour's ride will bring you down),
He fixes on his choice abode,
Not half a furlong from the road:
And so convenient does it lay,
The stages pass it ev'ry day:
And then so snug, so mighty pretty,
To have an house so near the city!
Take but your places at the Boar,
You're set down at the very door.
   Well then, suppose them fixed at last,
White-washing, painting, scrubbing past,
Hugging themselves in ease and clover,
With all the fuss of moving over;
Lo, a new heap of whims are bred,
And wanton in my lady's head:
   'Well, to be sure, it must be owned
It is a charming spot of ground;
So sweet a distance for a ride,
And all about so *countrified!*
'Twould come to but a trifling price
To make it quite a paradise;
I cannot bear those nasty rails,
Those ugly, broken, mouldy pales:

Suppose, my dear, instead of these,
We build a railing, all Chinese.
Although one hates to be exposed,
'Tis dismal to be thus inclosed;
One hardly any object sees –
I wish you'd fell those odious trees.
Objects continual passing by
Were something to amuse the eye,
But to be pent within the walls –
One might as well be at St Paul's.
Our house beholders would adore,
Was there a level lawn before,
Nothing its views to incommode,
But quite laid open to the road;
While ev'ry trav'ler in amaze
Should on our little mansion gaze,
And, pointing to the choice retreat,
Cry, "That's Sir Thrifty's country seat." '
　No doubt her arguments prevail,
For Madam's *taste* can never fail.
　Blest age! when all men may procure
The title of a connoisseur;
When noble and ignoble herd
Are governed by a single word;
Though, like the royal German dames,
It bears an hundred Christian names,
As Genius, Fancy, Judgement, Goût,
Whim, Caprice, Je-ne-sais-quoi, Virtù:
Which appellations all describe
Taste, and the modern *tasteful* tribe.
　Now bricklay'rs, carpenters and joiners,
With Chinese artists and designers,
Produce their schemes of alteration,
To work this wond'rous reformation.
The useful dome, which secret stood
Embosomed in the yew-tree's wood,

The trav'ler with amazement sees
A temple, Gothic, or Chinese,
With many a bell and tawdry rag on,
And crested with a sprawling dragon;
A wooden arch is bent astride
A ditch of water, four foot wide,
With angles, curves and zigzag lines,
From Halfpenny's exact designs.
In front, a level lawn is seen,
Without a shrub upon the green,
Where Taste would want its first great law,
But for the skulking, sly *ha-ha*,
By whose miraculous assistance,
You gain a prospect two fields' distance.
And now from Hyde-Park Corner come
The gods of Athens and of Rome.
Here squabby Cupids take their places,
With Venus and the clumsy Graces:
Apollo there, with aim so clever,
Stretches his leaden bow for ever;
And there, without the pow'r to fly,
Stands fixed a tip-toe Mercury.

   The villa thus completely graced,
All own that Thrifty has a Taste;
And Madam's female friends and cousins,
With common-council-men by dozens,
Flock ev'ry Sunday to the seat,
To stare about them, and to eat.

  London suburbs

GEORGE COLMAN, THE YOUNGER

from London Rurality

What would-be villas, range'd in dapper pride,
Usurp the fields, and choke the highway side!
Where the prig architect, with style in view,
Has dole'd his houses forth, in two by two;
And rear'd a row upon the plan, no doubt,
Of old men's jaws, with every third tooth out.
Or where, still greater lengths, in taste, to go,
He warps his tenements into a bow;
Nails a scant canvass, propt on slight deal sticks,
Nick-name'd veranda, to the first-floor bricks;
Before the whole, in one snug segment drawn,
Claps half a rood of turf he calls a lawn;
Then, chuckling at his lath-and-plaster bubble,
Dubs it the Crescent – and the rents are double. [...]

Here modest ostentation sticks a plate,
Or daubs Egyptian letters, on the gate,
Informing passengers 'tis 'Cowslip Cot',
Or 'Woodbine Lodge', or 'Mr Pummock's Grot'.
To beautify each close-wedge'd neighbour's door,
A stripe of garden aims at length, before;
Three thin, aquatick poplars, parch'd with drought,
(Vying with lines of lamp posts, fix'd without,)
Behind it pine, to decorate the grounds,
And mark with greater elegance their bounds.
Blest neighbourhood! – but three times blest! – thrice three!
When neighbours (as 'twill happen) disagree;
When grievances break forth, and deadly spite,
'Twixt those whom Fate, and bricklayers, would unite.

D. H. LAWRENCE

Flat Suburbs, S.W., in the Morning

The new red houses spring like plants
    In level rows
Of reddish herbage that bristles and slants
    Its square shadows.

The pink young houses show one side bright
    Flatly assuming the sun,
And one side shadow, half in sight,
    Half-hiding the pavement-run;

Where hastening creatures pass intent
    On their level way,
Threading like ants that can never relent
    And have nothing to say.

Bare stems of street lamps stiffly stand
    At random, desolate twigs,
To testify to a blight on the land
    That has stripped their sprigs.

   Croydon, now Greater London

JOHN BETJEMAN

Love in a Valley

Take me, Lieutenant, to that Surrey homestead!
    Red comes the winter and your rakish car,
Red among the hawthorns, redder than the hawberries
    And trails of old man's nuisance, and noisier far.
Far, far below me roll the Coulsdon woodlands,
    White down the valley curves the living rail,

Tall, tall, above me, olive spike the pinewoods,
   Olive against blue-black, moving in the gale.

Deep down the drive go the cushioned rhododendrons,
   Deep down, sand deep, drives the heather root,
Deep the spliced timber barked around the summer-house,
   Light lies the tennis-court, plaintain underfoot.
What a winter welcome to what a Surrey homestead!
   Oh! the metal lantern and white enamelled door!
Oh! the spread of orange from the gas-fire on the carpet!
   Oh! the tiny patter, sandalled footsteps on the floor!

Fling wide the curtains! – that's a Surrey sunset!'
   Low down the line sings the Addiscombe train,
Leaded are the windows lozenging the crimson,
   Drained dark the pines in resin-scented rain.
Portable Lieutenant! they carry you to China
   And me to lonely shopping in a brilliant arcade:
Firm hand, fond hand, switch the giddy engine!
   So for us a last time is bright light made.

   Surrey

JAMES THOMSON

Lines Written on Richmond Park

       Richmond, ev'n now,
Thy living landscape spreads beneath my feet,
Calm as the sleep of infancy – the song
Of Nature's vocalists, the blossom'd shrubs,
The velvet verdure, and the o'ershadowing trees,
The cattle wading in the clear smooth stream;
And, mirrored on its surface, the deep glow
Of sunset, the white smoke and yonder church,
Half hid by the green foliage of the grove –

These are thy charms, fair Richmond, and through these
The river, wafting many a graceful bark,
Glides swiftly onward like a lovely dream,
Making the scene a Paradise.

LOUIS MACNEICE

The Park

Through a glass greenly men as trees walking
Led by their dogs, trees as torrents
Loosed by the thaw, tulips as shriekmarks
(Yelps of delight), lovers as coracles
Riding the rapids: Spring as a spring
Releasing the jack-in-a-box of a fanfare.

Urban enclave of lawns and water,
Lacquered ducks and young men sculling,
Children who never had seen the country
Believing it this while those who had once
Known real country ignore the void
Their present imposes, their past exposes.

South and east lie the yellowed terraces
Grandiose, jerrybuilt, ghosts of gracious
Living, and north those different terraces
Where great white bears with extensile necks,
Convicted sentries, lope their beat,
No rest for their paws till the day they die.

Fossils of flesh, fossils of stucco:
Between them the carefully labelled flower beds
And the litter baskets, but also between them
Through a grille gaily men as music
Forcing the spring to loose the lid,
To break the bars, to find the world.

BERNARD SPENCER

Allotments: April

Cobbled with rough stone which rings my tread
The path twists through the squared allotments.
Blinking to glimpse the lark in the warming sun,
In what sense am I joining in
Such a hallooing, rousing April day,
Now that the hedges are so gracious and
Stick out at me moist buds, small hands, their opening
    scrolls and fans?

Lost to some of us the festival joy
At the bursting of the tomb, the seasonal mystery,
God walking again who lay all winter
As if in those long barrows built in the fields
To keep the root-crops warm. On squires' lawns
The booted dancers twirl. But what I hear
A spade slice in pebbled earth, swinging the nigger-coloured
    loam.

And the love-songs, the mediaeval grace,
The fluting lyrics, 'The only pretty ring-time,'
These have stopped singing. For love detonates like sap
Up into the limbs of men and bears all the seasons
And the starving and the cutting and hunts terribly through
    lives
To find its peace. But April comes as
Beast-smell flung from the fields, the hammers, the loud-
    speaking weir.

The rough voices of boys playing by the hedge
As manly as possible, their laughter, the big veins
Sprawled over the beet-leaf, light-red fires
Of flower pots heaped by the huts; they make a pause in

The wireless voice repeating pacts, persecutions,
And imprisonments and deaths and heaped violent deaths,
Impersonal now as figures in the city news.

Behind me, the town curves. Its parapeted edge,
With its burnt look, guards towards the river.
The worry about money, the eyeless work
Of those who do not believe, real poverty,
The sour doorways of the poor; April which
Delights the trees and fills the roads to the South,
Does not deny or conceal. Rather it adds

What more I am; excites the deep glands
And warms my animal bones as I go walking
Past the allotments and the singing water-meadows
Where hooves of cattle have plodded and cratered, and
Watch today go up like a single breath
Holding in its applause at masts of height
Two elms and their balanced attitude like dancers, their
   arms like dancers.

TOBIAS HILL

Draining the Grand Union

It happens quite suddenly,
the engineers doing their work
in the way important work is always done,

with no one noticing, until they've gone
and the canal with them. Its cold green
miles emptied quietly

as a gutter is emptied of rain.
The Grand Union Canal
has been removed, and left behind

are the skeletons of bicycles –
without wheels, without rust –
and twenty years of traffic cones
swollen, sheltering mussel shells
and torn-up letters, and lost coins

blackened or green with oxygen.
In the suntrap of a shopping trolley
an eel has worked its muscle
into soft brown knots
and died under the eyes of children
who watch its eyes turn into moons.

Behind the ten-foot doors
of the lock gates,
canal from here to Manchester
waits to find its level,

forcing green water
through the hinged black wood,
exploring in slow sheets
down old beams and bitumen.
There is the sour smell
of sun below the waterline

where a small man in pink Marigolds
rummages in the mud's cupboards.
Behind his back
the canal waits. Drips

drops. And up above,
a pair of tan-black dogs
watch it all from the footbridge,

their long, simple heads
full of the smell and the bright
shine of undiscovered country.

North-West London

FREDA DOWNIE

Her Garden

My grandmother grew tiny grapes and tiger-lilies,
But there is no sentimental cut to her garden
Through a fat album or remembered lane;
Only interior voyages made on London ferries

Paddling the Thames' wicked brew to Silvertown,
Where regular as boot boys, the factories
Blacked her house every day, obscured the skies
And the town's sweet name at the railway station.

Between ships parked at the end of the road
And factory gates, she kept her home against soot,
Kept her garden colours in spite of it –
Five square feet of bitterness in a paved yard

Turned to the silent flowering of her will,
Loaded with dusty beauty and natural odours,
Cinnamon lilies, and the vine roots hanging grapes,
Sour as social justice, on the wash-house wall.

Newham, East London

Cities

SYDNEY SMITH

'As one who, long in rural hamlets pent'

As one who, long in rural hamlets pent
(Where squires and parsons deep potations make,
With lengthen'd tale of fox, or timid hare,
Or antler'd stag, sore vext by hound and horn),
Forth issuing on a winter's morn, to reach
In chaise or coach the London Babylon
Remote, from each thing met conceives delight:
Or cab, or car, or evening muffin-bell,
Or lamps – each city-sight, each city-sound.

WILLIAM WORDSWORTH

Composed upon Westminster Bridge, September 3, 1802

Earth has not anything to show more fair:
Dull would he be of soul who could pass by
A sight so touching in its majesty:
This City now doth like a garment wear
The beauty of the morning; silent, bare,
Ships, towers, domes, theatres, and temples lie
Open unto the fields, and to the sky;
All bright and glittering in the smokeless air.
Never did sun more beautifully steep
In his first splendour valley, rock, or hill;
Ne'er saw I, never felt, a calm so deep!
The river glideth at his own sweet will:

Dear God! the very houses seem asleep;
And all that mighty heart is lying still!

   Central London

JOHN DAVIDSON

In the Isle of Dogs

While the water-wagon's ringing showers
Sweetened the dust with a woodland smell,
'Past noon, past noon, two sultry hours,'
Drowsily fell
From the schoolhouse clock
In the Isle of Dogs by Millwall Dock.

Mirrored in shadowy windows draped
With ragged net or half-drawn blind
Bowsprits, masts, exactly shaped
To woo or fight the wind,
Like monitors of guilt
By strength and beauty sent,
Disgraced the shameful houses built
To furnish rent.

From the pavements and the roofs
In shimmering volumes wound
The wrinkled heat;
Distant hammers, wheels and hoofs,
A turbulent pulse of sound,
Southward obscurely beat,
The only utterance of the afternoon,
Till on a sudden in the silent street
An organ-man drew up and ground
The Old Hundredth tune.

Forthwith the pillar of cloud that hides the past
Burst into flame,
Whose alchemy transmuted house and mast,
Street, dockyard, pier and pile:
By magic sound the Isle of Dogs became
A northern isle –
A green isle like a beryl set
In a wine-coloured sea,
Shadowed by mountains where a river met
The ocean's arm extended royally.

There also in the evening on the shore
An old man ground the Old Hundredth tune,
An old enchanter steeped in human lore,
Sad-eyed, with whitening beard, and visage lank:
Not since and not before,
Under the sunset or the mellowing moon,
Has any hand of man's conveyed
Such meaning in the turning of a crank.

Sometimes he played
As if his box had been
An organ in an abbey richly lit;
For when the dark invaded day's demesne,
And the sun set in crimson and in gold;
When idlers swarmed upon the esplanade,
And a late steamer wheeling towards the quay
Struck founts of silver from the darkling sea,
The solemn tune arose and shook and rolled
Above the throng,
Above the hum and tramp and bravely knit
All hearts in common memories of song.

Sometimes he played at speed;
Then the Old Hundredth like a devil's mass
Instinct with evil thought and evil deed,
Rang out in anguish and remorse. Alas!

That men must know both Heaven and Hell!
Sometimes the melody
Sang with the murmuring surge;
And with the winds would tell
Of peaceful graves and of the passing bell.
Sometimes it pealed across the bay
A high triumphal dirge,
A dirge
For the departing undefeated day.

A noble tune, a high becoming mate
Of the capped mountains and the deep broad firth;
A simple tune and great,
The fittest utterance of the voice of earth.

East London

OSCAR WILDE

Symphony in Yellow

An omnibus across the bridge
   Crawls like a yellow butterfly,
   And, here and there, a passer-by
Shows like a little restless midge.

Big barges full of yellow hay
   Are moved against the shadowy wharf,
   And, like a yellow silken scarf,
The thick fog hangs along the quay.

The yellow leaves begin to fade
   And flutter from the Temple elms,
   And at my feet the pale green Thames
Lies like a rod of rippled jade.

Thames embankment, Central London

WILLIAM MORRIS

from The Earthly Paradise ('Prologue')

Forget six counties overhung with smoke,
Forget the snorting steam and piston stroke,
Forget the spreading of the hideous town;
Think rather of the pack-horse on the down,
And dream of London, small and white and clean,
The clear Thames bordered by its gardens green;
Think, that below bridge, the green lapping waves
Smite some few keels that bear Levantine staves,
Cut from the yew-wood on the burnt-up hill,
And pointed jars that Greek hands toiled to fill,
And treasured scanty spice from some far sea,
Florence gold cloth, and Ypres napery,
And cloth of Bruges, and hogsheads of Guienne;
While nigh the thronged wharf Geoffrey Chaucer's pen
Moves over bills of lading – mid such times
Shall dwell the hollow puppets of my rhymes.

LOUIS MACNEICE

Birmingham

Smoke from the train-gulf hid by hoardings blunders
    upward, the brakes of cars
Pipe as the policeman pivoting round raises his flat hand,
    bars
With his figure of a monolith Pharaoh the queue of fidgety
    machines
(Chromium dogs on the bonnet, faces behind the triplex
    screens).

Behind him the streets run away between the proud glass of
    shops,
Cubical scent-bottles artificial legs arctic foxes and electric
    mops,
But beyond this centre the slumward vista thins like a
    diagram:
There, unvisited, are Vulcan's forges who doesn't care a
    tinker's damn.

Splayed outwards through the suburbs houses, houses for
    rest
Seducingly rigged by the builder, half-timbered houses with
    lips pressed
So tightly and eyes staring at the traffic through bleary haws
And only a six-inch grip of the racing earth in their concrete
    claws;
In these houses men as in a dream pursue the Platonic Forms
With wireless and cairn terriers and gadgets approximating
    to the fickle norms
And endeavour to find God and score one over the
    neighbour
By climbing tentatively upward on jerry-built beauty and
    sweated labour.

The lunch hour: the shops empty, shopgirls' faces relax
Diaphanous as green glass, empty as old almanacs
As incoherent with ticketed gewgaws tiered behind their
    heads
As the Burne-Jones windows in St Philip's broken by
    crawling leads;
Insipid colour, patches of emotion, Saturday thrills
(This theatre is sprayed with 'June') – the gutter take our old
    playbills,
Next week-end it is likely in the heart's funfair we shall pull
Strong enough on the handle to get back our money; or at
    any rate it is possible.

On shining lines the trams like vast sarcophagi move
Into the sky, plum after sunset, merging to duck's egg,
    barred with mauve
Zeppelin clouds, and Pentecost-like the cars' headlights bud
Out from sideroads and the traffic signals, crême-de-menthe
    or bull's blood,
Tell one to stop, the engine gently breathing, or to go on
To where like black pipes of organs in the frayed and fading
    zone
Of the West the factory chimneys on sullen sentry will all
    night wait
To call, in the harsh morning, sleep-stupid faces through the
    daily gate.

    Birmingham

ANONYMOUS (13TH CENTURY)

Durham

[translated from the Old English by Richard Hamer]

This city is renowned throughout all Britain,
Set on steep slopes and marvellously built
With rocks all round. A strongly running river
Flows past enclosed by weirs, and therein dwell
All kinds of fishes in the seething waters.
And there a splendid forest has grown up;
Many wild animals live in those places,
And countless beasts inhabit the deep dales.
Within that town, as is well-known to men,
There lies the blessed saint, the pious Cuthbert.
There also lies the head of chaste King Oswald,
England's protector, as does Bishop Aidan,
And the two noble lords, Eadberch and Eadfrith.
Therein with them are Bishop Athelwold,

The famous scholar Bede and Abbot Boisil
Who taught pure Cuthbert in his youthful days
Gladly, and he received his teaching well.
Inside the minster by the blessed saint
Are relics numberless; there multitudes
Of miracles take place, as books make known,
While there God's servant lies and waits for Judgment.

SIR WALTER SCOTT

from Marmion, Canto IV

Still on the spot Lord Marmion stay'd,
For fairer scene he ne'er survey'd.
   When sated with the martial show
   That peopled all the plain below,
   The wandering eye could o'er it go,
   And mark the distant city glow
      With gloomy splendour red;
   For on the smoke-wreaths, huge and slow,
   That round her sable turrets flow,
      The morning beams were shed,
   And ting'd them with a lustre proud,
   Like that which streaks a thunder-cloud.
Such dusky grandeur cloth'd the height,
Where the huge Castle holds its state,
   And all the steep slope down,
Whose ridgy back heaves to the sky,
Pil'd deep and massy, close and high,
   Mine own romantic town!
But northward far, with purer blaze,
On Ochil mountains fell the rays,
And as each heathy top they kiss'd,
It gleam'd a purple amethyst.
Yonder the shores of Fife you saw;

Here Preston-Bay and Berwick-Law:
    And, broad between them roll'd,
The gallant Frith the eye might note,
Whose islands on its bosom float,
    Like emeralds chas'd in gold.

Edinburgh from the Pentland Hills

VERNON WATKINS

Ode to Swansea

Bright town, tossed by waves of time to a hill,
Leaning Ark of the world, dense-windowed, perched
High on the slope of morning,
Taking fire from the kindling East:

Look where merchants, traders, and builders move
Through your streets, while above your chandlers' walls
Herring gulls wheel, and pigeons,
Mocking man and the wheelwright's art.

Prouder cities rise through the haze of time,
Yet, unenvious, all men have found is here.
Here is the loitering marvel
Feeding artists with all they know.

There, where sunlight catches a passing sail,
Stretch your shell-brittle sands where children play,
Shielded from hammering dockyards
Launching strange, equatorial ships.

Would they know you, could the returning ships
Find the pictured bay of the port they left
Changed by a murmuration,
Stained by ores in a nighthawk's wing?

Yes. Through changes your myth seems anchored here.
Staked in mud, the forsaken oyster beds
Loom; and the Mumbles lighthouse
Turns through gales like a seabird's egg.

Lundy sets the course of the painted ships.
Fishers dropping nets off the Gower coast
Watch them, where shag and cormorant
Perch like shades on the limestone rocks.

You I know, yet who from a different land
Truly finds the town of a native child
Nurtured under a rainbow,
Pitched at last on Mount Pleasant hill?

Stone-runged streets ascending to that crow's nest
Swinging East and West over Swansea Bay
Guard in their walls Cwmdonkin's
Gates of light for a bell to close.

Praise, but do not disturb, heaven's dreaming man
Not awakened yet from his sleep of wine.
Pray, while the starry midnight
Broods on Singleton's elms and swans.

ANONYMOUS

from Manchester's Improving Daily

c. 1830

This Manchester's a rare fine place,
   For trade and other such like movements;
What town can keep up such a race,
   As ours has done for prime improvements
For of late what sights of alterations,
Both streets and buldings changing stations,
That country folks, as they observe us,

Cry out, 'Laws! pickle and presarve us!'
    Sing hey, sing ho, sing hey down, gaily,
    Manchester's improving daily.

Once Oldham Jone, in his smock frock,
    I'th' town stop'd late one afternoon, sir,
And staring at th' infirmary clock,
    Said, Wounds, that must be th' harvest moon, sir;
And ecod, it's fix'd fast up i'th' place there,
And stands behind that nice clock-face there:
Well, this caps aw, for I'll be bound, sir,
They mak' it shine there aw th' year round, sir.
    Sing hey, etc.

Our fine town hall, that cost such cash,
    Is to all buildings quite a sample;
And they say, sir, that, to make a dash,
    'Twas copied from a Grecian temple:
But sure in Greece none e'er could view, sir,
Such a place built slanting on a brow, sir!
But Cross-Street, when there brass to spare is,
Must be rais'd and called the Town-Hall Terrace.
    Sing hey, etc.

Once Market-Street was called a lane,
    Old Toad-Lane too, a pretty pair, sir;
While Dangerous-Corner did remain,
    There was hardly room for a sedan chair, sir:
But now they both are open'd wide, sir,
And dashing shops plac'd on each side, sir:
And to keep up making old things new, sir,
They talk of levelling th' Mill-Brew, sir.
    Sing hey, etc.

Th' owd Stony-Knolls must be renew'd,
    And feel, in turn, improvement's power;
From there to Bury they'll mak' good
    A great hee-road by cutting lower:

The view from hence wur quite a show, sir,
And none but foot-folks o'er must go, sir,
Yet in Whitsun-week, as thick as grass is,
The Knolls wur fill'd wi' creawds of asses.
        Sing hey, etc.

Steam coaches soon will run from here
    To Liverpool and other places;
And their quicker rate and cheaper fare
    Will make some folks pull curious faces:
But though steam-dealers may be winners,
'Twill blow up all the whip-cord spinners;
And stable boys may grieve and weep, sir,
For horse-flesh soon will be dog cheap, sir.
        Sing hey, etc.

With bumping stones our streets wur paved,
    From earth like large peck-loaves up rising:
All jolts and shakings now are saved
    The town they're now McAdamizing:
And so smooth and soft is Cannon-Street, sir,
It suits the corns on tender feet sir:
And hookers-in, when times a'n't good there,
May fish about for eels i'th' mud there.
        Sing hey, etc.

Road and Rail

EDWARD THOMAS

Roads

I love roads:
The goddesses that dwell
Far along invisible
Are my favourite gods.

Roads go on
While we forget, and are
Forgotten like a star
That shoots and is gone.

On this earth 'tis sure
We men have not made
Anything that doth fade
So soon, so long endure:

The hill road wet with rain
In the sun would not gleam
Like a winding stream
If we trod it not again.

They are lonely
While we sleep, lonelier
For lack of the traveller
Who is now a dream only.

From dawn's twilight
And all the clouds like sheep
On the mountains of sleep
They wind into the night.

The next turn may reveal
Heaven: upon the crest
The close pine clump, at rest
And black, may Hell conceal.

Often footsore, never
Yet of the road I weary,
Though long and steep and dreary,
As it winds on for ever.

Helen of the roads,
The mountain ways of Wales
And the Mabinogion tales
Is one of the true gods,

Abiding in the trees,
The threes and fours so wise,
The larger companies,
That by the roadside be,

And beneath the rafter
Else uninhabited
Excepting by the dead;
And it is her laughter

At morn and night I hear
When the thrush cock sings
Bright irrelevant things,
And when the chanticleer

Calls back to their own night
Troops that make loneliness
With their light footsteps' press,
As Helen's own are light.

Now all roads lead to France
And heavy is the tread
Of the living; but the dead
Returning lightly dance:

Whatever the road bring
To me or take from me,
They keep me company
With their pattering,

Crowding the solitude
Of the loops over the downs,
Hushing the roar of towns
And their brief multitude.

THOMAS HARDY

The Roman Road

The Roman Road runs straight and bare
As the pale parting-line in hair
Across the heath. And thoughtful men
Contrast its days of Now and Then,
And delve, and measure, and compare;

Visioning on the vacant air
Helmed legionaries, who proudly rear
The Eagle, as they pace again
                    The Roman Road.

But no tall brass-helmed legionnaire
Haunts it for me. Uprises there
A mother's form upon my ken,
Guiding my infant steps, as when
We walked that ancient thoroughfare,
                    The Roman Road.

G. K. CHESTERTON

The Rolling English Road

Before the Roman came to Rye or out to Severn strode,
The rolling English drunkard made the rolling English road.
A reeling road, a rolling road, that rambles round the shire,
And after him the parson ran, the sexton and the squire;
A merry road, a mazy road, and such as we did tread
The night we went to Birmingham by way of Beachy Head.

I knew no harm of Bonaparte and plenty of the Squire,
And for to fight the Frenchman I did not much desire;
But I did bash their baggonets because they came arrayed
To straighten out the crooked road an English drunkard
    made,
Where you and I went down the lane with ale-mugs in our
    hands,
The night we went to Glastonbury by way of Goodwin
    Sands.

His sins they were forgiven him: or why do flowers run
Behind him: and the hedges all strengthening in the sun?
The wild thing went from left to right and knew not which
    was which,
But the wild rose was above him when they found him in the
    ditch.
God pardon us, nor harden us; we did not see so clear
The night we went to Bannockburn by way of Brighton Pier.

My friends, we will not go again or ape an ancient rage
Or stretch the folly of our youth to be the shame of age,
But walk with clearer eyes and ears this path that wandereth,
And see undrugged in evening light the decent inn of death;
For there is good news yet to hear and fine things to be seen,
Before we go to Paradise by way of Kensal Green.

SAMUEL TAYLOR COLERIDGE

Devonshire Roads

The indignant bard composed this furious ode,
As tired he dragg'd his way thro' Plimtree road!
Crusted with filth and stuck in mire
Dull sounds the bard's bemudded lyre;
Nathless revenge and ire the poet goad
To pour his imprecations on the road.

Curst road! whose execrable way
Was darkly shadow'd out in Milton's lay,
When the sad fiends thro' hell's sulphureous roads
Took the first survey of their new abodes;
Or when the fall'n Archangel fierce
Dared thro' the realms of night to pierce,
What time the bloodhound lured by human scent
Thro' all confusion's quagmires floundering went.

Nor cheering pipe. nor bird's shrill note
Around thy dreary paths shall float;
Their boding songs shall scritch-owls pour
To fright the guilty shepherds sore,
Led by the wandering fires astray
Through the dank horrors of thy way!
While they their mud-lost sandals hunt
May all the curses, which they grunt
In raging moan like goaded hog,
Alight upon thee, damnèd bog!

Plymtree, north-east of Exeter, Devon

WILLIAM BARNES

The White Road up athirt the Hill

When hot-beam'd zuns do strik right down,
An' burn our zweaty feäzen brown;
An' zunny slopes, a-lyèn nigh,
Be back'd by hills so blue's the sky;
Then, while the bells do sweetly cheem
Upon the champèn high-neck'd team,
How lively, wi' a friend, do seem
    The white road up athirt the hill.

The zwellèn downs, wi' chalky tracks
A-climmèn up their zunny backs,
Do hide green meäds an' zedgy brooks,
An' clumps o' trees wi' glossy rooks,
An' hearty vo'k to laugh an' zing,
An' parish-churches in a string,
Wi' tow'rs o' merry bells to ring,
    An' white roads up athirt the hills.

At feäst, when uncle's vo'k do come
To spend the day wi' us at hwome,
An' we do lay upon the bwoard
The very best we can avvword,
The wolder woones do talk an' smoke,
An' younger woones do plaÿ an' joke,
An' in the evenèn all our vo'k
    Do bring em gwaïn athirt the hill.

An' while the green do zwarm wi' wold
An' young, so thick as sheep in vwold,
The bellows in the blacksmith's shop,
An' miller's moss-green wheel do stop,
An' lwonesome in the wheelwright's shed

'S a-left the wheelless waggon-bed;
While zwarms o' comèn friends do tread
    The white road down athirt the hill.

An' when the windèn road so white,
A-climmèn up the hills in zight,
Do leäd to pleäzen, east or west,
The vu'st a-known, an' lov'd the best,
How touchèn in the zunsheen's glow,
Or in the sheädes that clouds do drow
Upon the zunburnt downs below,
    'S the white road up athirt the hill.

What peaceful hollows here the long
White roads do windy round among!
Wi' deäiry cows in woody nooks,
An' haymeäkers among their pooks,
An' housen that the trees do screen
From zun an' zight by boughs o' green!
Young blushèn beauty's hwomes between
    The white roads up athirt the hills.

Dorset

DEREK WALCOTT

Midsummer: Poem XXXV

Mud. Clods. The sucking heel of the rain-flinger.
Sometimes the gusts of rain veered like the sails
of dragon-beaked vessels dipping to Avalon
and mist. For hours, driving along
the skittering ridges of Wales, we carried the figure
of Langland's Plowman on the rain-seeded glass,
matching the tires with his striding heels,
while splintered puddles dripped from the roadside grass.

Once, in the drizzle, a crouched, clay-covered ghost
rose in his pivot, and the turning disk of the fields
with their ploughed stanzas sang of a freshness lost.
Villages began. We had crossed into England –
the fields, not their names, were the same. We found a caff,
parked in a thin drizzle, then crammed into a pew
of red leatherette. Outside, with thumb and finger,
a careful sun was picking the lint from things.
The sun brightened like a sign, the world was new
while the cairns, the castled hillocks, the stony kings
were scabbarded in sleep, yet what made me think
that the crash of chivalry in a kitchen sink
was my own dispossession? I could sense, from calf
to flinging wrist, my veins ache in a knot.
There was mist on the window. I rubbed it and looked out
at the helmets of wet cars in the parking lot.

Welsh/English border

ROBERT LOUIS STEVENSON

From a Railway Carriage

Faster than fairies, faster than witches,
Bridges and houses, hedges and ditches;
And charging along like troops in a battle,
All through the meadows the horses and cattle:
All of the sights of the hill and the plain
Fly as thick as driving rain:
And ever again, in the wink of an eye,
Painted stations whistle by.

Here is a child who clambers and scrambles,
All by himself and gathering brambles;
Here is a tramp who stands and gazes;
And there is the green for stringing the daisies!

Here is a cart run away in the road
Lumping along with man and load;
And here is a mill and there is a river.
Each a glimpse and gone for ever!

WILLIAM ALLINGHAM

Express

We move in elephantine row,
    The faces of our friends retire,
The roof withdraws, and curtsying flow
    The message-bearing lines of wire;
        With doubling, redoubling beat,
        Smoother we run and more fleet.

By flow'r-knots, shrubs, and slopes of grass,
    Cut walls of rock with ivy-stains,
Thro' winking arches swift we pass,
    And flying, meet the flying trains,
        Whirr – whirr – gone!
        And still we hurry on;

By orchards, kine in pleasant leas,
    A hamlet-lane, a spire, a pond,
Long hedgerows, counter-changing trees,
    With blue and steady hills beyond;
        (House, platform, post,
        Flash – and are lost!)

Smooth-edged canals, and mills on brooks;
    Old farmsteads, busier than they seem,
Rose-crusted or of graver looks,
    Rich with old tile and motley beam;
        Clay-cutting, slope, and ridge,
        The hollow rumbling bridge.

Gray vapour-surges, whirl'd in the wind
　Of roaring tunnels, dark and long,
Then sky and landscape unconfined,
　　Then streets again where workers throng
　　　　Come – go. The whistle shrill
　　　　Controls us to its will.

Broad vents, and chimneys tall as masts,
　With heavy flags of streaming smoke;
Brick mazes, fiery furnace-blasts,
　　Walls, waggons, gritty heaps of coke;
　　　　Through these our ponderous rank
　　　　Glides in with hiss and clank.

So have we sped our wondrous course
　Amid a peaceful busy land,
Subdued by long and painful force
　　Of planning head and plodding hand.
　　　　How much by labour can
　　　　The feeble race of man!

　　From Liverpool, southwards

PHILIP LARKIN

The Whitsun Weddings

That Whitsun, I was late getting away:
　Not till about
One-twenty on the sunlit Saturday
Did my three-quarters-empty train pull out,
All windows down, all cushions hot, all sense
Of being in a hurry gone. We ran
Behind the backs of houses, crossed a street
Of blinding windscreens, smelt the fish-dock; thence
The river's level drifting breadth began,
Where sky and Lincolnshire and water meet.

All afternoon, through the tall heat that slept
  For miles inland,
A slow and stopping curve southwards we kept.
Wide farms went by, short-shadowed cattle, and
Canals with floatings of industrial froth;
A hothouse flashed uniquely: hedges dipped
And rose: and now and then a smell of grass
Displaced the reek of buttoned carriage-cloth
Until the next town, new and nondescript,
Approached with acres of dismantled cars.

At first, I didn't notice what a noise
  The weddings made
Each station that we stopped at: sun destroys
The interest of what's happening in the shade,
And down the long cool platforms whoops and skirls
I took for porters larking with the mails,
And went on reading. Once we started, though,
We passed them, grinning and pomaded, girls
In parodies of fashion, heels and veils,
All posed irresolutely, watching us go,

As if out on the end of an event
  Waving goodbye
To something that survived it. Struck, I leant
More promptly out next time, more curiously,
And saw it all again in different terms:
The fathers with broad belts under their suits
And seamy foreheads; mothers loud and fat;
An uncle shouting smut; and then the perms,
The nylon gloves and jewellery-substitutes,
The lemons, mauves, and olive-ochres that

Marked off the girls unreally from the rest.
  Yes, from cafés
And banquet-halls up yards, and bunting-dressed
Coach-party annexes, the wedding-days

Were coming to an end. All down the line
Fresh couples climbed aboard: the rest stood round;
The last confetti and advice were thrown,
And, as we moved, each face seemed to define
Just what it saw departing: children frowned
At something dull; fathers had never known

Success so huge and wholly farcical;
    The women shared
The secret like a happy funeral;
While girls, gripping their handbags tighter, stared
At a religious wounding. Free at last,
And loaded with the sum of all they saw,
We hurried towards London, shuffling gouts of steam.
Now fields were building-plots, and poplars cast
Long shadows over major roads, and for
Some fifty minutes, that in time would seem

Just long enough to settle hats and say
    I nearly died,
A dozen marriages got under way.
They watched the landscape, sitting side by side
– An Odeon went past, a cooling tower,
And someone running up to bowl – and none
Thought of the others they would never meet
Or how their lives would all contain this hour.
I thought of London spread out in the sun,
Its postal districts packed like squares of wheat:

There we were aimed. And as we raced across
    Bright knots of rail
Past standing Pullmans, walls of blackened moss
Came close, and it was nearly done, this frail
Travelling coincidence; and what it held
Stood ready to be loosed with all the power
That being changed can give. We slowed again,
And as the tightened brakes took hold, there swelled

A sense of falling, like an arrow-shower
Sent out of sight, somewhere becoming rain.

From Hull to London

History

RICHARD JAMES

from Iter Lancastrense

   But greater wonder calls me hence: the deep
Low spongy mosses yet remembrance keep
Of Noah's flood: on numbers infinite
Of fir trees swains do in their cesses light;
And in some places where the sea doth beat
Down from the shore, 'tis wonder to relate
How many thousands of these trees now stand
Black broken on their roots, which once dry land
Did cover, whence turfs Neptune yields to show
He did not always to these borders flow.
We read in Caesar that no fir trees grew
Within this isle, if what he wrote be true.
But sure I am, that growing here, or sent
With storms of seas, these are an argument
That God, offended with earth's crimes, did rain
Till all once drowned was in a hurling main.
Hence, 'tis Sorayna, that on hills we find
And inland quarries, things, of sea-born kind,
Whelks, cockles, oysters: threescore miles from wale
Of sea, at Conington, was found a whale
Upon a high down's brow, whose ribs and bones
With chance and time were turned into stones;
And oft earth's bosom yields the rich prized horns
Of counter-poison sea-fish unicorns.

   Lancashire

A. E. HOUSMAN

'On Wenlock Edge the wood's in trouble'

On Wenlock Edge the wood's in trouble;
    His forest fleece the Wrekin heaves;
The gale, it plies the saplings double,
    And thick on Severn snow the leaves.

'Twould blow like this through holt and hanger
    When Uricon the city stood:
'Tis the old wind in the old anger,
    But then it threshed another wood.

Then, 'twas before my time, the Roman
    At yonder heaving hill would stare:
The blood that warms an English yeoman,
    The thoughts that hurt him, they were there.

There, like the wind through woods in riot,
    Through him the gale of life blew high;
The tree of man was never quiet:
    Then 'twas the Roman, now 'tis I.

The gale, it plies the saplings double,
    It blows so hard, 'twill soon be gone:
To-day the Roman and his trouble
    Are ashes under Uricon.

    Shropshire

RUDYARD KIPLING

Puck's Song

See you the ferny ride that steals
Into the oak-woods far?
O that was whence they hewed the keels
That rolled to Trafalgar.

And mark you where the ivy clings
To Bayham's mouldering walls?
O there we cast the stout railings
That stand around St Paul's.

See you the dimpled track that runs
All hollow through the wheat?
O that was where they hauled the guns
That smote King Philip's fleet.

(Out of the Weald, the secret Weald,
Men sent in ancient years,
The horse-shoes red at Flodden Field,
The arrows at Poitiers!)

See you our little mill that clacks,
So busy by the brook?
She has ground her corn and paid her tax
Ever since Domesday Book.

See you our stilly woods of oak,
And the dread ditch beside?
O that was where the Saxons broke
On the day that Harold died.

See you the windy levels spread
About the gates of Rye?
O that was where the Northmen fled,
When Alfred's ships came by.

See you our pastures wide and lone,
Where the red oxen browse?
O there was a City thronged and known,
Ere London boasted a house.

And see you, after rain, the trace
Of mound and ditch and wall?
O that was a Legion's camping-place,
When Cæsar sailed from Gaul.

And see you marks that show and fade,
Like shadows on the Downs?
O they are the lines the Flint Men made,
To guard their wondrous towns.

Trackway and Camp and City lost,
Salt Marsh where now is corn –
Old Wars, old Peace, old Arts that cease,
And so was England born!

She is not any common Earth,
Water or wood or air,
But Merlin's Isle of Gramarye,
Where you and I will fare!

East Sussex

MICHAEL BALDWIN

Chalk Horse

Men cut their Gods in the hills
The galloping Gods whose hooves
Go flying away in the grass
When the grass moves in the winds.

We walk our shadows astride
Those shimmering flanks at sunset

And ride with their muscled acres
Into revolving dark.

There as we stride away
While the rhythms run wild in our heart
How many words can we say
For the tulips we tune in the clay

Of our graver God, in the Park?

Uffington, Oxfordshire

JOHN MASEFIELD

Lollingdon Downs

Up on the downs the red-eyed kestrels hover,
Eyeing the grass.
The field-mouse flits like a shadow into cover
As their shadows pass.

Men are burning the gorse on the down's shoulder;
A drift of smoke
Glitters with fire and hangs, and the skies smoulder,
And the lungs choke.

Once the tribe did thus on the downs, on these downs, burning
Men in the frame,
Crying to the gods of the downs till their brains were turning
And the gods came.

And to-day on the downs, in the wind, the hawks, the grasses,
In blood and air,
Something passes me and cries as it passes,
On the chalk downland bare.

Oxfordshire

NORMAN NICHOLSON

Millom Old Quarry

'They dug ten streets from that there hole,' he said,
'Hard on five hundred houses.' He nodded
Down the set of the quarry and spat in the water
Making a moorhen cock her head
As if a fish had leaped. 'Half the new town
Came out of yonder – King Street, Queen Street, all
The houses round the Green as far as the slagbank,
And Market Street, too, from the Crown allotments
Up to the station Yard.' – 'But Market Street's
Brown freestone,' I said. 'Nobbut the facings;
We called them the Khaki Houses in the Boer War,
But they're Cumberland slate at the back.'

I thought of those streets still bearing their royal names
Like the coat-of-arms on a child's Jubilee Mug –
Noncomformist gables sanded with sun
Or branded with burning creeper; a smoke of lilac
Between the blue roofs of closet and coal-house:
So much that woman's blood gave sense and shape to
Hacked from this dynamited combe.
The rocks cracked to the pond, and hawthorns fell
In waterfalls of blossom. Shed petals
Patterned the scum like studs on the sole of a boot,
And stiff-legged sparrows skid down screes of gravel.

I saw the town's black generations
Packed in their caves of rock, as mussel or limpet
Washed by the tidal sky; then swept, shovelled
Back in the quarry again, a landslip of lintels
Blocking the gape of the tarn.
The quick turf pushed a green tarpaulin over
All that was mortal in five thousand lives.

Nor did it seem a paradox to one
Who held quarry and query, turf and town,
In the small lock of a recording brain.

    Cumbria

SEAMUS HEANEY

Toome

My mouth holds round
the soft blastings,
Toome, Toome,
as under the dislodged

slab of the tongue
I push into a souterrain
prospecting what new
in a hundred centuries'

loam, flints, musket-balls,
fragmented ware,
torcs and fish-bones.
till I am sleeved in

alluvial mud that shelves
suddenly under
bogwater and tributaries,
and elvers tail my hair.

    Co. Antrim, Northern Ireland

EDWIN MUIR

The Threefold Place

This is the place. The autumn field is bare,
　The row lies half-cut all the afternoon,
The birds are hiding in the woods, the air
　Dreams fitfully outworn with waiting. Soon

Out of the russet woods in amber mail
　Heroes come walking through the yellow sheaves,
Walk on and meet. And then a silent gale
　Scatters them on the field like autumn leaves.

Yet not a feathered stalk has stirred, and all
　Is still again, but for the birds that call
On every warrior's head and breast and shield.
　Sweet cries and horror on the field.

One field. I look again and there are three:
　One where the heroes fell to rest,
One where birds make of iron limbs a tree,
　Helms for a nest,
　And one where grain stands up like armies drest.

CHRISTOPHER NORTH

Battlefield

Preparing to enjoin, they do not see the clapboard,
the stacked blocks and timbers in the builder's yard
nor the dual-carriageway. Banners riffle in a slight breeze.

The infantry calmly take up their planned positions
as two anglers cycle by, one leaning back with hands
off the handlebars. It is late morning.

Archers form rank half in and half out a retail warehouse;
snorting cavalry shuffle amidst the screams of children
playing on the park swings. The tension is palpable.

An ice-cream van trills around the nearby estate.
The first cries across the car-park are ignored
by the shell-suit woman loading her boot.

The thunder of hooves and bellowed huzzahs
do not concern the kid clattering his skate-board
down the concrete ramp; nor the deadly waves of arrows.

Following ranks leap groaning bodies of the first
wielding axe and shield at massed formations
beside the filling station with its plastic flags.

The engagement is thickest where the speed bumps
put in last year, successfully calm the traffic.
There is terrible slaughter in the chemist's extended

cosmetics department. The new assistant frowns
as she works out how to use the electric cash register
and a spearman, head pumping blood, slumps across

the toiletries counter. A woman asks for cotton balls.
At the head of the bus queue two knights clang swords
hand to hand. A schoolgirl blows a pink bubble

as the single decker drones in past their foaming horses.
The conflict ebbs and flows through the overcast afternoon.
When the corner estate agent brings in his 'A' boards,

auxiliaries arrive across a field of rape. They clinch it.
There is a messy withdrawal down the back gardens
of 'Willow Ridge Crescent' and 'The Maltings'.

Panic sets in as the first home-bound executives turn
from the motorway. It ends in a rout by the sewage farm.
Cattle move towards a gate. The sodiums come on.

Victory cheers are unnoticed by plumed youths
gooning and looning around the corpses
strewn beside the vandalized memorial fountain.

Middle England

LOUIS MACNEICE

Wessex Guidebook

Hayfoot; strawfoot; the illiterate seasons
Still clump their way through Somerset and Dorset
While George the Third still rides his horse of chalk
From Weymouth and the new salt water cure
Towards Windsor and incurable madness. Inland
The ghosts of monks have grown too fat to walk
Through bone-dry ruins plugged with fossil sea-shells.

Thou shalt! Thou shalt not! In the yellow abbey
Inscribed beneath the crossing the Ten Commandments
Are tinted red by a Fifteenth Century fire;
On one round hill the yews still furnish bows
For Agincourt while, equally persistent,
Beneath another, in green-grassed repose,
Arthur still waits the call to rescue Britain.

Flake-tool; core-tool; in the small museum
Rare butterflies, green coins of Caracalla,
Keep easy company with the fading hand
Of one who chronicled a fading world;
Outside, the long roads, that the Roman ruler
Ruled himself out with, point across the land
To lasting barrows and long vanished barracks.

And thatchpoll numskull rows of limestone houses,
Dead from the navel down in plate glass windows,
Despise their homebrewed past, ignore the clock

On the village church in deference to Big Ben
Who booms round china dog and oaken settle
Announcing it is time and time again
To plough up tumuli, to damn the hindmost.

But hindmost, topmost, those illiterate seasons
Still smoke their pipes in swallow-hole and hide-out
As scornful of the tractor and the jet
As of the Roman road, or axe of flint,
Forgotten by the mass of human beings
Whom they, the Seasons, need not even forget
Since, though they fostered man, they never loved him.

Wessex

GEOFFREY HILL

The Laurel Axe

Autumn resumes the land, ruffles the woods
with smoky wings, entangles them. Trees shine
out from their leaves, rocks mildew to moss-green;
the avenues are spread with brittle floods.

Platonic England, house of solitudes,
rests in its laurels and its injured stone,
replete with complex fortunes that are gone,
beset by dynasties of moods and clouds.

It stands, as though at ease with its own world,
the mannerly extortions, languid praise,
all that devotion long since bought and sold,

the rooms of cedar and soft-thudding baize,
tremulous boudoirs where the crystals kissed
in cabinets of amethyst and frost.

T. S. ELIOT

Four Quartets: 'East Coker', Part I

In my beginning is my end. In succession
Houses rise and fall, crumble, are extended,
Are removed, destroyed, restored, or in their place
Is an open field, or a factory, or a by-pass.
Old stone to new building, old timber to new fires,
Old fires to ashes, and ashes to the earth
Which is already flesh, fur and faeces,
Bone of man and beast, cornstalk and leaf.
Houses live and die: there is a time for building
And a time for living and for generation
And a time for the wind to break the loosened pane
And to shake the wainscot where the field-mouse trots
And to shake the tattered arras woven with a silent motto.

In my beginning is my end. Now the light falls
Across the open field, leaving the deep lane
Shuttered with branches, dark in the afternoon,
Where you lean against a bank while a van passes,
And the deep lane insists on the direction
Into the village, in the electric heat
Hypnotised. In a warm haze the sultry light
Is absorbed, not refracted, by grey stone.
The dahlias sleep in the empty silence.
Wait for the early owl.
                              In that open field
If you do not come too close, if you do not come too close,
On a summer midnight, you can hear the music
Of the weak pipe and the little drum
And see them dancing around the bonfire
The association of man and woman
In daunsinge, signifying matrimonie –

A dignified and commodious sacrament.
Two and two, necessarye coniunction,
Holding eche other by the hand or the arm
Whiche betokeneth concorde. Round and round the fire
Leaping through the flames, or joined in circles,
Rustically solemn or in rustic laughter
Lifting heavy feet in clumsy shoes,
Earth feet, loam feet, lifted in country mirth
Mirth of those long since under earth
Nourishing the corn. Keeping time,
Keeping the rhythm in their dancing
As in their living in the living seasons
The time of the seasons and the constellations
The time of milking and the time of harvest
The time of the coupling of man and woman
And that of beasts. Feet rising and falling.
Eating and drinking. Dung and death.

   Dawn points, and another day
Prepares for heat and silence. Out at sea the dawn wind
Wrinkles and slides. I am here
Or there, or elsewhere. In my beginning.

  near Yeovil, Somerset

Divinity

WILLIAM BLAKE

from Milton

And did those feet in ancient time
Walk upon England's mountains green?
And was the holy Lamb of God
On England's pleasant pastures seen?

And did the Countenance Divine
Shine forth upon our clouded hills?
And was Jerusalem builded here
Among these dark Satanic Mills?

Bring me my Bow of burning gold:
Bring me my Arrows of desire:
Bring me my Spear: O clouds unfold!
Bring me my Chariot of fire.

I will not cease from Mental Fight,
Nor shall my Sword sleep in my hand
Till we have built Jerusalem
In England's green & pleasant Land.

WILLIAM WORDSWORTH

'The world is too much with us; late and soon'

The world is too much with us; late and soon,
Getting and spending, we lay waste our powers:
Little we see in Nature that is ours;
We have given our hearts away, a sordid boon!
This Sea that bares her bosom to the moon;

The winds that will be howling at all hours,
And are up-gathered now like sleeping flowers;
For this, for everything, we are out of tune;
It moves us not. – Great God! I'd rather be
A Pagan suckled in a creed outworn;
So might I, standing on this pleasant lea,
Have glimpses that would make me less forlorn;
Have sight of Proteus rising from the sea;
Or hear old Triton blow his wreathèd horn.

SAMUEL PALMER

'And now the trembling light'

And now the trembling light
Glimmers behind the little hills, and corn,
Ling'ring as loth to part: yet part thou must
And though than open day far pleasing more
(Ere yet the fields, and pearled cups of flowers
        Twinkle in the parting light;)
Thee night shall hide, sweet visionary gleam
That softly lookest through the rising dew;
        Till all like silver bright,
        The Faithful Witness, pure, and white,
        Shall look o'er yonder grassy hill,
        At this village, safe and still.
        All is safe and all is still
        Save what noise the watch-dog makes
        Or the shrill cock the silence breaks
                Now and then –
                And now and then –
                Hark! – Once again,
                The wether's bell
                To us doth tell
        Some little stirring in the fold.

Me thinks the ling'ring dying ray
　　Of twilight time doth seem more fair
And lights the soul up more than day,
　　When wide-spread sultry sunshines are.
Yet all is right, and all most fair,
　　For Thou, dear God, hast formed all;
Thou deckest ev'ry little flower,
　　Thou girdest ev'ry planet ball –
　　　　And mark'st when sparrows fall.
Thou pourest out the golden day
On corn-fields rip'ning in the sun
Up the side of some great hill
　　Ere the sickle has begun.

Shoreham, Kent

GERARD MANLEY HOPKINS

Hurrahing in Harvest

Summer ends now; now, barbarous in beauty, the stooks rise
Around; up above, what wind-walks! what lovely behaviour
Of silk-sack clouds! has wilder, wilful-wavier
Meal-drift moulded ever and melted across skies?

I walk, I lift up, I lift up heart, eyes,
Down all that glory in the heavens to glean our Saviour;
And, éyes, heárt, what looks, what lips yet gave you a
Rapturous love's greeting of realer, of rounder replies?

And the azurous hung hills are his world-wielding shoulder
Majestic – as a stallion stalwart, very-violet-sweet! –
These things, these things were here and but the beholder
Wanting; which two when they once meet,

The heart rears wings bold and bolder
And hurls for him, O half hurls earth for him off under his
    feet.

    Vale of Clwyd, North Wales

CHARLES TOMLINSON

Harvest

After the hay was baled and stacked in henges,
We walked through the circles in the moonlit field:
The moon was hidden from us by the ranges
Of hills that enclosed the meadows hay had filled.

But its light lay one suffusing undertone
That drew out the day and changed the pace of time:
It slowed to the pulse of our passing feet upon
Gleanings the baler had left on the ground to rhyme

With the colour of the silhouettes that arose,
Dark like the guardians of a frontier strayed across,
Into this in-between of time composed –
Sentries of Avalon, these megaliths of grass.

Yet it was time that brought us to this place,
Time that had ripened the grasses harvested here:
Time will tell us tomorrow that we paced
Last night in a field that is no longer there.

And yet it was. And time, the literalist,
The sense and the scent of it woven in time's changes,
Cannot put by that sweetness, that persistence
After the hay was baled and stacked in henges.

    Gloucestershire

ELIZABETH JENNINGS

Harvest and Consecration

After the heaped piles and the cornsheaves waiting
To be collected, gathered into barns,
After all fruits have burst their skins, the sating
    Season cools and turns,
And then I think of something that you said
Of when you held the chalice and the bread.

I spoke of Mass and thought of it as close
To how a season feels which stirs and brings
Fire to the hearth, food to the hungry house
    And strange, uncovered things –
God in a garden then in sheaves of corn
And the white bread a way to be reborn.

I thought of priest as midwife and as mother
Feeling the pain, feeling the pleasure too,
    All opposites together,
Until you said no one could feel such passion
And still preserve the power of consecration.

And it is true. How cool the gold sheaves lie,
Rich without need to ask for any more
Richness. The seed, the simple thing must die
    If only to restore
Our faith in fruitful, hidden things. I see
The wine and bread protect our ecstasy.

CHRISTOPHER FRY

from The Boy with a Cart, Act I

The people of South England:
In our fields, fallow and burdened, in grass and furrow,
In barn and stable, with scythe, flail, or harrow,
Sheepshearing, milking or mowing, on labour that's older
Than knowledge, with God we work shoulder to shoulder;
God providing, we dividing, sowing, and pruning;
Not knowing yet and yet sometimes discerning:
Discerning a little at Spring when the bud and shoot
With pointing finger show the hand at the root,
With stretching finger point the mood in the sky:
Sky and root in joint action; and the cry
Of the unsteady lamb allying with the brief
Sunlight, with the curled and cautious leaf.

    Coming out from our doorways on April evenings
    When to-morrow's sky is written on the slates
    We have discerned a little, we have learned
    More than the gossip that comes to us over our gates.
    We have seen old men cracking their memories for dry
      milk.
    We have seen old women dandling shadows;
    But coming out from our doorways, we have felt
    Heaven ride with Spring into the meadows.

We have felt the joint action of root and sky, of man
And God, when day first risks the hills, and when
The darkness hangs the hatchet in the barn
And scrapes the heavy boot against the iron:
In first and last twilight, before wheels have turned
Or after they are still, we have discerned:
Guessed at divinity working above the wind,
Working under our feet; or at the end

Of a furrow, watching the sun-dissolving lark
We have half-known, a little have known the work
That is with our work, as we have seen
The blackthorn hang where the Milky Way has been:
Flower and star spattering the sky
And the root touched by some divinity.

    Coming out from our doorways on October nights
    We have seen the sky unfreeze and a star drip
    Into the south: experienced alteration
    Beyond experience. We have felt the grip
    Of the hand on earth and sky in careful coupling
    Despite the jibbing, man destroying, denying,
    Disputing, or the late frost looting the land
    Of green. Despite flood and the lightning's rifle
    In root and sky we can discern the hand.

It is there in the story of Cuthman, the working together
Of man and God like root and sky; the son
Of a Cornish shepherd, Cuthman, the boy with a cart,
The boy we saw trudging the sheep-tracks with his mother
Mile upon mile over five counties; one
Fixed purpose biting his heels and lifting his heart.
We saw him; we saw him with a grass in his mouth, chewing
And travelling. We saw him building at last
A church among whortleberries. And you shall see
Now, in this place, the story of his going
And his building. – A thousand years in the past
There was a shepherd, and his son had three
Sorrows come together on him. Shadow
The boy. Follow him now as he runs in the meadow.

    Southern England

DERICK THOMSON (RUARAIDH MACTHÓMAIS)

Lewis in Summer

[translated by the author from his own Gaelic]

The atmosphere clear and transparent
as though the veil had been rent
and the Creator were sitting in full view of His people
eating potatoes and herring,
with no man to whom He can say grace.
Probably there's no other sky in the world
that makes it so easy for people
to look in on eternity;
you don't need philosophy
where you can make do with binoculars.

Outer Hebrides

TED HUGHES

Salmon-Taking Times

After a routing flood-storm, the river
Was a sounder of loud muddy pigs
Flushed out of hillsides. Tumbling hooligans
They jammed the old bends. Diabolical muscle,
Piglets, tusky boars, possessed, huge sows
Piling in the narrows.

                      I stayed clear. 'Swine
Bees and women cannot be turned.'

              But after
The warm shower
That just hazed and softened the daffodil buds

And clotted the primroses, a gauze
Struggles tenderly in the delighted current –
Clambers wetly on stones, and the river emerges
In glistenings, and gossamer, bridal veils,
And hovers over itself – there is a wedding
Delicacy –
                    so delicate
I touch it and its beauty-frailty crumples
To a smear of wet, a strengthless wreckage
Of dissolving membranes – and the air is ringing.

It is like a religious moment, slightly dazing.

It is like a shower of petals of eglantine.

JACK CLEMO

The Clay-Tip Worker

Our clay-dumps are converging on the land:
Each day a few more flowers are killed,
A few more mossy hollows filled
With gravel. Like a clutching hand
The refuse moves against the dower,
The flaunting pride and power
Of springtide beauty menacing the sod;
And it is joy to me
To lengthen thus a finger of God
That wars with Poetry.

I feel myself a priest,
Crusading from the tip-beams with my load
And pushing out along the iron lines
My gritty symbol of His new designs.
Creation's mood has ceased
Upon this ribbed height; here He has bestowed

Redemptive vision: I advance to pour
Sand, mud and rock upon the store
Of springtime loveliness idolaters adore.

The tarred rope winds across the mead,
Among the bushes and the weed,
Straight over grooved wheels from the sand-cone's ridge,
Back to the engine-house beside the bridge
I watch it draw the waggon up the rails,
Smack the surrounding foliage as it whirrs,
Daubing the ferns and furze
Till they droop black and battered, oily flails
Windblown against the turning spokes
Which catch and mangle frond and blossom, bend them
    over,
Spinning the puffy heads of clover
In dying blobs around the pulley-frames.
And here my faith acclaims
The righting of a balance, a full peace
Slipping from Nature's yokes,
Redemptive truth grey doctrines can release.

This sand-dump's base now licks a hedge
Whose snaky bramble-growths will bear
No flowers or fruit again; a few more days
And they'll be buried 'neath the wedge
Of settling gravel, rotting where
No naturalist may pry to mark their sleep.
The vomit then will creep
Up the sleek boughs of thorn trees that enwrap
The hedge-top, wound and smother them
Till splintered, jammed, they disappear, their sap
Bleeding and drying in the tomb I raise
High over root and soil and mouldering stem.

I love to see the sand I tip
Muzzle the grass and burst the daisy heads.

I watch the hard waves lapping out to still
The soil's rhythm for ever, and I thrill
With solitary song upon my lip,
Exulting as the refuse spreads:
'Praise God, the earth is maimed,
And there will be no daisies in that field
Next spring; it will not yield
A single bloom or grass blade: I shall see
In symbol potently
Christ's Kingdom there restored:
One patch of Poetry reclaimed
By Dogma: one more triumph for our Lord.'

Cornwall

R. S. THOMAS

Moorland

It is beautiful and still;
          the air rarefied
as the interior of a cathedral

expecting a presence. It is where, also,
          the harrier occurs,
materialising from nothing, snow-

soft, but with claws of fire,
          quartering the bare earth
for the prey that escapes it;

hovering over the incipient
          scream, here a moment, then
not here, like my belief in God.

Visions and Mysteries

ANONYMOUS

The Cliff of Alteran

[Irish, 12th century, translated by Brendan Kennelly]

As Sweeney ranged over Connaught
    He came to a lonely glen
Where a stream poured over a cliff
    And many holy men

Were gathered. Trees, heavy with fruit,
    Grew there by the score.
There were sheltering ivy bowers
    And apple trees galore.

Deer, hares and swine were there.
    On the warm cliff fat seals slept.
Sweeney watched while through his heart
    The raving madness swept.

    Connaught

WILLIAM LANGLAND

from Piers Plowman

[translated from the Middle English by E. Talbot Donaldson]

In a summer season when the sun was mild
I clad myself in clothes as I'd become a sheep;
In the habit of a hermit unholy of works
Walked wide in this world, watching for wonders.
And on a May morning, on Malvern Hills,

There befell me as by magic a marvelous thing:
I was weary of wandering and went to rest
At the bottom of a broad bank by a brook's side,
And as I lay lazily looking in the water
I slipped into a slumber, it sounded so pleasant.
There came to me reclining there a most curious dream
That I was in a wilderness, nowhere that I knew;
But as I looked into the east, up high toward the sun,
I saw a tower on a hill-top, trimly built,
A deep dale beneath, a dungeon tower in it,
With ditches deep and dark and dreadful to look at.
A fair field full of folk I found between them,
Of human beings of all sorts, the high and the low,
Working and wandering as the world requires.
   Some applied themselves to plowing, played very rarely,
Sowing seeds and setting plants worked very hard;
Won what wasters gluttonously consume.
And some pursued pride, put on proud clothing,
Came all got up in garments garish to see.
To prayers and penance many put themselves,
All for love of our Lord lived hard lives,
Hoping thereafter to have Heaven's bliss –
Such as hermits and anchorites that hold to their cells,
Don't care to go cavorting about the countryside,
With some lush livelihood delighting their bodies.
And some made themselves merchants – they managed
   better,
As it seems to our sight that such men prosper.
And some make mirth as minstrels can
And get gold for their music, guiltless, I think. [...]

Malvern Hills, West Midlands

WILLIAM BLAKE

from Jerusalem

The fields from Islington to Marybone,
To Primrose Hill and Saint John's Wood,
    Were builded over with pillars of gold,
And there Jerusalem's pillars stood.

Her Little-ones ran on the fields,
The Lamb of God among them seen,
    And fair Jerusalem his Bride,
Among the little meadows green.

Pancrass & Kentish-town repose
Among her golden pillars high,
    Among her golden arches which
Shine upon the starry sky.

The Jew's-harp-house & the Green Man,
The Ponds where Boys to bathe delight,
    The fields of Cows by Willan's farm,
Shine in Jerusalem's pleasant sight.

She walks upon our meadows green,
The Lamb of God walks by her side,
    And every English Child is seen
Children of Jesus & his Bride.

Forgiving trespasses and sins
Lest Babylon with cruel Og
    With Moral & Self-righteous Law
Should Crucify in Satan's Synagogue!

What are those golden Builders doing
Near mournful ever-weeping Paddington,
    Standing above that mighty Ruin
Where Satan the first victory won,

Where Albion slept beneath the Fatal Tree,
And the Druids' golden Knife
   Rioted in human gore,
In Offerings of Human Life?

   They groan'd aloud on London Stone,
They groan'd aloud on Tyburn's Brook,
   Albion gave his deadly groan,
And all the Atlantic Mountains shook.

   Albion's Spectre from his Loins
Tore forth in all the pomp of War:
   Satan his name: in flames of fire
He stretch'd his Druid Pillars far,

   Jerusalem fell from Lambeth's Vale
Down thro' Poplar & Old Bow,
   Thro' Malden & across the Sea,
In War & howling, death & woe.

North West London

T. S. ELIOT

Four Quartets: 'Little Gidding', Part I

Midwinter spring is its own season
Sempiternal though sodden towards sundown,
Suspended in time, between pole and tropic.
When the short day is brightest, with frost and fire,
The brief sun flames the ice, on pond and ditches,
In windless cold that is the heart's heat,
Reflecting in a watery mirror
A glare that is blindness in the early afternoon.
And glow more intense than blaze of branch, or brazier,
Stirs the dumb spirit: no wind, but pentecostal fire
In the dark time of the year. Between melting and freezing

The soul's sap quivers. There is no earth smell
Or smell of living thing. This is the spring time
But not in time's covenant. Now the hedgerow
Is blanched for an hour with transitory blossom
Of snow, a bloom more sudden
Than that of summer, neither budding nor fading,
Not in the scheme of generation.
Where is the summer, the unimaginable
Zero summer?

         If you came this way,
Taking the route you would be likely to take
From the place you would be likely to come from,
If you came this way in may time, you would find the hedges
White again, in May, with voluptuary sweetness.
It would be the same at the end of the journey,
If you came at night like a broken king,
If you came by day not knowing what you came for,
It would be the same, when you leave the rough road
And turn behind the pig-sty to the dull façade
And the tombstone. And what you thought you came for
Is only a shell, a husk of meaning
From which the purpose breaks only when it is fulfilled
If at all. Either you had no purpose
Or the purpose is beyond the end you figured
And is altered in fulfilment. There are other places
Which also are the world's end, some at the sea jaws,
Or over a dark lake, in a desert or a city –
But this is the nearest, in place and time,
Now and in England.

         If you came this way,
Taking any route, starting from anywhere,
At any time or at any season,
It would always be the same: you would have to put off
Sense and notion. You are not here to verify,
Instruct yourself, or inform curiosity

Or carry report. You are here to kneel
Where prayer has been valid. And prayer is more
Than an order of words, the conscious occupation
Of the praying mind, or the sound of the voice praying.
And what the dead had no speech for, when living,
They can tell you, being dead: the communication
Of the dead is tongued with fire beyond the language of the
    living.
Here, the intersection of the timeless moment
Is England and nowhere. Never and always.

Cambridgeshire

BASIL BUNTING

from Briggflatts, Part V

Winter wrings pigment
from petal and slough
but thin light lays
white next red on sea-crow wing,
gruff sole cormorant
whose grief turns carnival.
Even a bangle of birds
to bind sleeve to wrist
as west wind waves to east
a just perceptible greeting –
sinews ripple the weave,
threads flex, slew, hues meeting,
parting in whey-blue haze.

Mist sets lace of frost
on rock for the tide to mangle.
Day is wreathed in what summer lost.

Conger skimped at the ebb, lobster,
neither will I take, nor troll
roe of its like for salmon.
Let bass sleep, gentles
brisk, skim-grey,
group a nosegay
jostling on cast flesh,
frisk and compose decay
to side shot with flame,
unresting bluebottle wing. Sing,
strewing the notes on the air
as ripples skip in a shallow. Go
bare, the shore is adorned
with pungent weed loudly
filtering sand and sea.

Silver blades of surf
fall crisp on rustling grit,
shaping the shore as a mason
fondles and shapes his stone.

Shepherds follow the links,
sweet turf studded with thrift;
fell-born men of precise instep
leading demure dogs
from Tweed and Till and Teviotdale,
with hair combed back from the muzzle,
dogs from Redesdale and Coquetdale
taught by Wilson or Telfer.
Their teeth are white as birch,
slow under black fringe
of silent, accurate lips.
The ewes are heavy with lamb.
Snow lies bright on Hedgehope
and tacky mud about Till
where the fells have stepped aside

and the river praises itself,
silence by silence sits
and Then is diffused in Now.

Northumberland Coast

Spirits and Ghosts

WILLIAM WORDSWORTH

Resolution and Independence

I

There was a roaring in the wind all night;
The rain came heavily and fell in floods;
But now the sun is rising calm and bright;
The birds are singing in the distant woods;
Over his own sweet voice the Stock-dove broods;
The Jay makes answer as the Magpie chatters;
And all the air is filled with pleasant noise of waters.

II

All things that love the sun are out of doors;
The sky rejoices in the morning's birth;
The grass is bright with rain-drops; – on the moors
The hare is running races in her mirth;
And with her feet she from the plashy earth
Raises a mist; that, glittering in the sun,
Runs with her all the way, wherever she doth run.

III

I was a Traveller then upon the moor;
I saw the hare that raced about with joy;
I heard the woods and distant waters roar;
Or heard them not, as happy as a boy:
The pleasant season did my heart employ:
My old remembrances went from me wholly;
And all the ways of men, so vain and melancholy.

IV

But, as it sometimes chanceth, from the might
Of joy in minds that can no further go,
As high as we have mounted in delight
In our dejection do we sink as low;
To me that morning did it happen so;
And fears and fancies thick upon me came;
Dim sadness – and blind thoughts, I knew not, nor could
   name.

V

I heard the sky-lark warbling in the sky;
And I bethought me of the playful hare:
Even such a happy Child of earth am I;
Even as these blissful creatures do I fare;
Far from the world I walk, and from all care;
But there may come another day to me –
Solitude, pain of heart, distress, and poverty.

VI

My whole life I have lived in pleasant thought,
As if life's business were a summer mood;
As if all needful things would come unsought
To genial faith, still rich in genial good;
But how can He expect that others should
Build for him, sow for him, and at his call
Love him, who for himself will take no heed at all?

VII

I thought of Chatterton, the marvellous Boy,
The sleepless Soul that perished in his pride;
Of Him who walked in glory and in joy
Following his plough, along the mountain-side:
By our own spirits are we deified:

We Poets in our youth begin in gladness;
But thereof come in the end despondency and madness.

VIII

Now, whether it were by peculiar grace,
A leading from above, a something given,
Yet it befell, that, in this lonely place,
When I with these untoward thoughts had striven,
Beside a pool bare to the eye of heaven
I saw a Man before me unawares:
The oldest man he seemed that ever wore grey hairs.

IX

As a huge stone is sometimes seen to lie
Couched on the bald top of an eminence;
Wonder to all who do the same espy,
By what means it could thither come, and whence;
So that it seems a thing endued with sense:
Like a sea-beast crawled forth, that on a shelf
Of rock or sand reposeth, there to sun itself;

X

Such seemed this Man, not all alive nor dead,
Nor all asleep – in his extreme old age:
His body was bent double, feet and head
Coming together in life's pilgrimage;
As if some dire constraint of pain, or rage
Of sickness felt by him in times long past,
A more than human weight upon his frame had cast.

XI

Himself he propped, limbs, body, and pale face,
Upon a long grey staff of shaven wood:
And, still as I drew near with gentle pace,

Upon the margin of that moorish flood
Motionless as a cloud the old Man stood,
That heareth not the loud winds when they call;
And moveth all together, if it move at all.

XII

At length, himself unsettling, he the pond
Stirred with his staff, and fixedly did look
Upon the muddy water, which he conned,
As if he had been reading in a book:
And now a stranger's privilege I took;
And, drawing to his side, to him did say,
'This morning gives us promise of a glorious day.'

XIII

A gentle answer did the old Man make,
In courteous speech which forth he slowly drew:
And him with further words I thus bespake,
'What occupation do you there pursue?
This is a lonesome place for one like you.'
Ere he replied, a flash of mild surprise
Broke from the sable orbs of his yet-vivid eyes.

XIV

His words came feebly, from a feeble chest,
But each in solemn order followed each,
With something of a lofty utterance drest –
Choice word and measured phrase, above the reach
Of ordinary men; a stately speech;
Such as grave Livers do in Scotland use,
Religious men, who give to God and man their dues.

XV

He told, that to these waters he had come
To gather leeches, being old and poor:
Employment hazardous and wearisome!
And he had many hardships to endure:
From pond to pond he roamed, from moor to moor;
Housing, with God's good help, by choice or chance;
And in this way he gained an honest maintenance.

XVI

The old Man still stood talking by my side;
But now his voice to me was like a stream
Scarce heard; nor word from word could I divide;
And the whole body of the Man did seem
Like one whom I had met with in a dream;
Or like a man from some far region sent,
To give me human strength, by apt admonishment.

XVII

My former thoughts returned: the fear that kills;
And hope that is unwilling to be fed;
Cold, pain, and labour, and all fleshly ills;
And mighty Poets in their misery dead.
– Perplexed, and longing to be comforted,
My question eagerly did I renew,
'How is it that you live, and what is it you do?'

XVIII

He with a smile did then his words repeat;
And said that, gathering leeches, far and wide
He travelled; stirring thus about his feet
The waters of the pools where they abide.
'Once I could meet with them on every side;

But they have dwindled long by slow decay;
Yet still I persevere, and find them where I may.'

XIX

While he was talking thus, the lonely place,
The old Man's shape, and speech – all troubled me:
In my mind's eye I seemed to see him pace
About the weary moors continually,
Wandering about alone and silently.
While I these thoughts within myself pursued,
He, having made a pause, the same discourse renewed.

XX

And soon with this he other matter blended,
Cheerfully uttered, with demeanour kind,
But stately in the main; and when he ended,
I could have laughed myself to scorn to find
In that decrepit Man so firm a mind.
'God,' said I, 'be my help and stay secure;
I'll think of the Leech-gatherer on the lonely moor!'

MATTHEW ARNOLD

from The Scholar Gipsy

Go, for they call you, Shepherd, from the hill;
    Go, Shepherd, and untie the wattled cotes:
        No longer leave thy wistful flock unfed,
    Nor let thy bawling fellows rack their throats,
        Nor the cropp'd grasses shoot another head.
            But when the fields are still,

And the tired men and dogs all gone to rest,
  And only the white sheep are sometimes seen
    Cross and recross the strips of moon-blanch'd green;
      Come, Shepherd, and again renew the quest.

Here, where the reaper was at work of late,
  In this high field's dark corner, where he leaves
    His coat, his basket, and his earthen cruise,
  And in the sun all morning binds the sheaves,
    Then here, at noon, comes back his stores to use;
      Here will I sit and wait,
  While to my ear from uplands far away
    The bleating of the folded flocks is borne,
    With distant cries of reapers in the corn –
      All the live murmur of a summer's day.

Screen'd is this nook o'er the high, half-reap'd field,
  And here till sun-down, Shepherd, will I be.
    Through the thick corn the scarlet poppies peep
  And round green roots and yellowing stalks I see
    Pale blue convolvulus in tendrils creep:
      And air-swept lindens yield
  Their scent, and rustle down their perfum'd showers
    Of bloom on the bent grass where I am laid,
    And bower me from the August sun with shade;
      And the eye travels down to Oxford's towers:

And near me on the grass lies Glanvil's book –
  Come, let me read the oft-read tale again,
    The story of that Oxford scholar poor
  Of pregnant parts and quick inventive brain,
    Who, tir'd of knocking at Preferment's door,
      One summer morn forsook
  His friends, and went to learn the Gipsy lore,
    And roam'd the world with that wild brotherhood,
    And came, as most men deem'd, to little good,
      But came to Oxford and his friends no more.

But once, years after, in the country lanes,
　　Two scholars whom at college erst he knew
　　　Met him, and of his way of life enquir'd.
　　Whereat he answer'd, that the Gipsy crew,
　　　His mates, had arts to rule as they desir'd
　　　　The workings of men's brains;
　　And they can bind them to what thoughts they will:
　　　'And I,' he said, 'the secret of their art,
　　　When fully learn'd, will to the world impart:
　　　　But it needs heaven-sent moments for this skill.'

This said, he left them, and return'd no more,
　　But rumours hung about the country side
　　　That the lost Scholar long was seen to stray,
　　Seen by rare glimpses, pensive and tongue-tied,
　　　In hat of antique shape, and cloak of grey,
　　　　The same the Gipsies wore.
　　Shepherds had met him on the Hurst in spring:
　　　At some lone alehouse in the Berkshire moors,
　　　On the warm ingle bench, the smock-frock'd boors
　　　　Had found him seated at their entering,

But, mid their drink and clatter, he would fly:
　　And I myself seem half to know thy looks,
　　　And put the shepherds, Wanderer, on thy trace;
　　And boys who in lone wheatfields scare the rooks
　　　I ask if thou hast pass'd their quiet place;
　　　　Or in my boat I lie
　　Moor'd to the cool bank in the summer heats,
　　　Mid wide grass meadows which the sunshine fills,
　　　And watch the warm green-muffled Cumner hills,
　　　　And wonder if thou haunt'st their shy retreats.

For most, I know, thou lov'st retired ground.
　　Thee, at the ferry, Oxford riders blithe,
　　　Returning home on summer nights, have met
　　Crossing the stripling Thames at Bab-lock-hithe,

Trailing in the cool stream thy fingers wet,
   As the slow punt swings round:
And leaning backwards in a pensive dream,
   And fostering in thy lap a heap of flowers
   Pluck'd in shy fields and distant Wychwood bowers,
      And thine eyes resting on the moonlit stream.

And then they land, and thou art seen no more.
   Maidens who from the distant hamlets come
      To dance around the Fyfield elm in May,
   Oft through the darkening fields have seen thee roam,
      Or cross a stile into the public way.
         Oft thou hast given them store
   Of flowers – the frail-leaf'd, white anemone –
   Dark bluebells drench'd with dews of summer eves –
   And purple orchises with spotted leaves –
      But none has words she can report of thee.

And, above Godstow Bridge, when hay-time's here
   In June, and many a scythe in sunshine flames,
      Men who through those wide fields of breezy grass
   Where black-wing'd swallows haunt the glittering
         Thames,
      To bathe in the abandon'd lasher pass,
         Have often pass'd thee near
   Sitting upon the river bank o'ergrown:
      Mark'd thy outlandish garb, thy figure spare,
      Thy dark vague eyes, and soft abstracted air;
         But, when they came from bathing, thou wert gone.

At some lone homestead in the Cumner hills,
   Where at her open door the housewife darns,
      Thou hast been seen, or hanging on a gate
   To watch the threshers in the mossy barns.
      Children, who early range these slopes and late
         For cresses from the rills,
   Have known thee watching, all an April day,

The springing pastures and the feeding kine;
And mark'd thee, when the stars come out and shine,
Through the long dewy grass move slow away.

In Autumn, on the skirts of Bagley wood,
Where most the Gipsies by the turf-edg'd way
Pitch their smok'd tents, and every bush you see
With scarlet patches tagg'd and shreds of grey,
Above the forest ground call'd Thessaly –
The blackbird picking food
Sees thee, nor stops his meal, nor fears at all;
So often has he known thee past him stray
Rapt, twirling in thy hand a wither'd spray,
And waiting for the spark from Heaven to fall.

And once, in winter, on the causeway chill
Where home through flooded fields foot-travellers go,
Have I not pass'd thee on the wooden bridge
Wrapt in thy cloak and battling with the snow,
Thy face towards Hinksey and its wintry ridge?
And thou hast climb'd the hill
And gain'd the white brow of the Cumner range,
Turn'd once to watch, while thick the snowflakes fall,
The line of festal light in Christ-Church hall –
Then sought thy straw in some sequester'd grange.

But what – I dream! Two hundred years are flown
Since first thy story ran through Oxford halls,
And the grave Glanvil did the tale inscribe
That thou wert wander'd from the studious walls
To learn strange arts, and join a Gipsy tribe:
And thou from earth art gone
Long since, and in some quiet churchyard laid;
Some country nook, where o'er thy unknown grave
Tall grasses and white flowering nettles wave –
Under a dark red-fruited yew-tree's shade.

– No, no, thou hast not felt the lapse of hours.
  For what wears out the life of mortal men?
    'Tis that from change to change their being rolls:
'Tis that repeated shocks, again, again,
  Exhaust the energy of strongest souls,
    And numb the elastic powers.
Till having us'd our nerves with bliss and teen,
  And tir'd upon a thousand schemes our wit,
  To the just-pausing Genius we remit
    Our worn-out life, and are – what we have been.

Thou hast not liv'd, why should'st thou perish, so?
  Thou hadst *one* aim, *one* business, *one* desire:
    Else wert thou long since number'd with the dead –
Else hadst thou spent, like other men, thy fire.
  The generations of thy peers are fled,
    And we ourselves shall go;
But thou possessest an immortal lot,
  And we imagine thee exempt from age
  And living as thou liv'st on Glanvil's page,
    Because thou hadst – what we, alas, have not!

Oxford and environs

JOHN KEATS

La Belle Dame sans Merci

O, what can ail thee, knight at arms,
  Alone and palely loitering;
The sedge has withered from the lake,
  And no birds sing.

O, what can ail thee, knight at arms,
  So haggard and so woe-begone?
The squirrel's granary is full,
  And the harvest's done.

I see a lily on thy brow
　　With anguish moist and fever-dew,
And on thy cheeks a fading rose
　　Fast withereth too.

I met a lady in the meads,
　　Full beautiful – a faery's child,
Her hair was long, her foot was light,
　　And her eyes were wild.

I made a garland for her head,
　　And bracelets too, and fragrant zone,
She looked at me as she did love,
　　And made sweet moan.

I set her on my pacing steed
　　And nothing else saw all day long;
For sideways would she lean, and sing
　　A faery's song.

She found me roots of relish sweet,
　　And honey wild and manna dew;
And sure in language strange she said –
　　I love thee true.

She took me to her elfin grot,
　　And there she gazed and sighed full sore:
And there I shut her wild, wild eyes
　　With kisses four.

And there she lullèd me asleep,
　　And there I dreamed, ah woe betide,
The latest dream I ever dreamed
　　On the cold hill side.

I saw pale kings and princes too,
　　Pale warriors, death-pale were they all:
They cry'd – 'La belle Dame sans Merci
　　Hath thee in thrall!'

I saw their starved lips in the gloam
  With horrid warning gapèd wide,
And I awoke, and found me here
  On the cold hill side.

And this is why I sojourn here
  Alone and palely loitering,
Though the sedge is withered from the lake,
  And no birds sing.

THOMAS HARDY

Beeny Cliff

March 1870–March 1913

O the opal and the sapphire of that wandering western sea,
And the woman riding high above with bright hair flapping
  free –
The woman whom I loved so, and who loyally loved me.

The pale mews plained below us, and the waves seemed far
  away
In a nether sky, engrossed in saying their ceaseless babbling
  say,
As we laughed light-heartedly aloft on that clear-sunned
  March day.

A little cloud then cloaked us, and there flew an irised rain,
And the Atlantic dyed its levels with a dull misfeatured stain,
And then the sun burst out again, and purples prinked the
  main.

– Still in all its chasmal beauty bulks old Beeny to the sky,
And shall she and I not go there once again now March is
  nigh,
And the sweet things said in that March say anew there by
  and by?

What if still in chasmal beauty looms that wild weird
western shore,
The woman now is – elsewhere – whom the ambling pony
bore,
And nor knows nor cares for Beeny, and will laugh there
nevermore.

North Cornwall

CHARLES KINGSLEY

The Sands of Dee

'O Mary, go and call the cattle home,
    And call the cattle home,
    And call the cattle home
Across the sands of Dee;'
The western wind was wild and dank with foam,
    And all alone went she.

The western tide crept up along the sand,
    And o'er and o'er the sand,
    And round and round the sand,
    As far as eye could see.
The rolling mist came down and hid the land:
    And never home came she.

'Oh! is it weed, or fish, or floating hair –
    A tress of golden hair,
    A drownèd maiden's hair
Above the nets at sea?
Was never salmon yet that shone so fair
    Among the stakes on Dee.'

They rowed her in across the rolling foam,
    The cruel crawling foam,
    The cruel hungry foam,
  To her grave beside the sea:
But still the boatmen hear her call the cattle home
  Across the sands of Dee.

Cheshire

HILAIRE BELLOC

Ha'nacker Mill

Sally is gone that was so kindly
  Sally is gone from Ha'nacker Hill.
And the Briar grows ever since then so blindly
  And ever since then the clapper is still,
  And the sweeps have fallen from Ha'nacker Mill.

Ha'nacker Hill is in Desolation:
  Ruin a-top and a field unploughed.
And Spirits that call on a fallen nation
  Spirits that loved her calling aloud:
  Spirits abroad in a windy cloud.

Spirits that call and no one answers;
  Ha'nacker's down and England's done.
Wind and Thistle for pipe and dancers
  And never a ploughman under the Sun.
  Never a ploughman. Never a one.

Hallnacker Downs, West Sussex

RUDYARD KIPLING

The Way through the Woods

They shut the road through the woods
Seventy years ago.
Weather and rain have undone it again,
And now you would never know
There was once a road through the woods
Before they planted the trees.
It is underneath the coppice and heath
And the thin anemones.
Only the keeper sees
That, where the ring-dove broods,
And the badgers roll at ease,
There was once a road through the woods.

Yet, if you enter the woods
Of a summer evening late,
When the night-air cools on the trout-ringed pools
Where the otter whistles his mate,
(They fear not men in the woods,
Because they see so few.)
You will hear the beat of a horse's feet,
And the swish of a skirt in the dew,
Steadily cantering through
The misty solitudes,
As though they perfectly knew
The old lost road through the woods...
But there is no road through the woods.

Sussex

ROBERT BLOOMFIELD

The Fakenham Ghost

A Ballad

The lawns were dry in Euston Park;
(Here Truth inspires my Tale;)
The lonely footpath, still and dark,
Led over Hill and Dale.

Benighted was an ancient Dame,
And fearful haste she made
To gain the vale of Fakenham,
And hail its Willow shade.

Her footsteps knew no idle stops,
But follow'd faster still;
And echo'd to the darksome Copse
That whispere'd on the Hill;

Where clam'rous Rooks, yet scarcely hush'd,
Bespoke a peopled shade;
And many a wing the foliage brush'd,
And hov'ring circuits made.

The dappled herd of grazing Deer
That sought the Shades by day,
Now started from her path with fear,
And gave the Stranger way.

Darker it grew; and darker fears
Came o'er her troubled mind;
When now, a short quick step she hears
Come patting close behind.

She turn'd; it stopt! – nought could she see
Upon the gloomy plain!
But, as she strove the Sprite to flee,
She heard the same again.

Now terror seiz'd her quaking frame:
For, where the path was bare,
The trotting Ghost kept on the same!
She mutter'd many a pray'r.

Yet once again, amidst her fright,
She tried what sight could do;
When through the cheating glooms of night,
A Monster stood in view.

Regardless of whate'er she felt,
It follow'd down the plain!
She own'd her sins, and down she knelt,
And said her pray'rs again.

Then on she sped; and Hope grew strong,
The white park-gate in view;
Which pushing hard, so long it swung,
That Ghost and all pass'd through.

Loud fell the gate against the post!
Her heart-strings like to crack:
For, much she fear'd the grisly Ghost
Would leap upon her back.

Still on, pat, pat, the Goblin went,
As it had done before:–
Her strength and resolution spent,
She fainted at the door.

Out came her Husband, much surpris'd:
Out came her Daughter dear:
Good-natur'd souls! all unadvis'd
Of what they had to fear.

The Candle's gleam pierc'd through the night,
Some short space o'er the green;
And there the little trotting Sprite
Distinctly might be seen.

An Ass's Foal had lost its Dam
Within the spacious Park;
And, simple as the playful Lamb,
Had follow'd in the dark.

No Goblin he; no imp of sin:
No crimes had ever known.
They took the shaggy stranger in,
And rear'd him as their own.

His little hoofs would rattle round
Upon the Cottage floor;
The Matron learn'd to love the sound
That frighten'd her before.

A favourite the Ghost became;
And, 'twas his fate to thrive:
And long he liv'd and spread his fame,
And kept the joke alive.

For many a laugh went through the Vale;
And some conviction too:–
Each thought some other Goblin tale,
Perhaps, was just as true.

Suffolk

The Poet's Shadow

JOHN CLARE

'Look through the naked bramble and blackthorn'

Look through the naked bramble and blackthorn
And see the arum show its vivid green
Glossy and rich and some ink-spotted like the morn-
Ing sky with clouds – in sweetest neuks I've been
And seen the arum sprout its happy green
Full of spring visions and green thoughts
Dead leaves a-litter where its leaves are seen
Broader and brighter green from day to day
Beneath the hedges in their leafless spray

Here is the scenes the rural poet made
So famous in his songs – the very scenes
He painted in his words that warm and shade
In winter's wild waste and spring's young vivid greens
Alcove and shrubbery – and the tree that leans
With its overweight of Ivy – Yardley oak
The pheasant's nest and fields of blossomed beans
The bridge and avenue of thick-set oak
The wilderness – here Cowper's spirit spoke

   cf. Yardley Oak

SIDNEY KEYES

William Wordsworth

No room for mourning: he's gone out
Into the noisy glen, or stands between the stones

Of the gaunt ridge, or you'll hear his shout
Rolling among the screes, he being a boy again.
He'll never fail nor die
And if they laid his bones
In the wet vaults or iron sarcophagi
Of fame, he'd rise at the first summer rain
And stride across the hills to seek
His rest among the broken lands and clouds.
He was a stormy day, a granite peak
Spearing the sky; and look, about its base
Words flower like crocuses in the hanging woods,
Blank though the dalehead and the bony face.

Lake District

STEPHEN SPENDER

Worldsworth

Returned now, seventy years
Later, to the farmhouse
Beside the lake – finding
My way there as by instinct –
A sudden storm shuts down
The enormous view –
                    leaving
Only one drop of rain
Suspended from a leaf –

                    As through
The wrong end of a telescope
I look back to that day
Of August 1916
Our parents brought us here –
Because a Zeppelin,
Turned back from raiding London,

Damaged, across the coast,
Had jettisoned two bombs
Near Sheringham, our home.

                    *

I see in glassy miniature
Each precise particular:

        The van with us all in it
No sooner reaches the farmhouse
By Derwentwater than
We four children scramble out
To climb our first mountain:
CATBELLS its childish name –
With pelt of furze, fern, heather,
As tame for us to mount
As our donkey tethered by
The beach, at Sheringham.

                    *

Against the skyline, Michael
With arms and legs an X
Yells he has reached the top...

                    *

And all that summer was
Cornucopia that nature
Still pours profuse before me
Within my inmost eye
Like visions the old masters
Made frescoes of on walls:

Us rowing in our boat,
Us fishing, on the lake,
Us walking by the lake
Along the narrow road
A few feet from the water's

Rippling pellucid surface,
Distorted fish and weeds –

And on the road's far side
A ditch, and caves, where ferns
Unfurled heraldic tongues
Of glossy green which, under,
Concealed the dark brown spore.
But more than these I loved
The maiden hair fern with
Stalk fine as the coiled
Hairspring in my watch –
Its leaves minute green spots.

Then, from the road, a path
Led through a wood whose branches
Interweaving above
Seemed high as a cathedral
Sculpting out from shadow
Its own interior, within
Whose hush we stood, and watched
Under our feet the rain,
Dripping from that branched roof,
Collect into small puddles
On which huge black slugs drifted
Like barges on the Thames.

Beyond the wood, we came
Next to a clearing. Then
The rain stopped suddenly: the sky
Seemed one great sword of light
Raised above those bushes
Where berries, red and black,
Blazed like the crown jewels of
Some king much loved in legend
By his peace-loving people
(Among whom none were robbers),

Left on a hedge while he
Went hunting with his followers.

Beyond this there were fields
With slate walls between whose
Rough-hewn slabs, through shadows
Wedged between crevices,
Crystals like pinpoints pricked
Into the dark, their secrets.

But then the path traversed
The naked mountainside
Where, near it, lay the carcass
Of a dead ram, crawled over
By maggots, flies in swarms
As little caring whether
They battened upon eyes
Or guts or blood, as did
Those Zeppelins over London
Whether their bombs destroyed
Temples of stone, or flesh.

                    *

At dusk,
If there was no rain –
                    (great drops
Denting the flattened lake like boulders
Falling in molten lead,
Each one the centre of
Widening concentric circles) –

Our parents,
Seated in deck chairs on the lawn,
Read to each other poems

– The murmuring reached my bed –

Rhythms I knew called Wordsworth
Spreading through mountains, vales,
To fill, I thought, the world.
'*Worldsworth*', I thought, this peace
Of voices intermingling –
'Worldsworth', to me, a vow.

   Lake District

TED HUGHES

Emily Brontë

The wind on Crow Hill was her darling.
His fierce, high tale in her ear was her secret.
But his kiss was fatal.

Through her dark Paradise ran
The stream she loved too well
That bit her breast.

The shaggy sodden king of that kingdom
Followed through the wall
And lay on her love-sick bed.

The curlew trod in her womb.

The stone swelled under her heart.

Her death is a baby-cry on the moor.

   West Yorkshire

THOMAS HARDY

The Last Signal

(Oct. 11, 1886)
A memory of William Barnes

Silently I footed by an uphill road
That led from my abode to a spot yew-boughed;
Yellowly the sun sloped low down to westward,
          And dark was the east with cloud.

Then, amid the shadow of that livid sad east,
Where the light was least, and a gate stood wide,
Something flashed the fire of the sun that was facing it,
          Like a brief blaze on that side.

Looking hard and harder I knew what it meant –
The sudden shine sent from the livid east scene;
It meant the west mirrored by the coffin of my friend there,
          Turning to the road from his green,

To take his last journey forth – he who in his prime
Trudged so many a time from that gate athwart the land!
Thus a farewell to me he signalled on his grave-way,
          As with a wave of his hand.

          Winterborne-Carne Path

ELIZABETH JENNINGS

Hopkins in Wales

We know now how long that language,
Your language, had been dancing in you but
    Suppressed, held back by hard work, the debt
You owed to discipline. But no one, not one
    Stopped you looking, dissecting at a glance

A leaf, a tree's stump, while in your mind
    The long thought-over, now fermented
Ideas of Duns Scotus were waiting, the vintage
    Years about to be bottled at one sign, a word
From a Superior about the wreck you had read of.
    Worked-out ideas, your 'instress' and 'inscape',
Problems of prosody, 'Sprung Rhythm', came out dancing,
    Linked with that subject, and you wrote at last

    Guiltless, no squabble now between your vocation,
Endurance chosen as a priest, with art, two arts
    Now stretching within you with all the force of
Deliberations held back. And the discipline itself
    Appeared in selected stanzas, half-rhymes, senses once
        subdued
Unleashed into another order. A nun, a shipwreck
    Were set down, had happened but now would happen
Over and over in the committed, inexorable, also defenceless
    Way in which poems are always vulnerable. And every
        long look
At a leaf's individuality or the mark, his own, on a man's face
    Was dynamic. And the heroism heard of
Found place with all your admirations, while God's Presence
    Was granted a new kind of immanence in your lines.
        Doubtless

The no-understanding of others hurt but, far deeper
    And like the sea you wrote of, the fitness,
Inexorably of this exercise and joy, flowered in you, jetsam
    To others in time, acknowledged by you and by us
Years later. Let us hope you had some inkling of this
    As you rode through so many other poems until Dublin
Felled you like an axe or a wave into
    A desirable death, your work around you
Careful as carved stones simply waiting to be picked up,
    Wondered at, not static but dynamically precious,
Named by you, found by us, never diminishing.

MICHAEL HOFMANN

Myopia in Rupert Brooke Country

Birds, feathers, a few leaves, flakes of soot –
things start to fall. The stubble has been burned,
and the fields are striped in black and gold.
Elsewhere, the hay is still drying on long racks:
bulky men prancing about on slender hooves,
unconvincing as pantomime cattle ... A hedgehog
lies rolled over on its side like a broken castor.
Abandoned in one corner is a caravan that has
not been on holiday all year. Forever England...
A hot-air balloon sinks towards the horizon –
the amateur spirit or an advertising gimmick?
Quickly flames light it up, the primitive roar
of a kitchen geyser, and its calcified heart
gives a little skip, then slides down like tears.

ELIZABETH BARRETT BROWNING

from Aurora Leigh, Book I

Then, land! – then, England! oh, the frosty cliffs
Looked cold upon me. Could I find a home
Among those mean red houses through the fog?
And when I heard my father's language first
From alien lips which had no kiss for mine
I wept aloud, then laughed, then wept, then wept,
And some one near me said the child was mad
Through much sea-sickness. The train swept us on:
Was this my father's England? the great isle?
The ground seemed cut up from the fellowship
Of verdure, field from field, as man from man;

The skies themselves looked low and positive,
As almost you could touch them with a hand,
And dared to do it they were so far off
From God's celestial crystals; all things blurred
And dull and vague. Did Shakespeare and his mates
Absorb the light here? – not a hill or stone
With heart to strike a radiant colour up
Or active outline on the indifferent air. [...]

Whoever lives true life, will love true love.
I learnt to love that England. Very oft,
Before the day was born, or otherwise
Through secret windings of the afternoons,
I threw my hunters off and plunged myself
Among the deep hills, as a hunted stag
Will take the waters, shivering with the fear
And passion of the course. And when at last
Escaped, so many a green slope built on slope
Betwixt me and the enemy's house behind,
I dared to rest, or wander, in a rest
Made sweeter for the step upon the grass,
And view the grounds's most gentle dimplement,
(As if God's finger touched but did not press
In making England) such an up and down
Of verdure, – nothing too much up or down,
A ripple of land; such little hills, the sky
Can stoop to tenderly and the wheatfields climb;
Such nooks of valleys lined with orchises,
Fed full of noises by invisible streams;
And open pastures where you scarcely tell
White daisies from white dew, – at intervals
The mythic oaks and elm-trees standing out
Self-poised upon their prodigy of shade, –
I thought my father's land was worthy too
Of being my Shakespeare's.

  England (Shropshire/Herefordshire)

ARTHUR FREEMAN

The Reader Looks Up

See now how the English landscape lies
like an anthology open in the sun —
a rock-bound book, of even leaves
thumbed and unthumbed, of parts begun

and left undone, uncut, unread...
The Pastoral, e.g., to start:
once, all the streams were elegies,
and only such fish as chose to chart

an ideal course from source to weirs
swam there. In narcissistic pools
the imaged landscape rimed exact,
without the rules of riming schools.

Good things must end. A stylized knight
in stanzaic armor canters along
on a palfrey with dactylic feet.
Conventional blackbirds sing a song

of sovereigns, in the air like glass.
A purple patch of classic heather
bedecks each octosyllabic hillock
in a constancy of weather

courteously fair. Likewise
the Age of Romance closes out:
shared farms reform the epic flats
as paragraphs. Fat sluggish trout

are bred for sport by prosy squires,
while man-made poets prefer the town,
and practical crops lacquer the land
sack-yellow, and tobacco brown.

Wind thumbs the pages of my book
a quire at a time. The sun
sulks behind some symbolic clouds
as realistic rivers run

grim courses, bearing on their brim
the black newsprint of industry's
headlines: Where Thyrsis Lost His Sheep,
Morris Is Locating MGs.

All in a day. Clap shut the book.
What moral shall we draw tonight?
Say each age has its rhetoric,
which many edit, and few write.

   England

HUGH MACDIARMID

Skald's Death

I have known all the storms that roll.
I have been a singer after the fashion
Of my people – a poet of passion.
      All that is past.
Quiet has come into my soul.
Life's tempest is done.
      I lie at last
A bird cliff under a midnight sun.

   Coast of Scotland

Sounds

OLIVER GOLDSMITH

from The Deserted Village

   Sweet was the sound, when oft at evening's close,
Up yonder hill the village murmur rose;
There, as I past with careless steps and slow,
The mingling notes came soften'd from below;
The swain responsive as the milk-maid sung,
The sober herd that lowed to meet their young,
The noisy geese that gabbled o'er the pool,
The playful children just let loose from school,
The watch-dog's voice that bayed the whispering wind,
And the loud laugh that spoke the vacant mind,
These all in sweet confusion sought the shade,
And filled each pause the nightingale had made.
But now the sounds of population fail,
No cheerful murmurs fluctuate in the gale,
No busy steps the grass-grown foot-way tread,
For all the bloomy flush of life is fled.
All but yon widowed, solitary thing
That feebly bends beside the plashy spring;
She, wretched matron, forced in age, for bread,
To strip the brook with mantling cresses spread,
To pick her wintry faggot from the thorn,
To seek her nightly shed, and weep till morn;
She only left of all the harmless train,
The sad historian of the pensive plain.

  possibly Wiltshire

WILLIAM BLAKE

The Ecchoing Green

The Sun does arise,
And make happy the skies;
The merry bells ring
To welcome the Spring;
The skylark and thrush,
The birds of the bush,
Sing louder around
To the bells' chearful sound,
While our sports shall be seen
On the Ecchoing Green.

Old John, with white hair,
Does laugh away care,
Sitting under the oak,
Among the old folk.
They laugh at our play,
And soon they all say:
'Such, such were the joys
When we all, girls & boys,
In our youth time were seen
On the Ecchoing Green.'

Till the little ones, weary,
No more can be merry;
The sun does descend,
And our sports have an end.
Round the laps of their mothers
Many sisters and brothers,
Like birds in their nest,
Are ready for rest,
And sport no more seen
On the darkening Green.

SAMUEL TAYLOR COLERIDGE

The Eolian Harp

Composed at Clevedon, Somersetshire

My pensive Sara! thy soft cheek reclined
Thus on mine arm, most soothing sweet it is
To sit beside our Cot, our Cot o'ergrown
With white-flower'd Jasmin, and the broad-leav'd Myrtle,
(Meet emblems they of Innocence and Love!)
And watch the clouds, that late were rich with light,
Slow saddening round, and mark the star of eve
Serenely brilliant (such should Wisdom be)
Shine opposite! How exquisite the scents
Snatch'd from yon bean-field! and the world *so* hush'd!
The stilly murmur of the distant Sea
Tells us of silence.
                              And that simplest Lute,
Placed length-ways in the clasping casement, hark!
How by the desultory breeze caress'd,
Like some coy maid half yielding to her lover,
It pours such sweet upbraiding, as must needs
Tempt to repeat the wrong! And now, its strings
Boldlier swept, the long sequacious notes
Over delicious surges sink and rise,
Such a soft floating witchery of sound
As twilight Elfins make, when they at eve
Voyage on gentle gales from Fairy-Land,
Where Melodies round honey-dropping flowers,
Footless and wild, like birds of Paradise,
Nor pause, nor perch, hovering on untam'd wing!
O! the one Life within us and abroad,
Which meets all motion and becomes its soul,
A light in sound, a sound-like power in light,
Rhythm in all thought, and joyance every where –

Methinks, it should have been impossible
Not to love all things in a world so fill'd;
Where the breeze warbles, and the mute still air
Is Music slumbering on her instrument.

   And thus, my Love! as on the midway slope
Of yonder hill I stretch my limbs at noon,
Whilst through my half-clos'd eye-lids I behold
The sunbeams dance, like diamonds, on the main,
And tranquil muse upon tranquillity;
Full many a thought uncall'd and undetain'd,
And many idle flitting phantasies,
Traverse my indolent and passive brain,
As wild and various as the random gales
That swell and flutter on this subject Lute!
   And what if all of animated nature
Be but organic Harps diversely fram'd,
That tremble into thought, as o'er them sweeps
Plastic and vast, one intellectual breeze,
At once the Soul of each, and God of all?
   But thy more serious eye a mild reproof
Darts, O belovèd Woman! nor such thoughts
Dim and unhallow'd dost thou not reject,
And biddest me walk humbly with my God.
Meek Daughter in the family of Christ!
Well hast thou said and holily disprais'd
These shapings of the unregenerate mind;
Bubbles that glitter as they rise and break
On vain Philosophy's aye-babbling spring.
For never guiltless may I speak of him,
The Incomprehensible! save when with awe
I praise him, and with Faith that inly *feels*;
Who with his saving mercies healèd me,
A sinful and most miserable man,
Wilder'd and dark, and gave me to possess
Peace and this Cot, and thee, heart-honour'd Maid!

WILLIAM WORDSWORTH

from Poems on the Naming of Places

It was an April morning: fresh and clear
The Rivulet, delighting in its strength,
Ran with a young man's speed; and yet the voice
Of waters which the winter had supplied
Was softened down into a vernal tone.
The spirit of enjoyment and desire,
And hopes and wishes, from all living things
Went circling, like a multitude of sounds.
The budding groves seemed eager to urge on
The steps of June; as if their various hues
Were only hindrances that stood between
Them and their object: but, meanwhile, prevailed
Such an entire contentment in the air
That every naked ash, and tardy tree
Yet leafless, showed as if the countenance
With which it looked on this delightful day
Were native to the summer. – Up the brook
I roamed in the confusion of my heart,
Alive to all things and forgetting all.
At length I to a sudden turning came
In this continuous glen, where down a rock
The Stream, so ardent in its course before,
Sent forth such sallies of glad sound, that all
Which I till then had heard appeared the voice
Of common pleasure: beast and bird, the lamb,
The shepherd's dog, the linnet and the thrush
Vied with this waterfall, and made a song,
Which, while I listened, seemed like the wild growth
Or like some natural produce of the air,
That could not cease to be. [...]

Easedale, Lake District

JOHN DAVIDSON

In Romney Marsh

As I went down to Dymchurch Wall,
    I heard the South sing o'er the land;
I saw the yellow sunlight fall
    On knolls where Norman churches stand.

And ringing shrilly, taut and lithe,
    Within the wind a core of sound,
The wire from Romney town to Hythe
    Alone its airy journey wound.

A veil of purple vapour flowed
    And trailed its fringe along the Straits;
The upper air like sapphire glowed;
    And roses filled Heaven's central gates.

Masts in the offing wagged their tops;
    The swinging waves pealed on the shore;
The saffron beach, all diamond drops
    And beads of surge, prolonged the roar.

As I came up from Dymchurch Wall,
    I saw above the Downs' low crest
The crimson brands of sunset fall,
    Flicker and fade from out the west.

Night sank: like flakes of silver fire
    The stars in one great shower came down;
Shrill blew the wind; and shrill the wire
    Rang out from Hythe to Romney town.

The darkly shining salt sea drops
   Streamed as the waves clashed on the shore;
The beach, with all its organ stops
   Pealing again, prolonged the roar.

   Kent

VERNON WATKINS

Waterfalls

Always in that valley in Wales I hear the noise
   Of waters falling.
               There is a clump of trees
    We climbed for nuts; and high in the trees the boys
     Lost in the rookery's cries
       Would cross, and branches cracking under their
       knees

Would break, and make in the winter wood new gaps.
   The leafmould covering the ground was almost black,
    But speckled and striped were the nuts we threw in our
    caps,
     Milked from split shells and cups,
      Secret as chestnuts when they are tipped from a sack,

Glossy and new.
             Always in that valley in Wales
   I hear that sound, those voices. They keep fresh
    What ripens, falls, drops into darkness, fails,
     Gone when dawn shines on scales,
      And glides from village memory, slips through the
      mesh,

And is not, when we come again.
                              I look:
  Voices are under the bridge, and that voice calls,
     Now late, and answers;
                                   then, as the light twigs break
        Back, there is only the brook
            Reminding the stones where, under a breath, it falls.

  Wales

JOHN MONTAGUE

Windharp

for Patrick Collins

The sounds of Ireland,
that restless whispering
you never get away
from, seeping out of
low bushes and grass,
heatherbells and fern,
wrinkling bog pools,
scraping tree branches,
light hunting cloud,
sound hounding sight,
a hand ceaselessly
combing and stroking
the landscape, till
the valley gleams
like the pile upon
a mountain pony's coat.

  Ireland

JOHN KEATS

from To Autumn

Where are the songs of Spring? Ay, where are they?
    Think not of them, thou hast thy music too –
While barrèd clouds bloom the soft-dying day,
    And touch the stubble-plains with rosy hue:
Then in a wailful choir the small gnats mourn
    Among the river sallows, borne aloft
        Or sinking as the light wind lives or dies;
And full-grown lambs loud bleat from hilly bourn;
    Hedge-crickets sing; and now with treble soft
    The red-breast whistles from a garden-croft;
        And gathering swallows twitter in the skies.

    Winchester, Hampshire

TED HUGHES

Telegraph Wires

Take telegraph wires, a lonely moor,
And fit them together. The thing comes alive in your ear.

Towns whisper to towns over the heather.
But the wires cannot hide from the weather.

So oddly, so daintily made
It is picked up and played.

Such unearthly airs
The ear hears, and withers!

In the revolving ballroom of space,
Bowed over the moor, a bright face

Draws out of telegraph wires the tones
That empty human bones.

JOHN BETJEMAN

On Hearing the Full Peal of Ten Bells from Christ Church, Swindon, Wilts.

Your peal of ten ring over then this town,
Ring on any men nor ever ring them down.
This winter chill, let sunset spill cold fire
On villa'd hill and on Sir Gilbert's spire,
So new, so high, so pure, so broach'd, so tall.
Long run the thunder of the bells through all!

Oh still white headstones on these fields of sound
Hear you the wedding joybells wheeling round?
Oh brick-built breeding boxes of new souls,
Hear how the pealing through the louvres rolls!
Now birth and death-reminding bells ring clear,
Loud under 'planes and over changing gear.

   Wiltshire

Birds and Birdsong

JOHN CLARE

from The Shepherd's Calendar ('March')

Muffld in baffles leathern coat and gloves
The hedger toils oft scaring rustling doves
From out the hedgrows who in hunger browze
The chockolate berrys on the ivy boughs
And flocking field fares speckld like the thrush
Picking the red awe from the sweeing bush
That come and go on winters chilling wing
And seem to share no sympathy wi spring
The stooping ditcher in the water stands
Letting the furrowd lakes from off the lands
Or splashing cleans the pasture brooks of mud
Where many a wild weed freshens into bud
And sprouting from the bottom purply green
The water cresses neath the wave is seen
Which the old woman gladly drags to land
Wi reaching long rake in her tottering hand
The ploughman mawls along the doughy sloughs
And often stops their songs to clean their ploughs
From teazing twitch that in the spongy soil
Clings round the colter terryfying toil
The sower striding oer his dirty way
Sinks anckle deep in pudgy sloughs and clay
And oer his heavy hopper stoutly leans
Strewing wi swinging arms the pattering beans
Which soon as aprils milder weather gleams
Will shoot up green between the furroed seams
The driving boy glad when his steps can trace
The swelling edding as a resting place

Slings from his clotted shoes the dirt around
And feign woud rest him on the solid ground
And sings when he can meet the parting green
Of rushy balks that bend the lands between
While close behind em struts the nauntling crow
And daws whose heads seem powderd oer wi snow
To seek the worms – and rooks a noisey guest
That on the wind rockd elms prepares her nest
On the fresh furrow often drops to pull
The twitching roots and gathering sticks and wool
Neath trees whose dead twigs litter to the wind
And gaps where stray sheep left their coats behind
While ground larks on a sweeing clump of rushes
Or on the top twigs of the oddling bushes
Chirp their 'cree creeing' note that sounds of spring
And sky larks meet the sun wi flittering wing
Soon as the morning opes its brightning eye
Large clouds of sturnels blacken thro the sky
From oizer holts about the rushy fen
And reedshaw borders by the river Nen
And wild geese regiments now agen repair
To the wet bosom of broad marshes there
In marching coloms and attention all
Listning and following their ringleaders call
The shepherd boy that hastens now and then
From hail and snow beneath his sheltering den
Of flags or file leavd sedges tyd in sheaves
Or stubble shocks oft as his eye percieves
Sun threads struck out wi momentery smiles
Wi fancy thoughts his lonliness beguiles
Thinking the struggling winter hourly bye
As down the edges of the distant sky
The hailstorm sweeps – and while he stops to strip
The stooping hedgbriar of its lingering hip
He hears the wild geese gabble oer his head
And pleasd wi fancys in his musings bred

He marks the figurd forms in which they flye
And pausing follows wi a wandering eye
Likening their curious march in curves or rows
To every letter which his memory knows
While far above the solitary crane
Swings lonly to unfrozen dykes again
Cranking a jarring mellancholy cry
Thro the wild journey of the cheerless sky [...]

    Northamptonshire/Cambridgeshire

JOHN LYLY

from Campaspe

What bird so sings, yet so does wail?
Oh, 'tis the ravished nightingale.
Jug, jug, jug, jug, tereu, she cries,
And still her woes at midnight rise.
Brave prick-song! Who is 't now we hear?
None but the lark, so shrill and clear:
Now at heaven's gate she claps her wings,
The morn not waking till she sings!
Hark, hark, with what a pretty throat
Poor robin redbreast tunes his note!
Hark how the jolly cuckoos sing!

THOMAS RANDOLPH

On the Death of a Nightingale

Goe solitary wood, and henceforth be
Aequainted with no other Harmonie,
Then the Pyes chattering, or the shreeking note

Of bodeing Owles, and fatall Ravens throate.
Thy sweetest Chanters dead, that warbled forth
Layes, that might tempests calme, and still the North;
And call downe Angels from their glorious Spheare
To heare her Songs, and learne new Anthems there.
That soule is fled, and to *Elisium* gone;
Thou a poor desert left; goe then and runne,
Begge there to stand a grove, and if shee please
To sing againe beneath thy shadowy Trees;
The soules of happy Lovers crown'd with blisses
Shall flock about thee, and keepe time with kisses.

JOHN KEATS

Ode to a Nightingale

My heart aches, and a drowsy numbness pains
   My sense, as though of hemlock I had drunk,
Or emptied some dull opiate to the drains
   One minute past, and Lethe-wards had sunk:
'Tis not through envy of thy happy lot,
   But being too happy in thy happiness,
      That thou, light-wingèd Dryad of the trees,
         In some melodious plot
   Of beechen green, and shadows numberless,
      Singest of summer in full-throated ease.

O for a draught of vintage! that hath been
   Cooled a long age in the deep-delvèd earth,
Tasting of Flora and the country-green,
   Dance, and Provençal song, and sunburnt mirth!
O for a beaker full of the warm South!
   Full of the true, the blushful Hippocrene,
      With beaded bubbles winking at the brim,
         And purple-stainèd mouth;

That I might drink, and leave the world unseen,
  And with thee fade away into the forest dim:

Fade far away, dissolve, and quite forget
  What thou among the leaves hast never known,
The weariness, the fever, and the fret
  Here, where men sit and hear each other groan;
Where palsy shakes a few, sad, last grey hairs,
  Where youth grows pale, and spectre-thin, and dies;
    Where but to think is to be full of sorrow
      And leaden-eyed despairs;
  Where Beauty cannot keep her lustrous eyes,
    Or new Love pine at them beyond to-morrow.

Away! away! for I will fly to thee,
  Not charioted by Bacchus and his pards,
But on the viewless wings of Poesy,
  Though the dull brain perplexes and retards:
Already with thee! tender is the night,
  And haply the Queen-Moon is on her throne,
    Clustered around by all her starry Fays;
      But here there is no light,
  Save what from heaven is with the breezes blown
    Through verdurous glooms and winding mossy ways.

I cannot see what flowers are at my feet,
  Nor what soft incense hangs upon the boughs,
But, in embalmèd darkness, guess each sweet
  Wherewith the seasonable month endows
The grass, the thicket, and the fruit-tree wild;
  White hawthorn, and the pastoral eglantine;
    Fast fading violets covered up in leaves;
      And mid-May's eldest child,
  The coming musk-rose, full of dewy wine,
    The murmurous haunt of flies on summer eves.

Darkling I listen; and for many a time
  I have been half in love with easeful Death,

Called him soft names in many a musèd rhyme,
    To take into the air my quiet breath;
Now more than ever seems it rich to die,
    To cease upon the midnight with no pain,
        While thou art pouring forth thy soul abroad
            In such an ecstasy!
    Still wouldst thou sing, and I have ears in vain –
        To thy high requiem become a sod.

Thou wast not born for death, immortal Bird!
    No hungry generations tread thee down;
The voice I hear this passing night was heard
    In ancient days by emperor and clown:
Perhaps the self-same song that found a path
    Through the sad heart of Ruth, when, sick for home,
        She stood in tears amid the alien corn;
            The same that oft times hath
    Charmed magic casements, opening on the foam
    Of perilous seas, in faery lands forlorn.

Forlorn! the very word is like a bell
    To toll me back from thee to my sole self!
Adieu! the fancy cannot cheat so well
    As she is famed to do, deceiving elf.
Adieu! adieu! thy plaintive anthem fades
    Past the near meadows, over the still stream,
        Up the hill-side; and now 'tis buried deep
            In the next valley-glades:
    Was it a vision, or a waking dream?
        Fled is that music:– do I wake or sleep?

WILLIAM WORDSWORTH

'Yes it was the mountain Echo'

Yes it was the mountain Echo,
Solitary, clear, profound,
Answering to the shouting Cuckoo,
Giving to her sound for sound!

Unsolicited reply
To a babbling wanderer sent;
Like her ordinary cry,
Like – but oh, how different!

Hears not also mortal life?
Hear not we, unthinking Creatures!
Slaves of folly, love, or strife –
Voices of two different natures?

Have not we too? – yes, we have
Answers, and we know not whence;
Echoes from beyond the grave,
Recognised intelligence!

Such rebounds our inward ear
Catches sometimes from afar –
Listen, ponder, hold them dear;
For of God, – of God they are.

ALFRED, LORD TENNYSON

The Dying Swan

I

The plain was grassy, wild and bare,
Wide, wild, and open to the air,
Which had built up everywhere
   An under-roof of doleful grey.
With an inner voice the river ran,
Adown it floated a dying swan,
      And loudly did lament.
   It was the middle of the day.
Ever the weary wind went on,
      And took the reed-tops as it went.

II

Some blue peaks in the distance rose,
And white against the cold-white sky,
Shone out their crowning snows.
   One willow over the river wept,
And shook the wave as the wind did sigh;
Above in the wind was the swallow,
   Chasing itself at its own wild will,
   And far thro' the marish green and still
   The tangled water-courses slept,
Shot over with purple, and green, and yellow.

III

The wild swan's death-hymn took the soul
Of that waste place with joy
Hidden in sorrow: at first to the ear
The warble was low, and full and clear;

And floating about the under-sky,
Prevailing in weakness, the coronach stole
Sometimes afar, and sometimes anear;
But anon her awful jubilant voice,
With a music strange and manifold,
Flow'd forth on a carol free and bold;
As when a mighty people rejoice
With shawms, and with cymbals, and harps of gold,
And the tumult of their acclaim is roll'd
Thro' the open gates of the city afar,
To the shepherd who watcheth the evening star.
And the creeping mosses and clambering weeds,
And the willow-branches hoar and dank,
And the wavy swell of the soughing reeds,
And the wave-worn horns of the echoing bank,
And the silvery marish-flowers that throng
The desolate creeks and pools among,
Were flooded over with eddying song.

W. B. YEATS

The Wild Swans at Coole

The trees are in their autumn beauty,
The woodland paths are dry,
Under the October twilight the water
Mirrors a still sky;
Upon the brimming water among the stones
Are nine-and-fifty swans.

The nineteenth autumn has come upon me
Since I first made my count;
I saw, before I had well finished,
All suddenly mount
And scatter wheeling in great broken rings
Upon their clamorous wings.

I have looked upon those brilliant creatures,
And now my heart is sore.
All's changed since I, hearing at twilight,
The first time on this shore,
The bell-beat of their wings above my head,
Trod with a lighter tread.

Unwearied still, lover by lover,
They paddle in the cold
Companionable streams or climb the air;
Their hearts have not grown old;
Passion or conquest, wander where they will,
Attend upon them still.

But now they drift on the still water,
Mysterious, beautiful;
Among what rushes will they build,
By what lake's edge or pool
Delight men's eyes when I awake some day
To find they have flown away?

THOMAS HARDY

The Darkling Thrush

I leant upon a coppice gate
    When Frost was spectre-gray,
And Winter's dregs made desolate
    The weakening eye of day.
The tangled bine-stems scored the sky
    Like strings of broken lyres,
And all mankind that haunted nigh
    Had sought their household fires...

At once a voice arose among
    The bleak twigs overhead

In a full-hearted evensong
    Of joy illimited;
An agèd thrush, frail, gaunt, and small,
    In blast-beruffled plume,
Had chosen thus to fling his soul
    Upon the growing gloom.

So little cause for carollings
    Of such ecstatic sound
Was written on terrestrial things
    Afar or nigh around,
That I could think there trembled through
    His happy goodnight air
Some blessed Hope, whereof he knew
    And I was unaware.

EDWARD THOMAS

Adlestrop

Yes. I remember Adlestrop –
The name, because one afternoon
Of heat the express-train drew up there
Unwontedly. It was late June.

The steam hissed. Someone cleared his throat
No one left and no one came
On the bare platform. What I saw
Was Adlestrop – only the name

And willows, willow-herb, and grass,
And meadowsweet, and haycocks dry,
No whit less still and lonely fair
Than the high cloudlets in the sky.

And for that minute a blackbird sang
Close by, and round him, mistier,

Farther and farther, all the birds
Of Oxfordshire and Gloucestershire.

  Cotswolds

FRANCIS LEDWIDGE

The Herons

As I was climbing Ardan Mór
From the shore of Sheelin lake,
I met the herons coming down
Before the water's wake.

And they were talking in their flight
Of dreamy ways the herons go
When all the hills are withered up
Nor any waters flow.

ANNE RIDLER

Bempton Cliffs

Strangely quiet, the cliffs are, as we approach.
The sea swallows the sound until, suddenly,
As though a door were opened into a hall
(A prayer meeting, a gaggle of gossiping talkers)
It's there, around us. And the sky in shreds
With whirling birds.

Now I am earthbound in a city of fliers,
A rooted maypole, while about my head
The dancers weave their patterns, maypole ribbons
Of varying flight, and their incessant cries
Are skeins of sound, flung up into the air.

Law rules the dance; in all these comings and goings
None is aimless. And all comparisons –
Comic, anthropomorphic – that spring to mind
At the sight of guillemots, tier upon tier
In dinner-jackets, like a festival chorus,
Are out of place.
                    Comparisons anyhow
Die in astonishment when we reach the cliff
Where the great ocean birds are perched.

That was no tractor you heard, but the gannets' talk.

The gale-masters, precipitous plungers,
Brood here on their scraps of net
With smaller birds around them. Viking beak
With its armoured look, subdued for a mating kiss,
Domestic as a farmyard goose;
So close, it seems as though a hand stretched out
Could touch and stroke the saffron head.

   Humberside

WILLIAM WORDSWORTH

from There Was a Boy

There was a Boy; ye knew him well, ye cliffs
And islands of Winander! – many a time,
At evening, when the earliest stars began
To move along the edges of the hills,
Rising or setting, would he stand alone,
Beneath the trees, or by the glimmering lake;
And there, with fingers interwoven, both hands
Pressed closely palm to palm and to his mouth
Uplifted, he, as through an instrument,
Blew mimic hootings to the silent owls,

That they might answer him. – And they would shout
Across the watery vale, and shout again,
Responsive to his call, – with quivering peals,
And long halloos, and screams, and echoes loud
Redoubled and redoubled; concourse wild
Of jocund din! And, when there came a pause
Of silence such as baffled his best skill:
Then, sometimes, in that silence, while he hung
Listening, a gentle shock of mild surprise
Has carried far into his heart the voice
Of mountain-torrents; or the visible scene
Would enter unawares into his mind
With all its solemn imagery, its rocks,
Its woods, and that uncertain heaven received
Into the bosom of the steady lake.

Winander? Windermere?

Colour and the Painter's Eye

GERARD MANLEY HOPKINS

Pied Beauty

Glory be to God for dappled things –
  For skies of couple-colour as a brinded cow;
    For rose-moles all in stipple upon trout that swim;

Fresh fire-coal chestnut-falls; finches' wings;
  Landscape plotted and pieced – fold, fallow, and plough;
    And all trades, their gear and tackle and trim.

All things counter, original, spare, strange;
  Whatever is fickle, freckled (who knows how?)
    With swift, slow; sweet, sour; adazzle, dim;
He fathers-forth whose beauty is past change:
    Praise him.

North Wales

CHARLES TOMLINSON

A Meditation on John Constable

Painting is a science, and should be pursued as an inquiry into the laws of
nature. Why, then, may not landscape painting be considered as a branch
of natural philosophy, of which pictures are but the experiments?
                John Constable, *The History of Landscape Painting*

He replied to his own question, and with the unmannered
  Exactness of art; enriched his premises
By confirming his practice: the labour of observation
  In face of meteorological fact. Clouds

Followed by others, temper the sun in passing
   Over and off it. Massed darks
Blotting it back, scattered and mellowed shafts
   Break damply out of them, until the source
Unmasks, floods its retreating bank
   With raw fire. One perceives (though scarcely)
The remnant clouds trailing across it
   In rags, and thinned to a gauze.
But the next will dam it. They loom past
   And narrow its blaze. It shrinks to a crescent
Crushed out, a still lengthening ooze
   As the mass thickens, though cannot exclude
Its silvered-yellow. The eclipse is sudden,
   Seen first on the darkening grass, then complete
In a covered sky.
                  Facts. And what are they?
He admired accidents, because governed by laws,
   Representing them (since the illusion was not his end)
As governed by feeling. The end is our approval
   Freely accorded, the illusion persuading us
That it exists as a human image. Caught
   By a wavering sun, or under a wind
Which moistening among the outlines of banked foliage
   Prepares to dissolve them, it must grow constant;
Though there, ruffling and parted, the disturbed
   Trees let through the distance, like white fog
Into their broken ranks. It must persuade
   And with a constancy, not to be swept back
To reveal what it half-conceals. Art is itself
   Once we accept it. The day veers. He would have judged
Exactly in such a light, that strides down
   Over the quick stains of cloud-shadows
Expunged now, by its conflagration of colour.
   A descriptive painter? If delight
Describes, which wrings from the brush
   The errors of a mind, so tempered,

It can forgo all pathos; for what he saw
   Discovered what he was, and the hand – unswayed
By the dictation of a single sense –
   Bodied the accurate and total knowledge
In a calligraphy of present pleasure. Art
   Is complete when it is human. It is human
Once the looped pigments, the pin-heads of light
   Securing space under their deft restrictions
Convince, as the index of a possible passion,
   As the adequate gauge, both of the passion
And its object. The artist lies
   For the improvement of truth. Believe him.

   Dedham, Essex

WILLIAM BARNES

Green

Our zummer way to church did wind about
The cliff, where ivy on the ledge wer green.

Our zummer way to town did skirt the wood,
Where sheenèn leaves in tree an' hedge wer green.

Our zummer way to milkèn in the meäd,
Wer on by brook, where fluttrèn zedge wer green.

Our hwomeward ways did all run into one,
Where moss upon the roofstwones' edge were green.

   Dorset

RUTH PITTER

Dun-Colour

Subtle almost beyond thought are these dim colours,
The mixed, the all-including, the pervasive,
Earth's own delightful livery, banqueting
The eye with dimness that includes all brightness;
Complexity which the mind sorts out, as the sunlight
Resolves into many purities the mingled
Dun fleeces of the moorland; the quartz sparkles,
The rosy heath glows, the mineral-like mosses
And the heathbells and the myriad lichens
Start each into the eye a separate splendour:
So in the mind's sun bloom the dim dun-colours.

The dry vermilion glow of familiar redbreast
Is not his real glory: that is the greenish,
Light-toned, light-dissembling, eye-deceiving
Dun of his smooth-sloped back, and on his belly
The whitish dun is laid to deceive the shadow:
In the dear linnet the olive-dun is lovely,
And the primrose-duns in the yellowhammer: but most
    beguiling,
Perhaps because of the perfect shape, is the ash-dun,
That quietest, most urbane, unprofaneable colour
Reserved as her livery of beauty to the hedge-sparrow.
There is a royal azure in her blood,
As her eggs prove, and in her nature gold,
For her children's throats are kingcups; but she veils them,
Mingled and blended, in her rare dun-colour.

For the rose-duns, and the blue-duns, look to the finches:
For the clear clear brown-duns, to the fallow deer
(How the sudden tear smarts in the eye wearied of cities)
And for all these and more to the many toadstools,

Which alone have the violet-dun, livid yet lovely:
But the most delicate duns are seen in the gentle
Monkeys from the great forests, the silvan spirits:
Wonderful! that these, almost our brothers,
Should be dressed so rarely, in sulphurous-dun and greenish;
O that a man had grassy hair like these dryads!
O that I too were attired in such dun-colours.

ROBERT BROWNING

from Christmas Eve

IV

There was a lull in the rain, a lull
    In the wind too; the moon was risen,
And would have shone out pure and full,
    But for the ramparted cloud-prison,
Block on block built up in the West,
For what purpose the wind knows best,
Who changes his mind continually.
And the empty other half of the sky
Seemed in its silence as if it knew
What, any moment, might look through
A chance gap in that fortress massy:—
    Through its fissures you got hints
    Of the flying moon, by the shifting tints,
Now, a dull lion-colour, now, brassy
Burning to yellow, and whitest yellow,
Like furnace-smoke just ere flames bellow,
All a-simmer with intense strain
To let her through, – then blank again,
At the hope of her appearance failing.
Just by the chapel, a break in the railing
Shows a narrow path directly across;

'Tis ever dry walking there, on the moss –
Besides, you go gently all the way uphill. [...]

VI

For lo, what think you? suddenly
The rain and the wind ceased, and the sky
Received at once the full fruition
Of the moon's consummate apparition.
The black cloud-barricade was riven,
Ruined beneath her feet, and driven
Deep in the West; while, bare and breathless,
   North and South and East lay ready
For a glorious thing that, dauntless, deathless,
   Sprang across them and stood steady.
'Twas a moon-rainbow, vast and perfect,
From heaven to heaven extending, perfect
As the mother-moon's self, full in face.
It rose, distinctly at the base
   With its seven proper colours chorded,
Which still, in the rising, were compressed,
Until at last they coalesced,
   And supreme the spectral creature lorded
In a triumph of whitest white, –
Above which intervened the night.
But above night too, like only the next,
   The second of a wondrous sequence,
   Reaching in rare and rarer frequence,
Till the heaven of heavens were circumflexed,
Another rainbow rose, a mightier,
Fainter, flushier and flightier, –
Rapture dying along its verge.
Oh, whose foot shall I see emerge,
Whose, from the straining topmost dark.
On to the keystone of that arc?

P. J. KAVANAGH

And Light Fading

It's like a de Chirico drawing. The sun going,
A boy on a big grey horse with his bare ankles showing,
A little boy below exclaiming at the hunter's huge feet:
Eyes of saffron heifers reflecting yellow light,
Anxious, standing back from the yard gate:
Garish among the ochre fallows
And high bare fields with scooped lavender shadows
A green surprising triangle of winter wheat.

The lane winds up and long. Winter hedgerows
Burn, lemon-green and coral, trap a black bag or sack that
blows
Sometimes in a wind above the lane.
Boys and big grey horse and fields and man:
Black plastic like a broken bird, flapping, cracking:
Coloured lane climbing away, and turning, narrowing, and
light fading.

Sustained by Nature

WILLIAM WORDSWORTH

Lines Composed a Few Miles above Tintern Abbey,
on Revisiting the Banks of the Wye during a Tour.
July 13, 1798

Five years have past; five summers, with the length
Of five long winters! and again I hear
These waters, rolling from their mountain-springs
With a soft inland murmur. – Once again
Do I behold these steep and lofty cliffs,
That on a wild secluded scene impress
Thoughts of more deep seclusion; and connect
The landscape with the quiet of the sky.
The day is come when I again repose
Here, under this dark sycamore, and view
These plots of cottage-ground, these orchard-tufts,
Which at this season, with their unripe fruits,
Are clad in one green hue, and lose themselves
'Mid groves and copses. Once again I see
These hedge-rows, hardly hedge-rows, little lines
Of sportive wood run wild: these pastoral farms,
Green to the very door; and wreaths of smoke
Sent up, in silence, from among the trees!
With some uncertain notice, as might seem
Of vagrant dwellers in the houseless woods,
Or of some Hermit's cave, where by his fire
The Hermit sits alone.
                              These beauteous forms,
Through a long absence, have not been to me
As is a landscape to a blind man's eye:
But oft, in lonely rooms, and 'mid the din

Of towns and cities, I have owed to them
In hours of weariness, sensations sweet,
Felt in the blood, and felt along the heart;
And passing even into my purer mind,
With tranquil restoration:– feelings too
Of unremembered pleasure: such, perhaps,
As have no slight or trivial influence
On that best portion of a good man's life,
His little, nameless, unremembered, acts
Of kindness and of love. Nor less, I trust,
To them I may have owed another gift,
Of aspect more sublime; that blessed mood,
In which the burden of the mystery,
In which the heavy and the weary weight
Of all this unintelligible world,
Is lightened:– that serene and blessed mood,
In which the affections gently lead us on, –
Until, the breath of this corporeal frame
And even the motion of our human blood
Almost suspended, we are laid asleep
In body, and become a living soul:
While with an eye made quiet by the power
Of harmony, and the deep power of joy,
We see into the life of things.
                         If this
Be but a vain belief, yet, oh! how oft –
In darkness and amid the many shapes
Of joyless daylight; when the fretful stir
Unprofitable, and the fever of the world,
Have hung upon the beatings of my heart –
How oft, in spirit, have I turned to thee,
O sylvan Wye! thou wanderer through the woods,
How often has my spirit turned to thee!

    And now, with gleams of half-extinguished thought,
With many recognitions dim and faint,

And somewhat of a sad perplexity,
The picture of the mind revives again:
While here I stand, not only with the sense
Of present pleasure, but with pleasing thoughts
That in this moment there is life and food
For future years. And so I dare to hope,
Though changed, no doubt, from what I was when first
I came among these hills; when like a roe
I bounded o'er the mountains, by the sides
Of the deep rivers, and the lonely streams,
Wherever nature led: more like a man
Flying from something that he dreads, than one
Who sought the thing he loved. For nature then
(The coarser pleasures of my boyish days,
And their glad animal movements all gone by)
To me was all in all. – I cannot paint
What then I was. The sounding cataract
Haunted me like a passion: the tall rock,
The mountain, and the deep and gloomy wood,
Their colours and their forms, were then to me
An appetite; a feeling and a love,
That had no need of a remoter charm,
By thought supplied, nor any interest
Unborrowed from the eye. – That time is past,
And all its aching joys are now no more,
And all its dizzy raptures. Not for this
Faint I, nor mourn nor murmur; other gifts
Have followed; for such loss, I would believe,
Abundant recompense. For I have learned
To look on nature, not as in the hour
Of thoughtless youth; but hearing oftentimes
The still, sad music of humanity,
Nor harsh nor grating, though of ample power
To chasten and subdue. And I have felt
A presence that disturbs me with the joy
Of elevated thoughts; a sense sublime

Of something far more deeply interfused,
Whose dwelling is the light of setting suns,
And the round ocean and the living air,
And the blue sky, and in the mind of man:
A motion and a spirit, that impels
All thinking things, all objects of all thought,
And rolls through all things. Therefore am I still
A lover of the meadows and the woods,
And mountains; and of all that we behold
From this green earth; of all the mighty world
Of eye, and ear, – both what they half create,
And what perceive; well pleased to recognize
In nature and the language of the sense,
The anchor of my purest thoughts, the nurse,
The guide, the guardian of my heart, and soul
Of all my moral being.
              Nor perchance,
If I were not thus taught, should I the more
Suffer my genial spirits to decay:
For thou art with me here upon the banks
Of this fair river; thou my dearest Friend,
My dear, dear Friend; and in thy voice I catch
The language of my former heart, and read
My former pleasures in the shooting lights
Of thy wild eyes. Oh! yet a little while
May I behold in thee what I was once,
My dear, dear Sister! and this prayer I make,
Knowing that Nature never did betray
The heart that loved her; 'tis her privilege,
Through all the years of this our life, to lead
From joy to joy: for she can so inform
The mind that is within us, so impress
With quietness and beauty, and so feed
With lofty thoughts, that neither evil tongues,
Rash judgements, nor the sneers of selfish men,
Nor greetings where no kindness is, nor all

The dreary intercourse of daily life,
Shall e'er prevail against us, or disturb
Our cheerful faith, that all which we behold
Is full of blessings. Therefore let the moon
Shine on thee in thy solitary walk;
And let the misty mountain-winds be free
To blow against thee: and, in after years,
When these wild ecstasies shall be matured
Into a sober pleasure; when thy mind
Shall be a mansion for all lovely forms,
Thy memory be as a dwelling-place
For all sweet sounds and harmonies; oh! then,
If solitude, or fear, or pain, or grief,
Should be thy portion, with what healing thoughts
Of tender joy wilt thou remember me,
And these my exhortations! Nor, perchance –
If I should be where I no more can hear
Thy voice, nor catch from thy wild eyes these gleams
Of past existence – wilt thou then forget
That on the banks of this delightful stream
We stood together; and that I, so long
A worshipper of Nature, hither came
Unwearied in that service: rather say
With warmer love – oh! with far deeper zeal
Of holier love. Nor wilt thou then forget,
That after many wanderings, many years
Of absence, these steep woods and lofty cliffs,
And this green pastoral landscape, were to me
More dear, both for themselves and for thy sake!

   Wye Valley

HENRY VAUGHAN

Retirement

Fresh fields and woods! the earth's fair face!
God's footstool and man's dwelling place!
I ask not why the first believer
Did love to be a country liver,
Who to secure pious content
Did pitch by groves and wells his tent,
Where he might view the boundless skie,
And all those glorious lights on high,
With flying meteors, mists, and show'rs,
Subjected hills, trees, meads, and flow'rs,
And ev'ry minute bless the King,
And wise Creator of each thing.

I ask not why he did remove
To happy Mamre's holy grove,
Leaving the cities of the plain
To Lot and his successless train.
All various lusts in cities still
Are found; they are the thrones of ill;
The dismal sinks, where blood is spill'd,
Cages with much uncleanness fill'd.
But rural shades are the sweet sense
Of piety and innocence;
They are the meek's calm region, where
Angels descend and rule the sphere;
Where Heaven lies leaguer, and the Dove
Duely as dew comes from above.
If Eden be on earth at all,
'Tis that which we the country call.

near Brecon, Powys

SAMUEL TAYLOR COLERIDGE

from Fears in Solitude

A green and silent spot, amid the hills,
A small and silent dell! O'er stiller place
No singing sky-lark ever poised himself.
The hills are heathy, save that swelling slope,
Which hath a gay and gorgeous covering on,
All golden with the never-bloomless furze,
Which now blooms most profusely: but the dell,
Bathed by the mist, is fresh and delicate
As vernal cornfield, or the unripe flax,
When, through its half-transparent stalks, at eve,
The level sunshine glimmers with green light.
O! 'tis a quiet spirit-healing nook!
Which all, methinks, would love; but chiefly he,
The humble man, who, in his youthful years,
Knew just so much of folly, as had made
His early manhood more securely wise!
Here he might lie on fern or withered heath,
While from the singing-lark (that sings unseen
The minstrelsy that solitude loves best),
And from the sun, and from the breezy air
Sweet influences trembled o'er his frame;
And he, with many feelings, many thoughts,
Made up a meditative joy, and found
Religious meanings in the forms of nature!
And so, his senses gradually wrapt
In a half sleep, he dreams of better worlds,
And dreaming hears thee still, O singing-lark;
That singest like an angel in the clouds!

WILLIAM SHAKESPEARE

from As You Like It, Act II, Scene i

[*Enter Duke Senior, Amyens, and two or three Lords like Forresters.*]

   Duke Senior:
Now my Coe-mates, and brothers in exile
Hath not old custome made this life more sweete
Then that of painted pompe? Are not these woods
More free from perill then the envious Court?
Heere feele we not the penaltie of Adam,
The seasons difference, as the Icie phange
And churlish chiding of the winters winde,
Which when it bites and blowes upon my body
Even till I shrinke with cold, I smile, and say
This is no flattery: these are counsellors
That feelingly perswade me what I am:
Sweet are the uses of adversitie
Which like the toad, ougly and venemous,
Weares yet a precious Jewell in his head:
And this our life exempt from publike haunt,
Findes tongues in trees, bookes in the running brookes,
Sermons in stones, and good in every thing.

   Forest of Arden

IDRIS DAVIES

'There was a dreamer in the mining town'

There was a dreamer in the mining town
Who wandered in the evening to the hills
To lie among grass, and gaze until the day

Had faded into night.
And good it was to breathe the mountain air,
The clean, sweet mountain air, and listen
To a hundred larks make song above the world;
To see the grasses shine and stir and sway,
And watch the blue mists gather in the south;
To smell the mountain herbs at dusk...
O fine it was to be alive and young
And feel the beauty of the summer hills,
To lose the puny self, forget the drab
And heavy toil beneath the massy earth.

There in the dusk the dreamer dreamed
Of shining lands, and love unhampered
By the callous economics of a world
Whose god is Mammon.
There in the mountain dusk the dream was born,
The spirit fired, and the calm disturbed
By the just anger of the blood.
Wilder than the politician's yellow tongue
And stronger than the demagogue's thunder,
The insistent language of the dream would ring
Through the dear and secret places of the soul.
O fresher than the April torrent, the words of indignation
Would clothe themselves with beauty, and be heard
Among the far undying echoes of the world.

And slowly the west would lose its crimson curves,
The larks descend, the hidden plover cry,
And the vast night would darken all the hills.

South Wales

NORMAN MACCAIG

Landscape and I

Landscape and I get on together well.
Though I'm the talkative one, still he can tell
His symptoms of being to me, the way a shell
Murmurs of oceans.

Loch Rannoch lapses dimpling in the sun.
Its hieroglyphs of light fade one by one
But re-create themselves, their message done,
For ever and ever.

That sprinkling lark jerked upward in the blue
Will daze to nowhere but leave himself in true
Translation – hear his song cascading through
His disappearance.

The hawk knows all about it, shaking there
An empty glove on steep chutes of the air
Till his yellow foot cramps on a squeal, to tear
Smooth fur, smooth feather.

This means, of course, Schiehallion in my mind
Is more than mountain. In it he leaves behind
A meaning, an idea, like a hind
Couched in a corrie.

So then I'll woo the mountain till I know
The meaning of the meaning, no less. Oh,
There's a Schiehallion anywhere you go.
The thing is, climb it.

W. R. RODGERS

Field Day

The old farmer, nearing death, asked
To be carried outside and set down
Where he could see a certain field
'And then I will cry my heart out,' he said.

It troubles me, thinking about that man;
What shape was the field of his crying
In Donegal?

I remember a small field in Down, a field
Within fields, shaped like a triangle.
I could have stood there and looked at it
All day long.

And I remember crossing the frontier between
France and Spain at a forbidden point, and seeing
A small triangular field in Spain,
And stopping
Or walking in Ireland down any rutted by-road
To where it hit the highway, there was always
At this turning-point and abutment
A still centre, a V-shape of grass
Untouched by cornering traffic,
Where country lads larked at night.

I think I know what the shape of the field was
That made the old man weep.

Childhood

THOMAS GRAY

from Ode on a Distant Prospect of Eton College

Ye distant spires, ye antique towers,
That crown the wat'ry glade,
Where grateful Science still adores
Her Henry's holy Shade;
And ye, that from the stately brow
Of Windsor's heights th'expanse below
Of grove, of lawn, of mead survey,
Whose turf, whose shade, whose flowers among
Wanders the hoary Thames along
His silver-winding way.

   Ah happy hills, ah pleasing shade,
Ah fields belov'd in vain,
Where once my careless childhood stray'd,
A stranger yet to pain!
I feel the gales, that from ye blow,
A momentary bliss bestow,
As waving fresh their gladsome wing,
My weary soul they seem to soothe,
And redolent of joy and youth,
To breathe a second spring.

   Say, Father Thames, for thou hast seen
Full many a sprightly race
Disporting on thy margent green
The paths of pleasure trace,
Who foremost now delight to cleave
With pliant arm thy glassy wave?
The captive linnet which enthrall?

What idle progeny succeed
To chase the rolling circle's speed,
Or urge the flying ball?

   While some on earnest business bent
Their murm'ring labours ply
'Gainst graver hours, that bring constraint
To sweeten liberty:
Some bold adventurers disdain
The limits of their little reign,
And unknown regions dare descry:
Still as they run they look behind,
They hear a voice in every wind,
And snatch a fearful joy.

   Berkshire

WILLIAM WORDSWORTH

from The Prelude, Book I

   Fair seed-time had my soul, and I grew up
Foster'd alike by beauty and by fear;
Much favor'd in my birthplace, and no less
In that beloved Vale to which, erelong,
I was transplanted. Well I call to mind
('Twas at an early age, ere I had seen
Nine summers) when upon the mountain slope
The frost and breath of frosty wind had snapp'd
The last autumnal crocus, 'twas my joy
To wander half the night among the Cliffs
And the smooth Hollows, where the woodcocks ran
Along the open turf. In thought and wish
That time, my shoulder all with springes hung,
I was a fell destroyer. On the heights
Scudding away from snare to snare, I plied

My anxious visitation, hurrying on,
Still hurrying, hurrying onward; moon and stars
Were shining o'er my head; I was alone,
And seem'd to be a trouble to the peace
That was among them. Sometimes it befel
In these night-wanderings, that a strong desire
O'erpower'd my better reason, and the bird
Which was the captive of another's toils
Became my prey; and, when the deed was done
I heard among the solitary hills
Low breathings coming after me, and sounds
Of undistinguishable motion, steps
Almost as silent as the turf they trod.
Nor less in springtime when on southern banks
The shining sun had from his knot of leaves
Decoy'd the primrose flower, and when the Vales
And woods were warm, was I a plunderer then
In the high places, on the lonesome peaks
Where'er, among the mountains and the winds,
The Mother Bird had built her lodge. Though mean
My object, and inglorious, yet the end
Was not ignoble. Oh! when I have hung
Above the raven's nest, by knots of grass
And half-inch fissures in the slippery rock
But ill sustain'd, and almost, as it seem'd,
Suspended by the blast which blew amain,
Shouldering the naked crag; Oh! at that time,
While on the perilous ridge I hung alone,
With what strange utterance did the loud dry wind
Blow through my ears! the sky seem'd not a sky
Of earth, and with what motion mov'd the clouds!

SAMUEL TAYLOR COLERIDGE

Sonnet to the River Otter

Dear native brook! wild streamlet of the west!
  How many various-fated years have past,
  What happy, and what mournful hours, since last
I skimmed the smooth thin stone along thy breast,
Numbering its light leaps! yet so deep imprest
Sink the sweet scenes of childhood, that mine eyes
  I never shut amid the sunny ray,
But straight with all their tints thy waters rise,
  Thy crossing plank, thy marge with willows grey,
And bedded sand that veined with various dyes
Gleamed through thy bright transparence! On my way,
  Visions of childhood! oft have ye beguiled
Lone manhood's cares, yet waking fondest sighs:
  Ah! that once more I were a careless child!

  Ottery St Mary, Devon

GEORGE ELIOT

from Brother and Sister

Our brown canal was endless to my thought;
And on its banks I sat in dreamy peace,
Unknowing how the good I loved was wrought,
Untroubled by the fear that it would cease.

Slowly the barges floated into view
Rounding a grassy hill to me sublime
With some Unknown beyond it, whither flew
The parting cuckoo toward a fresh spring time.

The wide-arched bridge, the scented elder-flowers,
The wondrous watery rings that died too soon,
The echoes of the quarry, the still hours
With white robe sweeping-on the shadeless noon,

    Were but my growing self, are part of me,
    My present Past, my root of piety.

    ? Warwickshire

DYLAN THOMAS

Fern Hill

Now as I was young and easy under the apple boughs
About the lilting house and happy as the grass was green,
    The night above the dingle starry,
        Time let me hail and climb
    Golden in the heydays of his eyes,
And honoured among wagons I was prince of the apple towns
And once below a time I lordly had the trees and leaves
        Trail with daisies and barley
    Down the rivers of the windfall light.

And as I was green and carefree, famous among the barns
About the happy yard and singing as the farm was home,
    In the sun that is young once only,
        Time let me play and be
    Golden in the mercy of his means,
And green and golden I was huntsman and herdsman, the
    calves
Sang to my horn, the foxes on the hills barked clear and cold,
        And the sabbath rang slowly
    In the pebbles of the holy streams.

All the sun long it was running, it was lovely, the hay
Fields high as the house, the tunes from the chimneys, it was air
    And playing, lovely and watery
        And fire green as grass.
    And nightly under the simple stars
As I rode to sleep the owls were bearing the farm away,
All the moon long I heard, blessed among stables, the night-
  jars
    Flying with the ricks, and the horses
        Flashing into the dark.

And then to awake, and the farm, like a wanderer white
With the dew, come back, the cock on his shoulder: it was all
    Shining, it was Adam and maiden,
        The sky gathered again
    And the sun grew round that very day.
So it must have been after the birth of the simple light
In the first, spinning place, the spellbound horses walking
  warm
    Out of the whinnying green stable
        On to the fields of praise.

And honoured among foxes and pheasants by the gay house
Under the new made clouds and happy as the heart was long,
    In the sun born over and over,
        I ran my heedless ways,
    My wishes raced through the house high hay
And nothing I cared, at my sky blue trades, that time allows
In all his tuneful turning so few and such morning songs
    Before the children green and golden
        Follow him out of grace,

Nothing I cared, in the lamb white days, that time would
  take me
Up to the swallow thronged loft by the shadow of my hand,
    In the moon that is always rising,
        Nor that riding to sleep

I should hear him fly with the high fields
And wake to the farm forever fled from the childless land.
Oh as I was young and easy in the mercy of his means,
    Time held me green and dying
  Though I sang in my chains like the sea.

Llangain, Carmarthenshire

EDWIN MUIR

Childhood

Long time he lay upon the sunny hill,
  To his father's house below securely bound.
Far off the silent, changing sound was still,
  With the black islands lying thick around.

He saw each separate height, each vaguer hue,
  Where the massed islands rolled in mist away,
And though all ran together in his view
  He knew that unseen straits between them lay.

Often he wondered what new shores were there.
  In thought he saw the still light on the sand,
The shallow water clear in tranquil air,
  And walked through it in joy from strand to strand.

Over the sound a ship so slow would pass
  That in the black hill's gloom it seemed to lie.
The evening sound was smooth like sunken glass,
  And time seemed finished ere the ship passed by.

Grey tiny rocks slept round him where he lay,
  Moveless as they, more still as evening came,
The grasses threw straight shadows far away,
  And from the house his mother called his name.

Orkney

W. S. GRAHAM

Loch Thom

I

Just for the sake of recovering
I walked backward from fifty-six
Quick years of age wanting to see,
And managed not to trip or stumble
To find Loch Thom and turned round
To see the stretch of my childhood
Before me. Here is the loch. The same
Long-beaked cry curls across
The heather-edges of the water held
Between the hills a boyhood's walk
Up from Greenock. It is the morning.

And I am here with my mammy's
Bramble jam scones in my pocket.
The Firth is miles and I have come
Back to find Loch Thom maybe
In this light does not recognise me.

This is a lonely freshwater loch.
No farms on the edge. Only
Heather grouse-moor stretching
Down to Greenock and One Hope
Street or stretching away across
Into the blue moors of Ayrshire.

II

And almost I am back again
Wading the heather down to the edge
To sit. The minnows go by in shoals
Like iron-filings in the shallows.

My mother is dead. My father is dead
And all the trout I used to know
Leaping from their sad rings are dead.

III

I drop my crumbs into the shallow
Weed for the minnows and pinheads.
You see that I will have to rise
And turn round and get back where
My running age will slow for a moment
To let me on. It is a colder
Stretch of water than I remember.

The curlew's cry travelling still
Kills me fairly. In front of me
The grouse flurry and settle. GOBACK
GOBACK GOBACK FAREWELL LOCH THOM.

near Greenock, Strathclyde

LOUIS MACNEICE

Carrickfergus

I was born in Belfast between the mountain and the gantries
    To the hooting of lost sirens and the clang of trams:
Thence to Smoky Carrick in County Antrim
    Where the bottle-neck harbour collects the mud which
    jams

The little boats beneath the Norman castle,
    The pier shinging with lumps of crystal salt;
The Scotch Quarter was a line of residential houses
    But the Irish Quarter was a slum for the blind and halt.

The brook ran yellow from the factory stinking of chlorine,
  The yarn-mill called its funeral cry at noon;
Our lights looked over the lough to the lights of Bangor
  Under the peacock aura of a drowning moon.

The Norman walled this town against the country
  To stop his ears to the yelping of his slave
And built a church in the form of a cross but denoting
  The list of Christ on the cross in the angle of the nave.

I was the rector's son, born to the anglican order,
  Banned for ever from the candles of the Irish poor;
The Chichesters knelt in marble at the end of a transept
  With ruffs about their necks, their portion sure.

The war came and a huge camp of soldiers
  Grew from the ground in sight of our house with long
Dummies hanging from gibbets for bayonet practice
  And the sentry's challenge echoing all day long;

A Yorkshire terrier ran in and out by the gate-lodge
  Barred to civilians, yapping as if taking affront:
Marching at ease and singing 'Who Killed Cock Robin?'
  The troops went out by the lodge and off to the Front.

The steamer was camouflaged that took me to England –
  Sweat and khaki in the Carlisle train;
I thought that the war would last for ever and sugar
  Be always rationed and that never again

Would the weekly papers not have photos of sandbags
  And my governess not make bandages from moss
And people not have maps above the fireplace
  With flags on pins moving across and across –

Across the hawthorn hedge the noise of bugles,
  Flares across the night,
Somewhere on the lough was a prison ship for Germans,
  A cage across their sight.

I went to school in Dorset, the world of parents
　　Contracted into a puppet world of sons
Far from the mill girls, the smell of porter, the salt-mines
　　And the soldiers with their guns.

　　Co. Antrim, Northern Ireland

FRANCIS SCARFE

Tyne Dock

The summer season at Tyne Dock
Lifted my boyhood in a crane
Above the shaggy mining town,
Above the slaghills and the rocks,
Above the middens in backlanes
And wooden hen-huts falling down.

Grass grew vermilion in the streets
Where the blind pit-ponies pranced
And poppies screamed by butchers' stalls
Where bulls kicked sparks with dying feet,
And in the naked larks I sensed
A cruel god beneath it all.

Over the pithead wheel the moon
Was clean as a girl's face in school;
I envied the remote old man
Who lived there, quiet and alone,
While in the kitchen the mad spool
Unwound, as Annie's treadle ran.

Squat fishing-smacks swung down the Tyne
And windwards their wide tan sails spread
With bobbling lights red on the wave,
While with their lanterns to the mine

The pitmen clogged, and by my bed
Night kneeled, and all the day forgave.

The boyish season is still there
For clapping hands and leaping feet
Across the slagheaps and the dunes,
And still it breaks into my care
Though I will never find the street,
Nor find the old, impulsive tune,
Nor ever lose that child's despair.

    Tyneside

GEOFFREY HILL

from Mercian Hymns

VI

The princes of Mercia were badger and raven. Thrall to
their freedom, I dug and hoarded. Orchards fruited above
clefts. I drank from honeycombs of chill sandstone.

'A boy at odds in the house, lonely among brothers.' But I,
who had none, fostered a strangeness; gave myself to
unattainable toys.

Candles of gnarled resin, apple-branches, the tacky
mistletoe. 'Look' they said and again 'look'. But I ran
slowly; the landscape flowed away, back to its source.

In the schoolyard, in the cloakrooms, the children boasted
their scars of dried snot; wrists and knees garnished with
impetigo.

VII

Gasholders, russet among fields. Milldams, marlpools that lay unstirring. Eel-swarms. Coagulations of frogs: once, with branches and half-bricks, he battered a ditchful; then sidled away from the stillness and silence.

Ceolred was his friend and remained so, even after the day of the lost fighter: a biplane, already obsolete and irreplaceable, two inches of heavy snub silver. Ceolred let it spin through a hole in the classroom-floorboards, softly, into the rat-droppings and coins.

After school he lured Ceolred, who was sniggering with fright, down to the old quarries, and flayed him. Then, leaving Ceolred, he journeyed for hours, calm and alone, in his private derelict sandlorry named *Albion*.

Nature's Influence on Character and Mood

SIR WALTER SCOTT

from The Lay of the Last Minstrel, Canto VI

O Caledonia! stern and wild,
Meet nurse for a poetic child!
Land of brown heath and shaggy wood,
Land of the mountain and the flood,
Land of my sires! what mortal hand
Can e'er untie the filial band,
That knits me to thy rugged strand!
Still, as I view each well known scene,
Think what is now, and what hath been,
Seems as, to me, of all bereft,
Sole friends thy woods and streams were left;
And thus I love them better still,
Even in extremity of ill.
By Yarrow's stream still let me stray,
Though none should guide my feeble way;
Still feel the breeze down Ettricke break,
Although it chill my withered cheek;
Still lay my head by Teviot Stone,
Though there, forgotten and alone,
The Bard may draw his parting groan.

Scottish Borders

SIR ALEXANDER GRAY

Scotland

Here in the Uplands
The soil is ungrateful;
The fields, red with sorrel,
Are stony and bare.
A few trees, wind-twisted –
Or are they but bushes? –
Stand stubbornly guarding
A home here and there.

Scooped out like a saucer,
The land lies before me;
The waters, once scattered,
Flow orderedly now
Through fields where the ghosts
Of the marsh and the moorland
Still ride the old marches,
Despising the plough.

The marsh and the moorland
Are not to be banished;
The bracken and heather,
The glory of broom,
Usurp all the balks
And the fields' broken fringes,
And claim from the sower
Their portion of room.

This is my country,
The land that begat me.
These windy spaces
Are surely my own.
And those who here toil

In the sweat of their faces
Are flesh of my flesh,
And bone of my bone.

Hard is the day's task –
Scotland, stern Mother –
Wherewith at all times
Thy sons have been faced:
Labour by day,
And scant rest in the gloaming,
With Want an attendant,
Not lightly outpaced.

Yet do thy children
Honour and love thee.
Harsh is thy schooling,
Yet great is the gain:
True hearts and strong limbs,
The beauty of faces,
Kissed by the wind
And caressed by the rain.

 Lairhillock, Kincardine

JOHN GRAY

On the South Coast of Cornwall

There lives a land beside the western sea
The sea-salt makes not barren, for its hills
Laugh even in winter time; the bubbly rills
Dance down their grades, and fill with melody
The fishers' hearts; for these, where'er they be,
Sing out salt choruses; the land-breeze fills
Their sweetened lungs with wine which it distils
From emerald fat field and gorse gold lea.

Like a thrown net leans out the ample bay.
The fishers' huddled cabins crowd and wedge,
Greedy, against the rugged treacherous edge
Of their great liquid mine renewed alway.
The fishers have no thought but of the strong
Sea, whence their food, their crisp hair, and their song.

ROBERT HERRICK

To Dean-bourn, a Rude River in Devon

Dean-bourn, farewell; I never look to see
Dean, or thy warty incivility.
Thy rocky bottom, that doth tear thy streams,
And makes them frantic, ev'n to all extremes,
To my content I never should behold,
Were thy streams silver, or thy rocks all gold.
Rocky thou art; and rocky we discover
Thy men; and rocky are thy ways all over.
O men, O manners; now, and ever known
To be a rocky generation!
A people currish, churlish as the seas,
And rude (almost) as rudest savages –
With whom I did, and may re-sojourn when
Rocks turn to rivers, rivers turn to men.

Devon

JOHN DAVIDSON

A Northern Suburb

Nature selects the longest way,
    And winds about in tortuous grooves;
A thousand years the oaks decay;
    The wrinkled glacier hardly moves.

But here the whetted fangs of change
    Daily devour the old demesne –
The busy farm, the quiet grange,
    The wayside inn, the village green.

In gaudy yellow brick and red,
    With rooting pipes, like creepers rank,
The shoddy terraces o'erspread
    Meadow, and garth, and daisied bank.

With shelves for rooms the houses crowd,
    Like draughty cupboards in a row –
Ice-chests when wintry winds are loud,
    Ovens when summer breezes blow.

Roused by the fee'd policeman's knock,
    And sad that day should come again,
Under the stars the workmen flock
    In haste to reach the workmen's train.

For here dwell those who must fulfil
    Dull tasks in uncongenial spheres,
Who toil through dread of coming ill,
    And not with hope of happier years –

The lowly folk who scarcely dare
 Conceive themselves perhaps misplaced,
Whose prize for unremitting care
 Is only not to be disgraced.

 North London

WILLIAM COWPER

'The heart is hard in nature...'

The heart is hard in nature, and unfit
For human fellowship, as being void
Of sympathy, and therefore dead alike
To love and friendship both, that is not pleased
With sight of animals enjoying life
Nor feels their happiness augment his own.
The bounding fawn, that darts across the glade
When none pursues, through mere delight of heart,
And spirits buoyant with excess of glee;
The horse as wanton, and almost as fleet
That skims the spacious meadow at full speed,
Then stops and snorts, and, throwing high his heels,
Starts to the voluntary race again;
The very kine that gambol at high noon,
The total herd receiving first from one
That leads the dance a summons to be gay,
Though wild their strange vagaries, and uncouth
Their efforts, yet resolved with one consent
To give such act and utterance as they may
To ecstasy too big to be suppress'd –
These, and a thousand images of bliss
With which kind Nature graces every scene,
Where cruel man defeats not her design,
Impart to the benevolent, who wish

All that are capable of pleasure, pleased,
A far superior happiness to theirs,
The comfort of a reasonable joy.

ELIZABETH JENNINGS

Introduction to a Landscape

Difficult not to see significance
In any landscape we are charged to watch,
Impossible not to set all seasons there
Fading like movements in a music one
To other, slow spring into the fast rage
Of summer that takes possession of a place
Leaving the residue of time to autumn
Rather than just a used and ravished landscape.

And never long able to see the place
As it must be somewhere itself beyond
Any regard of the ecstatic gazer
Or any human attitude of mind,
We blame all human happiness or grief
Upon a place, make figures of our feeling
And move them, as a story-teller might
Move modern heroes into ancient legends,
Into the solid and receptive land.

For who can keep a grief as pure grief
Or hold a happiness against the heart?
Noble indeed to impute our worthiest thoughts
To a serene and splendid countryside,
And therefore logical to let our loathing
See a storm looming in the summer light,
The hills about to learn of landslides and
The entire landscape be quite swallowed up
In a surrender – a type of our death.

Pride, National and Local

WILLIAM SHAKESPEARE

from Richard II, Act II, Scene i

> *John of Gaunt*
> This royal throne of kings, this sceptered isle,
> This earth of majesty, this seat of Mars,
> This other Eden, demi-paradise;
> This fortress built by Nature for herself
> Against infection and the hand of war;
> This happy breed of men, this little world;
> This precious stone set in the silver sea,
> Which serves it in the office of a wall,
> Or as a moat defensive to a house,
> Against the envy of less happier lands;
> This blessed plot, this earth, this realm, this England,
> This nurse, this teeming womb of royal kings [...]

SAMUEL TAYLOR COLERIDGE

from Fears in Solitude

> 'O dear Britain! O my Mother Isle!
> Needs must thou prove a name most dear and holy
> To me a son, a brother, and a friend,
> A husband and a father! who revere
> All bonds of natural love, and find them all
> Within the limits of thy rocky shores.
> O native Britain! O my Mother Isle!
> How shouldst thou prove aught else but dear and holy
> To me, who from thy lakes and mountain-hills,

Thy clouds, thy quiet dales, thy rocks and seas,
Have drunk in all my intellectual life,
All sweet sensations, all ennobling thoughts,
All adoration of the God in nature,
All lovely and all honourable things,
Whatever makes this mortal spirit feel
The joy and greatness of its future being?
There lives nor form nor feeling in my soul
Unborrowed from my country...'

RUDYARD KIPLING

A Charm

(Introduction to 'Rewards and Fairies')

Take of English earth as much
As either hand may rightly clutch.
In the taking of it breathe
Prayer for all who lie beneath.
Not the great nor well-bespoke,
But the mere uncounted folk
Of whose life and death is none
Report or lamentation.
   Lay that earth upon thy heart,
   And thy sickness shall depart!

It shall sweeten and make whole
Fevered breath and festered soul.
It shall mightily restrain
Over-busied hand and brain.
It shall ease thy mortal strife
'Gainst the immortal woe of life,
Till thyself, restored, shall prove
By what grace the Heavens do move.

Take of English flowers these —
Spring's full-facèd primroses,
Summer's wild wide-hearted rose,
Autumn's wall-flower of the close,
And, thy darkness to illume,
Winter's bee-thronged ivy-bloom.
Seek and serve them where they bide
From Candlemas to Christmas-tide,
    For these simples, used aright,
    Can restore a failing sight.

These shall cleanse and purify
Webbed and inward-turning eye;
These shall show thee treasure hid
Thy familiar fields amid;
And reveal (which is thy need)
Every man a King indeed!

IVOR GURNEY

By Severn

If England, her spirit lives anywhere
It is by Severn, by hawthorns, and grand willows.
Earth heaves up twice a hundred feet in air
And ruddy clay falls scooped out to the weedy shallows.
There in the brakes of May Spring has her chambers,
Robing-rooms of hawthorn, cowslip, cuckoo flower —
Wonder complete changes for each square joy's hour,
Past thought miracles are there and beyond numbers.
If for the drab atmospheres and managed lighting
In London town, Oriana's playwrights had
Wainlode her theatre and then coppice clad
Hill for her ground of sauntering and idle waiting.
Why, then I think, our chieftest glory of pride

(The Elizabethans of Thames, South and Northern side)
Would nothing of its needing be denied,
And her sons praises from England's mouth again be outcried.

Cotswolds

JOHN EARL

Northumbrian Place-names

(Winner of the Underwater Folk Dance and Recital Section of the
Northumbrian Offshore Plankton Appreciation Society's annual festival)

If I were a bogle, I'd bogle in Ogle,
I'd bogle in Ogle all day;
I'd bogle in Ogle without any trouble,
I'd bogle my life away.

If I were a buller, I'd buller in Wooler,
I'd buller in Wooler all day;
I'd buller in Wooler, I'd quite lose my colour,
I'd be duller in Wooler that day.

If I were a pulgham, I'd puff'em in Ulgham
I'd puff 'em in Ulgham all day;
I'd puff and I'd huff, and I'd pulg and I'd hulg,
And I'd blow all their houses away.

If I were a fritter, I'd fritter in Snitter,
I'd fritter my time away;
I'd prob'ly drop litter, and drink pints of bitter,
Then sleep it all off in the hay.

If I were a getholm, I'd get 'em in Yetholm,
I'd get 'em in Yetholm, all day;
I'd getholm, I'd vetholm, I'd really upsetholm,
I'd getholm and then run away.

If I lived in Whittingham
I might end up hittingham.

If I lived in Berwick
I'd swing from a derrick.

It would be a disaster
To live in Craster.
I'd have to smoke kippers
And eat seal flippers.

If I lived in Cambois,
I'd have to be famis.
(It'd have to be famis
because if it was famous,
I'd not live in Cambois,
I'd live in Camus.)

HUGH MACDIARMID

Scotland Small?

Scotland small? Our multiform, our infinite Scotland *small*?
Only as a patch of hillside may be a cliché corner
To a fool who cries 'Nothing but heather!' where in
    September another
Sitting there and resting and gazing round
Sees not only heather but blaeberries
With bright green leaves and leaves already turned scarlet,
Hiding ripe blue berries; and amongst the sage-green leaves
Of the bog-myrtle the golden flowers of the tormentil shining;
And on the small bare places, where the little Blackface sheep
Found grazing, milkworts blue as summer skies;
And down in neglected peat-hags, not worked
In living memory, sphagnum moss in pastel shades
Of yellow, green, and pink; sundew and butterwort

And nodding harebells vying in their colour
With the blue butterflies that poise themselves delicately
   upon them,
And stunted rowans with harsh dry leaves of glorious colour.
'Nothing but heather!' – How marvellously descriptive! And
   incomplete!

SORLEY MACLEAN (SOMHAIRLE MACGILL-EAIN)

Hallaig

'Time, the deer, is in the wood of Hallaig'
[translated by the author from his own Gaelic]

The window is nailed and boarded
through which I saw the West
and my love is at the Burn of Hallaig,
a birch tree, and she has always been

between Inver and Milk Hollow,
here and there about Baile-chuirn:
she is a birch, a hazel,
a straight, slender young rowan.

In Screapadal of my people
where Norman and Big Hector were,
their daughters and their sons are a wood
going up beside the stream.

Proud tonight the pine cocks
crowing on the top of Cnoc an Ra,
straight their backs in the moonlight –
they are not the wood I love.

I will wait for the birch wood
until it comes up by the cairn,
until the whole ridge from Beinn na Lice
will be under its shade.

If it does not, I will go down to Hallaig,
to the Sabbath of the dead,
where the people are frequenting,
every single generation gone.

They are still in Hallaig,
MacLeans and MacLeods,
all who were there in the time of Mac Gille Chaluim
the dead have been seen alive.

The men lying on the green
at the end of every house that was,
the girls a wood of birches,
straight their backs, bent their heads.

Between the Leac and Fearns
the road is under mild moss
and the girls in silent bands
go to Clachan as in the beginning,

and return from Clachan
from Suisnish and the land of the living;
each one young and lift-stepping,
without the heartbreak of the tale.

From the Burn of Fearns to the raised beach
that is clear in the mystery of the hills,
there is only the congregation of the girls
keeping up the endless walk,

coming back to Hallaig in the evening,
in the dumb living twilight,
filling the steep slopes,
their laughter a mist in my ears,

and their beauty a film on my heart
before the dimness comes on the kyles,
and when the sun goes down behind Dun Cana
a vehement bullet will come from the gun of Love;

and will strike the deer that goes dizzily,
sniffing at the grass-grown ruined homes;
his eye will freeze in the wood,
his blood will not be traced while I live.

PATRICK KAVANAGH

Stony Grey Soil

O stony grey soil of Monaghan
The laugh from my love you thieved;
You took the gay child of my passion
And gave me your clod-conceived.

You clogged the feet of my boyhood
And I believed that my stumble
Had the poise and stride of Apollo
And his voice my thick-tongued mumble.

You told me the plough was immortal!
O green-life-conquering plough!
Your mandril strained, your coulter blunted
In the smooth lea-field of my brow.

You sang on steaming dunghills
A song of cowards' brood,
You perfumed my clothes with weasel itch,
You fed me on swinish food.

You flung a ditch on my vision
Of beauty, love and truth.
O stony grey soil of Monaghan
You burgled my bank of youth!

Lost the long hours of pleasure
All the women that love young men.
O can I still stroke the monster's back
Or write with unpoisoned pen

His name in these lonely verses
Or mention the dark fields where
The first gay flight of my lyric
Got caught in a peasant's prayer.

Mullahinsha, Drummeril, Black Shanco –
Wherever I turn I see
In the stony grey soil of Monaghan
Dead loves that were born for me.

Co. Monaghan, Ireland

JOHN HEWITT

Ulster Names

I take my stand by the Ulster names,
each clean hard name like a weathered stone;
Tyrella, Rostrevor, are flickering flames:
the names I mean are the Moy, Malone,
Strabane, Slieve Gullion and Portglenone.

Even suppose that each name were freed
from legend's ivy and history's moss,
there'd be music still in, say, Carrick-a-rede,
though men forget it's the rock across
the track of the salmon from Islay and Ross.

The names of a land show the heart of the race;
they move on the tongue like the lilt of a song.
You say the name and I see the place –
Drumbo, Dungannon, Annalong.
Barony, townland, we cannot go wrong.

You say Armagh, and I see the hill
with the two tall spires or the square low tower;
the faith of Patrick is with us still;

his blessing falls in a moonlit hour,
when the apple orchards are all in flower.

You whisper Derry. Beyond the walls
and the crashing boom and the coiling smoke,
I follow that freedom which beckons and calls
to Colmcille, tall in his grove of oak,
raising his voice for the rhyming folk.

County by county you number them over;
Tyrone, Fermanagh ... I stand by a lake,
and the bubbling curlew, the whistling plover
call over the whins in the chill daybreak
as the hills and the waters the first light take.

Let Down be famous for care-tilled earth,
for the little green hills and the harsh grey peaks,
the rocky bed of the Lagan's birth,
the white farm fat in the August weeks.
There's one more county my pride still seeks.

You give it the name and my quick thoughts run
through the narrow towns with their wheels of trade,
to Glenballyemon, Glenaan, Glendun,
from Trostan down to the braes of Layde,
for there is the place where the pact was made.

But you have as good a right as I
to praise the place where your face is known,
for over us all is the selfsame sky;
the limestone's locked in the strength of the bone,
and who shall mock at the steadfast stone?

So it's Ballinamallard, it's Crossmaglen,
it's Aughnacloy, it's Donaghadee,
it's Magherafelt breeds the best of men,
I'll not deny it. But look for me
on the moss between Orra and Slievenanee.

POSTSCRIPT, 1984
Those verses surfaced thirty years ago
when time seemed edging to a better time,
most public voices tamed, those loud untamed
as seasonal as tawdry pantomime,
and over my companionable land
placenames still lilted like a childhood rime.

The years deceived; our unforgiving hearts,
by myth and old antipathies betrayed,
flared into sudden acts of violence
in daily shocking bulletins relayed,
and through our dark dream-clotted consciousness
hosted like banners in some black parade.

Now with compulsive resonance they toll:
Banbridge, Ballykelly, Darkley, Crossmaglen,
summoning pity, anger and despair,
by grief of kin, by hate of murderous men
till the whole tarnished map is stained and torn,
not to be read as pastoral again.

   Northern Ireland

SEAMUS HEANEY

Broagh

Riverback, the long rigs
ending in broad docken
and a canopied pad
down to the ford.

The garden mould
bruised easily, the shower
gathering in your heelmark
was the black O

in *Broagh*,
its low tattoo
among the windy boortrees
and rhubarb-blades

ended almost
suddenly, like that last
gh the strangers found
difficult to manage.

South Derry

R. S. THOMAS

Reservoirs

There are places in Wales I don't go:
Reservoirs that are the subconscious
Of a people, troubled far down
With gravestones, chapels, villages even;
The serenity of their expression
Revolts me, it is a pose
For strangers, a watercolour's appeal
To the mass, instead of the poem's
Harsher conditions. There are the hills,
Too; gardens gone under the scum
Of the forests; and the smashed faces
Of the farms with the stone trickle
Of their tears down the hills' side.

Where can I go, then, from the smell
Of decay, from the putrefying of a dead
Nation? I have walked the shore
For an hour and seen the English
Scavenging among the remains
Of our culture, covering the sand

Like the tide and, with the roughness
Of the tide, elbowing our language
Into the grave that we have dug for it.

   Llyn Trewelyn, y Bala

Secret and Special Places

SAMUEL TAYLOR COLERIDGE

This Lime-Tree Bower My Prison

Well, they are gone, and here must I remain,
This lime-tree bower my prison! I have lost
Beauties and feelings, such as would have been
Most sweet to my remembrance even when age
Had dimmed mine eyes to blindness! They, meanwhile,
Friends, whom I never more may meet again,
On springy heath, along the hill-top edge,
Wander in gladness, and wind down, perchance,
To that still roaring dell, of which I told;
The roaring dell, o'erwooded, narrow, deep,
And only speckled by the midday sun;
Where its slim trunk the ash from rock to rock
Flings arching like a bridge; – that branchless ash,
Unsunned and damp, whose few poor yellow leaves
Ne'er tremble in the gale, yet tremble still,
Fanned by the waterfall! and there my friends
Behold the dark green file of long lank weeds,
That all at once (a most fantastic sight!)
Still nod and drip beneath the dripping edge
Of the blue clay-stone.

                Now, my friends emerge
Beneath the wide wide heaven – and view again
The many-steepled track magnificent
Of hilly fields and meadows, and the sea,
With some fair bark, perhaps, whose sails light up
The slip of smooth clear blue betwixt two isles
Of purple shadow! Yes! they wander on
In gladness all; but thou, methinks, most glad,

My gentle-hearted Charles! for thou hast pined
And hungered after Nature, many a year,
In the great city pent, winning thy way
With sad yet patient soul, through evil and pain
And strange calamity! Ah! slowly sink
Behind the western ridge, thou glorious sun!
Shine in the slant beams of the sinking orb,
Ye purple heath-flowers! richlier burn, ye clouds!
Live in the yellow light, ye distant groves!
And kindle, thou blue ocean! So my friend
Struck with deep joy may stand, as I have stood,
Silent with swimming sense; yea, gazing round
On the wide landscape, gaze till all doth seem
Less gross than bodily; and of such hues
As veil the Almighty Spirit, when yet He makes
Spirits perceive His presence.

                   A delight
Comes sudden on my heart, and I am glad
As I myself were there! Nor in this bower,
This little lime-tree bower, have I not marked
Much that has soothed me. Pale beneath the blaze
Hung the transparent foliage; and I watched
Some broad and sunny leaf, and loved to see
The shadow of the leaf and stem above
Dappling its sunshine! And that walnut-tree
Was richly tinged, and a deep radiance lay
Full on the ancient ivy, which usurps
Those fronting elms, and now, with blackest mass
Makes their dark branches gleam a lighter hue
Through the late twilight: and though now the bat
Wheels silent by, and not a swallow twitters,
Yet still the solitary humble-bee
Sings in the bean-flower! Henceforth I shall know
That Nature ne'er deserts the wise and pure,
No plot so narrow, be but Nature there,
No waste so vacant, but may well employ

Each faculty of sense, and keep the heart
Awake to love and beauty! and sometimes
'Tis well to be bereft of promised good,
That we may lift the soul, and contemplate
With lively joy the joys we cannot share.
My gentle-hearted Charles! when the last rook
Beat its straight path along the dusky air
Homewards, I blest it! deeming, its black wing
(Now a dim speck, now vanishing in light)
Had cross'd the mighty orb's dilated glory,
While thou stood'st gazing; or when all was still,
Flew creeking o'er thy head, and had a charm
For thee, my gentle-hearted Charles, to whom
No sound is dissonant which tells of Life.

    Nether Stowey, Somerset

WILLIAM BARNES

My Orcha'd in Linden Lea

'Ithin the woodlands, flow'ry gleäded,
  By the woak tree's mossy moot,
The sheenèn grass-bleädes, timber-sheäded,
  Now do quiver under voot;
An' birds do whissle auver head,
An' water's bubblèn in its bed,
An' there vor me the apple tree
Do leän down low in Linden Lea.

When leaves that leätely wer a-springèn
  Now do feäde 'ithin the copse,
An' painted birds do hush their zingèn
  Up upon the timber's tops;
An' brown-leav'd fruit's a-turnèn red,
In cloudless zunsheen, auver head,

Wi' fruit vor me, the apple tree
Do leän down low in Linden Lea.

Let other vo'k meäke money vaster
   In the aïr o' dark-room'd towns,
I don't dread a peevish meäster;
   Though noo man do heed my frowns,
I be free to goo abrode,
Or teäke my hwomeward road
To where, vor me, the apple tree
Do leän down low in Linden Lea.

WILLIAM WORDSWORTH

from The Prelude, Book I

   And in the frosty season, when the sun
Was set, and visible for many a mile
The cottage windows through the twilight blaz'd,
I heeded not the summons:– happy time
It was, indeed, for all of us; to me
It was a time of rapture: clear and loud
The village clock toll'd six; I wheel'd about,
Proud and exulting, like an untired horse,
That cares not for his home. – All shod with steel,
We hiss'd along the polish'd ice, in games
Confederate, imitative of the chace
And woodland pleasures, the resounding horn,
The Pack loud bellowing, and the hunted hare.
So through the darkness and the cold we flew,
And not a voice was idle; with the din,
Meanwhile, the precipices rang aloud,
The leafless trees, and every icy crag
Tinkled like iron, while the distant hills
Into the tumult sent an alien sound

Of melancholy, not unnoticed, while the stars,
Eastward, were sparkling clear, and in the west
The orange sky of evening died away.

   Not seldom from the uproar I retired
Into a silent bay, or sportively
Glanced sideway, leaving the tumultuous throng,
To cut across the image of a star
That gleam'd upon the ice: and oftentimes
When we had given our bodies to the wind,
And all the shadowy banks, on either side,
Came sweeping through the darkness, spinning still
The rapid line of motion; then at once
Have I, reclining back upon my heels,
Stopp'd short, yet still the solitary Cliffs
Wheeled by me, even as if the earth had roll'd
With visible motion her diurnal round;
Behind me did they stretch in solemn train
Feebler and feebler, and I stood and watch'd
Till all was tranquil as a dreamless sleep.

   Lake District

ARTHUR HUGH CLOUGH

from The Bothie of Tober-na-Vuolich

   There is a stream, I name not its name, lest inquisitive
     tourist
Hunt it, and make it a lion, and get it at last into guide-
     books,
Springing far off from a loch unexplored in the folds of great
     mountains,
Falling two miles through rowan and stunted alder, enveloped
Then for four more in a forest of pine, where broad and ample

Spreads, to convey it, the glen with heathery slopes on both
    sides:
Broad and fair the stream, with occasional falls and narrows;
But, where the glen of its course approaches the vale of the
    river,
Met and blocked by a huge interposing mass of granite,
Scarce by a channel deep-cut, raging up, and raging onward,
Forces its flood through a passage so narrow a lady would
    step it.
There, across the great rocky wharves, a wooden bridge goes,
Carrying a path to the forest; below, three hundred yards, say,
Stepping-stones and a cart-track cross in the open valley.
    But in the interval here the boiling pent-up water
Frees itself by a final descent, attaining a bason,
Ten feet wide and eighteen long, with whiteness and fury
Occupied partly, but mostly pellucid, pure, a mirror;
Beautiful there for the colour derived from green rocks under;
Beautiful, most of all, where beads of foam uprising
Mingle their clouds of white with the delicate hue of the
    stillness.
Cliff over cliff for its sides, with rowan and pendent birch
    boughs,
Here it lies, unthought of above at the bridge and pathway,
Still more enclosed from below by wood and rocky projection.
You are shut in, left alone with yourself and perfection of
    water,
Hid on all sides, left alone with yourself and the goddess of
    bathing.
    Here, the pride of the plunger, you stride the fall and clear it;
Here, the delight of the bather, you roll in beaded sparklings,
Here into pure green depth drop down from lofty ledges.
    Hither, a month agone, they had come, and discovered it;
    hither
(Long a design, but long unaccountably left unaccomplished,)
Leaving the well-known bridge and pathway above to the
    forest,

Turning below from the track of the carts over stone and
    shingle,
Piercing a wood, and skirting a narrow and natural causeway
Under the rocky wall that hedges the bed of the streamlet,
Rounded a craggy point, and saw on a sudden before them
Slabs of rock, and a tiny beach, and perfection of water,
Picture-like beauty, seclusion sublime, and the goddess of
    bathing.

   Inverness-shire

BERNARD SPENCER

At 'The Angler'

The apple trees were all 'salaams' of clusters
in those walled gardens where the mown
grass, what with rains and years, took dents like peaches;
the bent old roofs, the trees, that grass
went on so with their lives there, we alone
seemed to be short of time to pass.

The world was summer and a doze, that pasturing
country so lazily inclined
down to the willow-wept, the swan-sailed river
and the eighteenth-century villages;
quelled river voices seeped the back of the mind
fooling the ear with distances.

And if rain rattled all night on the leaves,
the great night-crescent of the weir,
swollen with rainfall, growling its white tons
seemed to call pardon on our crime
of parting, cause more deep than now or here
talking to our short from its long time.

Lovers, we had our share of the ideal;
again, next day, with end of storm
how swans curved near as if to bring good omens
to us and – so love made it seem
there and then certain – in their trance of calm
blazed a white Always from that stream.

DANTE GABRIEL ROSSETTI

Silent Noon

Your hands lie open in the long fresh grass, –
    The finger-points look through like rosy blooms:
    Your eyes smile peace. The pasture gleams and glooms
'Neath billowing skies that scatter and amass.
All round our nest, far as the eye can pass,
    Are golden kingcup-fields with silver edge
    Where cow-parsley skirts the hawthorn-hedge.
'Tis visible silence, still as the hour-glass.

Deep in the sun-searched growths the dragon-fly
Hangs like a blue thread loosened from the sky: –
    So this winged hour is dropped to us from above.
Oh! clasp we to our hearts, for deathless dower
This close-companioned inarticulate hour
    When twofold silence was the song of love.

W. B. YEATS

The Lake Isle of Innisfree

I will arise and go now, and go to Innisfree,
And a small cabin build there, of clay and wattles made:
Nine bean-rows will I have there, a hive for the honey-bee,
And live alone in the bee-loud glade.

And I shall have some peace there, for peace comes dropping
  slow,
Dropping from the veils of the morning to where the cricket
  sings;
There midnight's all a glimmer, and noon a purple glow,
And evening full of the linnet's wings.

I will arise and go now, for always night and day
I hear lake water lapping with low sounds by the shore;
While I stand on the roadway, or on the pavements grey,
I hear it in the deep heart's core.

EDWARD THOMAS

The Combe

The Combe was ever dark, ancient and dark.
Its mouth is stopped with bramble, thorn, and briar;
And no one scrambles over the sliding chalk
By beech and yew and perishing juniper
Down the half precipices of its sides, with roots
And rabbit holes for steps. The sun of Winter,
The moon of Summer, and all the singing birds
Except the missel-thrush that loves juniper,
Are quite shut out. But far more ancient and dark
The Combe looks since they killed the badger there,
Dug him out and gave him to the hounds,
That most ancient Briton of English beasts.

JOHN FULLER

Bog

Kneeling for marshfruit like spilled
Beads bedded in displaying moss
I notice a licked frog dragging
His drenched fatigues up and through
The barring spears and stalks of orange
Bog asphodel as if in terror
Of unknown purposes, as though
I were a weight of sky, a whole
Universe of beak and gullet,
And not, as I am, a mere slider
And stumbler like him, damp to the hips,
Reaching for tussocks, scrabbling for almost
Nothing: these little speckled fruits,
Chill marbles of a forgotten tourney,
Aching playthings of a lost garden
That has always been mostly water,
A place of utter loneliness,
Terrain of the asphodel and of the frog.

   Lleyn Peninsula, North Wales

NORMAN MACCAIG

Summer Farm

Straws like tame lightnings lie about the grass
And hang zigzag on hedges. Green as glass
The water in the horse-trough shines.
Nine ducks go wobbling by in two straight lines.

A hen stares at nothing with one eye,
Then picks it up. Out of an empty sky
A swallow falls and, flickering through
The barn, dives up again into the dizzy blue.

I lie, not thinking, in the cool, soft grass,
Afraid of where a thought might take me –
This grasshopper with plated face
Unfolds his legs and finds himself in space.

Self under self, a pile of selves I stand
Threaded on time, and with metaphysic hand
Lift the farm like a lid and see
Farm within farm, and in the centre, me.

SEAMUS HEANEY

Settings: XXIV

Deserted harbour stillness. Every stone
Clarified and dormant under water,
The harbour wall a masonry of silence.

Fullness. Shimmer. Laden high Atlantic
The moorings barely stirred in, very slight
Clucking of the swell against boat boards.

Perfected vision: cockle minarets
Consigned down there with green-slicked bottle glass,
Shell-debris and a reddened bud of sandstone.

Air and ocean known as antecedents
Of each other. In apposition with
Omnipresence, equilibrium, brim.

near Ballyconneely, Co. Galway, Ireland

Homesickness and Wanderlust

ROBERT BROWNING

Home-Thoughts, from Abroad

I

Oh, to be in England
Now that April's there,
And whoever wakes in England
Sees, some morning, unaware,
That the lowest boughs and the brush-wood sheaf
Round the elm-tree bole are in tiny leaf,
While the chaffinch sings on the orchard bough
In England – now!

II

And after April, when May follows,
And the whitethroat builds, and all the swallows!
Hark, where my blossomed pear-tree in the hedge
Leans to the field and scatters on the clover
Blossoms and dewdrops – at the bent spray's edge –
That's the wise thrush; he sings each song twice over,
Lest you should think he never could recapture
The first fine careless rapture!
And though the fields look rough with hoary dew,
All will be gay when noontide wakes anew
The buttercups, the little children's dower
– Far brighter than this gaudy melon-flower!

RUDYARD KIPLING

In Springtime

My garden blazes brightly with the rose-bush and the peach,
   And the *köil* sings above it, in the *siris* by the well,
From the creeper-covered trellis comes the squirrel's
     chattering speech,
   And the blue jay screams and flutters where the cheery
   sat-bhai dwell.
But the rose has lost its fragrance, and the *köil's* note is
     strange;
   I am sick of endless sunshine, sick of blossom-burdened
   bough.
Give me back the leafless woodlands where the winds of
     Springtime range –
   Give me back one day in England, for it's Spring in England
   now!

Through the pines the gusts are booming, o'er the brown
     fields blowing chill,
   From the furrow of the ploughshare streams the fragrance
   of the loam,
And the hawk nests on the cliffside and the jackdaw in the hill,
   And my heart is back in England 'mid the sights and sounds
   of Home.
But the garland of the sacrifice this wealth of rose and peach
     is,
   Ah! *köil*, little *köil*, singing on the *siris* bough,
In my ears the knell of exile your ceaseless bell like speech is –
   Can *you* tell me aught of England or of Spring in England
   now?

   köil: Indian bell-bird; *sat-bhai*: Indian starling

LADY MARY WORTLEY MONTAGU

from Verses Written in the Chiosk of the British
Palace, at Pera, Overlooking the City of
Constantinople, Dec. 26, 1717

Give me, great God! said I, a little farm,
In summer shady, and in winter warm;
Where a clear spring gives birth to murmuring brooks,
By nature gliding down the mossy rocks.
Not artfully by leaden pipes conveyed,
Or greatly falling in a forced cascade,
Pure and unsullied winding through the shade.
All bounteous Heaven has added to my prayer,
A softer climate and a purer air.
   Our frozen isle now chilling winter binds,
Deformed by rains, and rough with blasting winds;
The withered woods grow white with hoary frost,
By driving storms their verdant beauty lost;
The trembling birds their leafless covert shun,
And seek in distant climes a warmer sun:
The water nymphs their silent urns deplore,
Even Thames, benumbed, 's a river now no more:
The barren meads no longer yield delight,
By glistening snows made painful to the sight.
   Here summer reigns with one eternal smile,
Succeeding harvests bless the happy soil;
Fair fertile fields, to whom indulgent Heaven
Has every charm of every season given.
No killing cold deforms the beauteous year,
The springing flowers no coming winter fear.
But as the parent rose decays and dies,
The infant buds with brighter colours rise,
And with fresh sweets the mother's scent supplies.

RUPERT BROOKE

from The Old Vicarage, Grantchester

Just now the lilac is in bloom,
All before my little room;
And in my flower-beds, I think,
Smile the carnation and the pink;
And down the borders, well I know,
The poppy and the pansy blow . . .
Oh! there the chestnuts, summer through,
Beside the river make for you
A tunnel of green gloom, and sleep
Deeply above; and green and deep
The stream mysterous glides beneath,
Green as a dream and deep as death.
– Oh, damn! I know it! and I know
How the May fields all golden show,
And when the day is young and sweet,
Gild gloriously the bare feet
That run to bathe . . .
                              Du lieber Gott!
Here am I, sweating, sick, and hot,
And there the shadowed waters fresh
Lean up to embrace the naked flesh.
Temperamentvoll German Jews
Drink beer around; – and *there* the dews
Are soft beneath a morn of gold.
Here tulips bloom as they are told;
Unkempt about those hedges blows
An English unofficial rose;
And there the unregulated sun
Slopes down to rest when day is done,
And wages a vague unpunctual star,
A slippered Hesper; and there are

Meads towards Haslingfield and Coton
Where *das Betreten*'s not *verboten*.

εἴθε γενοίμην ... would I were
In Grantchester, in Grantchester! –
Some, it may be, can get in touch
With Nature there, or Earth, or such.
And clever modern men have seen
A Faun a-peeping through the green,
And felt the Classics were not dead,
To glimpse a Naiad's reedy head,
Or hear the Goat-foot piping low:...
But these are things I do not know.
I only know that you may lie
Day-long and watch the Cambridge sky,
And, flower-lulled in sleepy grass,
Hear the cool lapse of hours pass,
Until the centuries blend and blur
In Grantchester, in Grantchester...

near Cambridge

IVOR GURNEY

Song

(Severn meadows)

Only the wanderer
  Knows England's graces,
Or can anew see clear
  Familiar faces.

And who loves joy as he
   That dwells in shadows?
Do not forget me quite,
   O Severn meadows.

   Cotswolds

A. E. HOUSMAN

'Into my heart an air that kills'

Into my heart an air that kills
   From yon far country blows:
What are those blue remembered hills,
   What spires, what farms are those?

That is the land of lost content,
   I see it shining plain,
The happy highways where I went
   And cannot come again.

   Shropshire

ROBERT BURNS

My Heart's in the Highlands

My heart's in the Highlands, my heart is not here;
My heart's in the Highlands a chasing the deer;
Chasing the wild deer, and following the roe;
My heart's in the Highlands, wherever I go. –

Farewell to the Highlands, farewell to the North;
The birth-place of valour, the country of worth:
Wherever I wander, wherever I rove,
The hills of the Highlands for ever I love. –

Farewell to the mountains high cover'd with snow;
Farewell to the Straths and green valleys below:
Farewell to the forests and wild-hanging woods;
Farewell to the torrents and loud-pouring floods. –

My heart's in the Highlands, my heart is not here,
My heart's in the Highlands a chasing the deer:
Chasing the wild deer, and following the roe;
My heart's in the Highlands, wherever I go. –

Scottish Highlands

PATRICK KAVANAGH

Kerr's Ass

We borrowed the loan of Kerr's big ass
To go to Dundalk with butter,
Brought him home the evening before the market
An exile that night in Mucker.

We heeled up the cart before the door,
We took the harness inside –
The straw-stuffed straddle, the broken breeching
With bits of bull-wire tied;

The winkers that had no choke-band,
The collar and the reins...
In Ealing Broadway, London Town
I name their several names

Until a world comes to life –
Morning, the silent bog,
And the God of imagination waking
In a Mucker fog.

Dundalk, Ireland

GEORGE GORDON, LORD BYRON

from Don Juan, Canto II

I can't but say it is an awkward sight
   To see one's native land receding through
The growing waters; it unmans one quite,
   Especially when life is rather new:
I recollect Great Britain's coast looks white,
   But almost every other country's blue,
When gazing on them, mystified by distance,
We enter on our nautical existence.

ANONYMOUS

from The Seafarer

[translated from the Anglo-Saxon by Harold Massingham]

Now England's glades unwinter brilliantly,
The sun's a gold-giver in every village,
Daisies galore, small glory of meadows,
All thrill my conviction to voyage.
Also the sorrow-tones of remote cuckoos
Bode badly. That same bluff citizen
Knows next to nothing of anxious solitudes. –
And yet my heart-boat tugs at harbour ropes,
I imagine already the plunging whales,
Sea-distances surge through my dissatisfaction,
Already the gannet screams to itself
Over forlorn water, kingdom of roaming whales,
All, all irresistible to this sea-yearning.

JOHN KEATS

from Epistle to My Brother George

E'en now I am pillow'd on a bed of flowers
That crown a lofty cliff, which proudly towers
Above the ocean waves. The stalks and blades
Chequer my tablet with their quivering shades.
On one side is a field of drooping oats,
Through which the poppies show their scarlet coats,
So pert and useless, that they bring to mind
The scarlet-coats that pester human-kind.
And on the other side, outspread is seen
Ocean's blue mantle streak'd with purple and green.
Now 'tis I see a canvas'd ship, and now
Mark the bright silver curling round her prow.
I see the lark down-dropping to his nest,
And the broad winged sea-gull never at rest;
For when no more he spreads his feathers free,
His breast is dancing on the restless sea.

written at Margate, Kent

ALFRED, LORD TENNYSON

Audley Court

'The Bull, the Fleece are cramm'd, and not a room
For love or money. Let us picnic there
At Audley Court.'
                          I spoke, while Audley feast
Humm'd like a hive all round the narrow quay,
To Francis, with a basket on his arm,
To Francis just alighted from the boat,

And breathing of the sea. 'With all my heart,'
Said Francis. Then we shoulder'd thro' the swarm,
And rounded by the stillness of the beach
To where the bay runs up its latest horn.
　　We left the dying ebb that faintly lipp'd
The flat red granite; so by many a sweep
Of meadow smooth from aftermath we reach'd
The griffin-guarded gates, and pass'd thro' all
The pillar'd dusk of sounding sycamores,
And cross'd the garden to the gardener's lodge,
With all its casements bedded, and its walls
And chimneys muffled in the leafy vine.
　　There, on a slope of orchard, Francis laid
A damask napkin wrought with horse and hound,
Brought out a dusky loaf that smelt of home,
And, half-cut-down, a pasty costly-made,
Where quail and pigeon, lark and leveret lay,
Like fossils of the rock, with golden yolks
Imbedded and injellied; last, with these,
A flask of cider from his father's vats,
Prime, which I knew; and so we sat and eat,
And talk'd old matters over; who was dead,
Who married, who was like to be, and how
The races went, and who would rent the hall:
Then touch'd upon the game, how scarce it was
This season; glancing thence, discuss'd the farm,
The four-field system, and the price of grain;
And struck upon the corn-laws, where we split,
And came again together on the king
With heated faces; till he laugh'd aloud;
And, while the blackbird on the pippin hung
To hear him, clapt his hand in mine and sang –
　　'Oh! who would fight and march and countermarch,
Be shot for sixpence in a battle-field,
And shovell'd up into a bloody trench
Where no one knows? but let me live my life.

'Oh! who would cast and balance at a desk,
Perch'd like a crow upon a three-legg'd stool,
Till all his juice is dried, and all his joints
Are full of chalk? but let me live my life.

'Who'd serve the state? for if I carved my name
Upon the cliffs that guard my native land,
I might as well have traced it in the sands;
The sea wastes all: but let me live my life.

'Oh! who would love? I woo'd a woman once,
But she was sharper than an eastern wind,
And all my heart turn'd from her, as a thorn
Turns from the sea: but let me live my life.'

He sang his song, and I replied with mine:
I found it in a volume, all of songs,
Knock'd down to me, when old Sir Robert's pride,
His books – the more the pity, so I said –
Came to the hammer here in March – and this –
I set the words, and added names I knew.

'Sleep, Ellen Aubrey, sleep, and dream of me:
Sleep, Ellen, folded in thy sister's arm,
And sleeping, haply dream her arm is mine.

'Sleep, Ellen, folded in Emilia's arm;
Emilia, fairer than all else but thou,
For thou art fairer than all else that is.

'Sleep, breathing health and peace upon her breast:
Sleep, breathing love and trust against her lip:
I go to-night: I come to-morrow morn.

'I go, but I return. I would I were
The pilot of the darkness and the dream.
Sleep, Ellen Aubrey, love, and dream of me.'

So sang we each to either, Francis Hale,
The farmer's son who lived across the bay,
My friend; and I, that having wherewithal,
And in the fallow leisure of my life
A rolling stone of here and everywhere,
Did what I would; but ere the night we rose

And saunter'd home beneath a moon, that, just
In crescent, dimly rain'd about the leaf
Twilights of airy silver, till we reach'd
The limit of the hills; and as we sank
From rock to rock upon the glooming quay,
The town was hush'd beneath us: lower down
The bay was oily-calm; the harbour-buoy
With one green sparkle ever and anon
Dipt by itself, and we were glad at heart.

suggested by Abbey Park, Torquay, Devon

Acknowledgements

The editor and publishers gratefully acknowledge the following for permission to reproduce copyright material in this book.

W. H. AUDEN: to Faber and Faber Ltd for 'The summer holds upon its glittering back', 'O lurcher-loving collier, black as night,' and 'In Praise of Limestone'. MICHAEL BALDWIN: to Michael Baldwin for 'The Map' and 'Chalk Horse'. GEORGE BARKER: to Faber and Faber Ltd for 'Morning in Norfolk'. HILAIRE BELLOC: to The Peters Fraser and Dunlop Group Limited on behalf of The Estate of Hilaire Belloc for 'Ha'nacker Mill' from Complete Verse. JOHN BETJEMAN: to John Murray (Publishers) Ltd for 'The Planster's Vision', 'The Small Towns of Ireland', 'Love in a Valley', 'A Lincolnshire Tale', 'On hearing the Full Peal of Ten Bells' and 'Henley on Thames' from Collected Poems. LAURENCE BINYON: to The Society of Authors, on behalf of the Laurence Binyon Estate for 'The Burning of the Leaves'. GEORGE MACKAY BROWN: to John Murray (Publishers) Ltd for 'Dead Fires' from Selected Poems. BASIL BUNTING: to Bloodaxe Books Ltd for 'Briggflats', 'Stones trip Couquet burn', 'Weeping oaks grieve, chestnuts raise', 'At Briggflats Meetinghouse' and 'Gin the Goodwife stint' from Complete Poems (Bloodaxe Books, 1999). C. K. CHESTERTON: to A. P. Watt Ltd on behalf of the The Royal Literary Fund for 'The Rolling English Road' from Collected Poems. AMY CLAMPITT: to Faber and Faber Ltd for 'The Hurricane and Charlotte Mew' from Collected Poems by Amy Clampitt, copyright © 1997 by the Estate of Amy Clampitt; to Random House, Inc., for reprinting rights in Canada. GILLIAN CLARKE: to Carcanet Press Ltd for 'East Moors' from Collected Poems. JACK CLEMO: to Bloodaxe Books Ltd for 'The Clay Tip Worker' from Selected Poems (Bloodaxe Books,1988). C. DAY LEWIS: to The Random House Group for 'Seen from the Train', '1954', 'Poem 12' and 'Poem 5' from The Complete Poems (Sinclair-Stevenson, 1992), copyright © 1992 in this edition and the estate of C. Day Lewis. WALTER DE LA MARE: to The Society of Authors as the representative of the Literary Trustees of Walter de la Mare for 'Solitude' from The Complete Poems (1969; USA, 1970). FREDA DOWNIE: to Bloodaxe Books Ltd for 'Her Garden' from Collected Poems, edited by George Szirtes (Bloodaxe Books, 1995). DOUGLAS DUNN: to Faber and Faber Ltd for 'Washing the Coins', 'Gardeners' and 'Loch Music'. T. S. ELIOT: to Faber and Faber

Ltd for 'East Coker' (Part I), 'Little Gidding' (Part I) and 'Rannoch, by Glencoe'. ARTHUR FREEMAN: to the author for kind permission to reprint 'The Reader Looks Up'. JOHN FULLER: to Chatto and Windus for 'Cairn' and 'Bog' from Collected Poems. IVOR GURNEY: to Oxford University Press for 'Cotswold Ways', 'Feeling a Tree', 'Tewkesbury', 'By Severn' and 'Song', from The Collected Poems, edited by P. J. Kavanagh (1982). LAVINIA GREENLAW: to Faber and Faber Ltd for 'River History'. THOM GUNN: to Faber and Faber Ltd for 'Flooded Meadows'. TONY HARRISON: to the author for kind permission to reprint 'The Earthen Lot', 'National Trust' and 'History Classes'. SEAMUS HEANEY: to Faber and Faber Ltd for 'The Peninsula', 'Toome', 'Broagh', 'Whinlands', 'Sweeney Astray' and 'Settings: xxiv'. JOHN HEATH-STUBBS: to David Higham Associates for 'The Green Man's Last Will and Testament' from Collected Poems 1943–1987 (Carcanet Press Ltd). TOBIAS HILL: to Carcanet Press Ltd for 'Draining the Grand Union' from Zoo (Oxford University Press). MICHAEL HOFMANN: to Faber and Faber Ltd for 'Myopia in Rupert Brooke Country'. A. E. HOUSMAN: to The Society of Authors as the literary representative of the Estate of A. E. Housman for 'Hughey Steeple', 'Into my heart an air that kills' and 'On Wenlock Edge' from A Shropshire Lad. TED HUGHES: to Faber and Faber Ltd for 'Dee', 'Salmon - Taking Times', 'Vrow Hill', 'Emily Bronte', 'Rain', 'Wind', 'Moors', 'Sir Gawain and the Green Knight' and 'Coming Down through Somerset'. ELZABETH JENNINGS: to David Higham Associates for 'Hopkins in Wales' from Growing Points (Carcanet Press). PATRICK KAVANAGH: to Peter Fallon, Literary Agent of Loughcrew, Oldcastle, Co. Meath, Ireland, on behalf of the Trustees of the Estate of Patrick Kavanagh for 'The Great Hunger' (Part XIII), 'Kerr's Ass' and 'Stony Grey Soil'. P. J. KAVANAGH: to Carcanet Press Ltd for 'And Light Fading' from Collected Poems. GENE KEMP: to Faber and Faber Ltd for extract from 'The Mink War'. RUDYARD KIPLING: to A. P. Watt Ltd on behalf of The National Trust for Places of Historic Interest or Natural Beauty for 'The River's Tale', 'Sussex', 'A Charm', 'Pucks Song', 'The Land', 'The Way through the Woods' and 'In Springtime'. PHILIP LARKIN: to Faber and Faber Ltd for 'Going, Going', 'Here' and 'The Whitsun Weddings'. D. H. LAWRENCE: to Laurence Pollinger on behalf of the Estate of Frieda Lawrence Ravagli for 'The North Country', 'The Rainbow' and 'Flat Suburbs, S.W., in the Morning' from The Complete Poems. NORMAN MACCAIG: to Chatto & Windus for 'Looking Down on Glen Canisp', 'July Evening', 'Summer Farm', 'Landscape and I' and Firewood, from Collected Poems. HUGH MACDIARMID: to Carcanet Press Ltd for 'Scald's Death - Scotland Small' from Complete Poems. SORLEY MACLEAN: to Carcanet Press Ltd for 'Hallaig' from From Wood to

Ridge. LOUIS MACNEICE: to David Higham Associates for 'Under the Mountain', 'The Park', 'Carrickfergus', 'Birmingham' and 'Wessex Guidebook' from *Collected Poems* (Faber and Faber). DEREK MAHON: to The Gallery Press for 'The Mayo Tao' and 'North Wind: Portrush' from *Collected Poems* (The Gallery Press, 1999), by kind permission of the author. JOHN MASEFIELD: to The Society of Authors as the literary representative of the Estate of John Masefield for 'Reynard the Fox'. HAROLD MASSINGHAM: to the author for kind permission to reprint 'Winter in Wensleydale' and 'The Seafarer'. GLYN MAXWELL: to Gillon Aitken Associates Ltd for 'Hilles Edge' from *The Breakage* (Faber and Faber), copyright © Glyn Maxwell, reprinted with the permission of Gillon Aitken Associates Ltd. JOHN MONTAGUE: to The Gallery Press for 'Windharp' from *Collected Poems* (The Gallery Press, 1995), by kind permission of the author. ANDREW MOTION: to Faber and Faber Ltd for 'Fresh Water' (Part 1). EDWIN MUIR: to Faber and Faber Ltd for 'Childhood' and 'The Threefold Place'. NORMAN NICHOLSON: to Faber and Faber Ltd for 'Weeds', 'Rock Face', 'Millom Old Quarry', and 'Five Rivers'; to David Higham Associates for 'Scafell Pike' and 'Windscale' from *Collected Poems* (Faber and Faber). CHRISTOPHER NORTH: to the author for kind permission to reprint 'Battlefield'. DOUGLAS OLIVER: to the author for kind permission to reprint 'Again in Dorset'. KATHERINE PIERPOINT: to Faber and Faber Ltd for 'The Twist in the River' and 'Saltmarsh and Skylark'. RUTH PITTER: to Enitharmon Press for 'Dun-Colour' from *Collected Poems* (Enitharmon Press, 1996). SYLVIA PLATH: to Faber and Faber Ltd for 'Blackberrying'. ANNE RIDLER: to Carcanet Press Ltd for 'Bempton Cliffs' *from New and Selected Poems*. MICHAEL ROBERTS: to Carcanet Press Ltd for 'Langdale: Nightfall January 4' from *Selected Poetry & Prose*. W. R. RODGERS: to The Gallery Press for 'An Irish Lake', 'Field Day' and 'Armagh' from *Poems* (The Gallery Press, 1993) by kind permission of the author. STEVIE SMITH: to James MacGibbon for kind permission to reprint 'The River Humber'. BERNARD SPENCER: to Oxford University Press for 'Allotments: April' and 'At The Angler', from *Collected Poems*, edited by Roger Bowen (1981) © Mrs Anne Humphreys, 1981. STEPHEN SPENDER: to Faber and Faber Ltd for 'The Pylons' and 'Wordsworth'. DYLAN THOMAS: to David Higham Associates for 'Poem in October' and 'Fern Hill' from *Collected Poems* (J. M. Dent). R. S. THOMAS: to The Orion Publishing Group Ltd for 'The Belfry', 'The Village', 'Reservoirs' and 'A Peasant' from *Collected Poems 1945–1990*. CHARLES TOMLINSON: to Carcanet Press Ltd for 'Harvest: A Meditation on John Constable' from *Selected Poems: Annunciations*. DEREK WALCOTT: to Faber & Faber Ltd for 'xxxv' from 'Midsummer' from *Collected Poems 1958–1986* by Derek Walcott,

Index of Poets

Allingham, William (1824–89), 252
Anonymous, 20, 35, 57, 83, 125, 238, 241, 281, 413
Arnold, Matthew (1822–88), 50, 294
Auden, W. H. (1907–73), 119, 204

Baldwin, Michael (b 1930), 260
Barnes, William (1801–86), 71, 182, 249, 346, 397
Belloc, Hilaire (1870–1953), 303
Betjeman, Sir John (1906–84), 51, 205, 215, 225, 329
Binyon, Laurence (1869–1945), 82
Bisset, James, 91
Blake, William (1757–1827), 20, 270, 283, 321
Bloomfield, Robert (1766–1823), 305
Brontë, Emily (1818–1845), 61, 74
Brooke, Rupert (1887–1915), 409
Brown, George Mackay (1921–1996), 187
Browne, William (1591–1643), 36
Browning, Elizabeth Barrett (1806–61), 12, 316
Browning, Robert (1812–89), 348, 406
Bunting, Basil (1900–85), 34, 76, 143, 188, 286
Burns, Robert (1759–96), 35, 411
Byron, George Gordon, Lord (1788–1824), 413

Cavendish, Margaret, Duchess of Newcastle (1624?–74), 147
Chesterton, G. K. (1875–1936), 247
Clampitt, Amy (1920–94), 111
Clare, John (1793–1864), 11, 65, 77, 164, 179, 308, 330
Clarke, Gillian (b 1937), 198
Clemo, Jack (b 1916), 278
Clough, A. H. (1819–61), 399
Coleridge, Hartley (1796–1849), 67
Coleridge, S. T. (1772–1834), 21, 248, 322, 357, 365, 382, 395
Colman, George, the Younger (1762–1836), 224
Cowper, William (1731–1800), 89, 101, 158, 380
Crabbe, George (1754–1832), 159

Dafydd ap Gwilym (c1320–c1380), 71
Dalton, John (1709–63), 194
Davidson, John (1857–1909), 233, 325, 379

Davies, Idries (1905–53), 70, 214, 358
Dekker, Thomas (1570?–1632), 156
Diaper, William (1685–1717), 46
Downie, Freda (1929–93), 231
Drayton, Michael (1563–1631), 45
Dunbar, William (1456?–1513?), 29
Dunn, Douglas (b 1942), 91, 167
Dyer, John (1699–1757), 5, 189

Earl, John (b 1949), 385
Eliot, George (1819–80), 365
Eliot, T. S. (1888–1965), 64, 268, 284
Elliott, Ebenezer (1781–1849), 152

Fanthorpe, U. A. (b 1929), 41, 99, 177
Finch, Anne, Countess of Winchilsea (1661–1720), 77
Freeman, Arthur (b 1938), 318
Fry, Christopher (b 1907), 275
Fuller, John (b 1937), 118, 404

Goldsmith, Oliver (1730?–74), 178, 200, 320
Graham, W. S. (1918–86), 369
Gray, Sir Alexander (1882–1967), 376
Gray, John (1866–1934), 377
Gray, Thomas (1716–71), 135, 362
Gunn, Thom (b 1929), 47
Gurney, Ivor (1890–1937), 14, 107, 216, 384, 410

Hannay, Patrick (d 1629?), 189
Hardy, Thomas (1840–1928), 37, 115, 173, 247, 301, 314, 339
Harrison, Tony (b 1937), 143, 197
Heaney, Seamus (b 1939), 56, 64, 263, 392, 405
Heath-Stubbs, John (b 1918), 207
Hedderwick, John (1814–97), 161
Herrick, Robert (1591–1674), 378
Hewitt, John (1927–87), 390
Hill, Geoffrey (b 1932), 267, 373
Hill, Tobias (b 1970), 229
Hofmann, Michael (b 1957), 316
Hood, Thomas (1799–1845), 211
Hopkins, Gerard Manley (1844–89), 76, 97, 106, 272, 344
Housman, A. E. (1859–1936), 139, 258, 411
Hughes, Ted (1930–98), 67, 72, 152, 172, 277, 313, 328
Hurdis, James (1763–1801), 74, 170

James, Richard (1592–1638), 257
Jennings, Elizabeth (b 1926), 274, 314, 381
Jonson, Ben (1572–1637), 131

Kavanagh, Patrick (1905–67), 164, 389, 412
Kavanagh, P. J. (b 1931), 350
Keats, John (1795–1821), 299, 328, 333, 414
Kemp, Gene (b 1926), 113
Keyes, Sidney (1922–43), 308
Kingsley, Charles (1819–75), 302
Kipling, Rudyard (1865–1936), 174, 259, 304, 383, 407

Langland, William (c1330–c1386), 281
Lanyer, Aemilia (1569–1645), 100
Larkin, Philip (1922–85), 205, 253
Lawrence, D. H. (1885–1930), 70, 193, 225
Ledwidge, Francis (1891–1917), 341
Lewis, C. Day (1904–72), 196
Lloyd, Robert (1733–64), 220
Lyly, John (1554–1606), 332

MacCaig, Norman (1910–96), 24, 184, 360, 404
MacDiarmid, Hugh (1892–1978), 122, 319, 386
Maclean, Sorley (Somhairle Macgill-Eain) (1911–96), 387
MacNeice, Louis (1907–63), 22, 227, 236, 266, 370
Mahon, Derek (b 1941), 17, 54
Mangan, James Clarence (1803–49), 126
Marvell, Andrew (1621–74), 87, 125
Masefield, John (1878–1967), 151, 261
Massingham, Harold (b 1932), 85
Maxwell, Glyn (b 1963), 23
Mew, Charlotte (1869–1928), 110
Milton, John (1608–74), 3
Montagu, Lady Mary Wortley (1690–1762), 408
Montague, John (b 1929), 327
Moore, Sir Jonas (1617–79), 98
Morris, William (1834–96), 236
Motion, Andrew (b 1952), 30
Muir, Edwin (1887–1950), 264, 368

Nicholson, Norman (1914–87), 25, 32, 117, 262
North, Christopher (b 1945), 264

O'Sullivan, Seamas (1879–1958), 69

Palmer, Samuel (1805–81), 271
The 'Pearl' Poet (14th century), 59
Pierpoint, Katherine (b 1961), 48

Pitter, Ruth (1897–1992), 347
Plath, Sylvia (1932–63), 53
Pope, Alexander (1688–1744), 133, 145

Raine, Katherine (b 1908), 117, 142
Randolph, Thomas (1605–1635), 332
Ridler, Anne (b 1912), 341
Rodgers, W. R. (1909–69), 43, 218, 361
Rossetti, D. G. (1828–82), 402

Sackville-West, V. (1892–1962), 133, 169
Scarfe, Francis (b 1911), 372
Scott, John (1730–83), 47
Scott, Sir Walter (1771–1832), 130, 239, 375
Shakespeare, William (1564–1616), 52, 155, 16203, 358, 382
Sidney, Sir Philip (1554–1586), 112
Smith, Ian Crichton (1928–98), 183
Smith, Stevie (1902–71), 31
Smith, Sydney, 232
Southey, Robert (1774–1843), 92
Spencer, Bernard (1909–63), 228, 401
Spender, Sir Stephen (1909–95), 203, 309
Spenser, Edmund (c1552–99), 28, 154
Stallworthy, Jon (b 1935), 80, 96
Stevenson, R. L. (1850–94), 63, 251
Strode, William (1602?–45), 18
Swinburne, A. C. (1837–1909), 94

Tennyson, Alfred, Lord (1809–92), 39, 81, 337, 414
Thomas, Dylan (1914–53), 14, 366
Thomas, Edward (1878–1917), 80, 96, 105, 140, 146, 244, 340, 403
Thomas, R. S. (b 1913), 135, 166, 210, 280, 393
Thomson, Derick (Ruaraidh MacThómais) (b 1921), 277
Thomson, James (1700–48), 150, 226
Tomlinson, Charles (b 1927), 273, 344
Vaughan, Henry (1621–95), 38, 73, 356

Walcott, Derek (b 1930), 250
Watkins, Vernon (1906–67), 240, 326
White, Gilbert (1720–93), 9
Whitehead, William (1715–85), 90
Wilde, Oscar (1854–1900), 235
Wordsworth, William (1770–1850), 1, 26, 44, 129, 201, 232, 270, 289, 324, 336, 342, 351, 363, 398

Yeats, W. B. (1865–1939), 338, 402
Young, Andrew (1885–1971), 79
Young, Douglas (1913–73), 104

Index of Places

English places are arranged under counties where possible. Entries for Ireland, Northern Ireland, Scotland and Wales are under each country.

Avon, Bath, 124

Berkshire, 145, 362
Birmingham, 236
Buckinghamshire
Horton, 3
Stoke Poges, 135

Cambridgeshire, 77, 164, 284, 330
Helpston, 11, 65, 179
near Cambridge, 409
Cheshire, 302
Cornwall, 51, 278
Carne, 314
North, 301
Cotswolds, 107, 340, 384, 410
east of Gloucester, 14
near Burford, Oxfordshire, 18
Cumberland, 92
Cumbria, 32, 117, 143, 194, 262
Scafell Pike, 25
Whitehaven, 32

Devon, 36, 67, 378
Dartmoor, 113
North, 53
Ottery St Mary, 365
Plymtree, north-east of Exeter, 248
Torquay, Abbey Park, 414
Dorset, 115, 173, 249, 346
Bagber Common, 182
Sturminster Newton, 37
Winterborne, 314

East Sussex, 259
England, 318
Middle, 264
South-east, 111
Southern, 275
at the time of Edward the Confessor, 99
Essex, 47
Dedham, 344

Fens, The, 45, 98

Gloucestershire, 216, 273
Cheltenham and Cirencester, 177
near Stroud, 23

Hampshire
Selborne, 9
Winchester, 328
Herefordshire, 316
Hope End Colwall, 12
Humberside, 341

Ireland, Republic of, 215, 327
County Cork, 126
County Galway, near Ballyconneely, 405
County Mayo, 17
Connaught, 281
Slievemore, Achill Island, 22
Dundalk, 412
Westmeath, Coole, 338
Isle of Wight, near Bonchurch, 94

Kent, 50, 52, 169, 325
Margate, 414
Penshurst, 112
Shoreham, 271

Lake District, 201, 308, 309, 398
Black Crag, 26
Easedale, 324
Lancashire, 257
Liverpool, 252
London, 41, 255
Central, 232
Thames embankment, 235
East, 233
Newham, 231
Greater, Croydon, 225
North, 379
North-West, 229, 283
River Thames, 29
suburbs, 220

Malvern Hills, 281

Norfolk, near Blakeney, 48
North, the, 193
industrial towns, 189
Northamptonshire, 164, 330
Helpston, *see under* Cambridgeshire
Northamptonshire/Buckinghamshire
border, Yardley Chase, 101

Northern Ireland, 43, 390
  County Antrim, 54, 263, 370
  County Armagh, 218
  County Down, 56
  County Monaghan, 164, 389
  Donegal, 69
  South Derry, 39
Northumberland, 34
  Coast, 286
  Newbiggin-by-the-Sea, 143
Northumbria, 188

Oxfordshire, 261
  and environs, 294
  near Burford, 18
  near Oxford, 106
  Nuneham Coultanay, 90
  Uffington, 260

Scotland
  Ayrshire, 36
  Borders, 35, 375
  Central, 97
  Coast, 319
  Edinburgh, from the Pentland Hills, 239
  Glasgow, near, 161
  Highlands, 24, 411
    Rannoch Moor, 64
  Inner Hebrides, Canna, 117, 142
  Inverness-shire, 399
  Kincardine, Lairhillock, 376
  Orkney, 187, 368
  Outer Hebrides, 277
  Pentland Hills, 63, 239
  Raasay Island, Hallaig, 387
  Renfrewshire, 167
  Strathclyde, near Greenock, 369
  Sutherland, 183, 184
  West Coast, Iona, 57
Shropshire, 12, 139, 258, 316, 411
Somerset, 151, 152
  Alfoxden, 1
  near Weston-super-Mare, 46
  near Yeovil, 268
  Nether Stowey, 21, 395
Staffordshire, North Lud's Church,
  Blackbrook Valley, 59
Stirlingshire, 97

Suffolk
  Aldeburgh, 159
  Fakenham, 305
Surrey, 189, 225
Sussex, 174, 304

Thames River
  at London, 29
  source, 31
Thames Valley, 28
Tyneside, 372

Ullswater, 26, 44

Wales, 20, 166, 326
  Cardiganshire (now Dyfed), New Quay,
    14
  Carmarthenshire
    Grongar Hill, by Llandeilo, 5
    Llangain, 366
  Mid-Glamorgan, 214
  Montgomery, Tregynon, 210
  North, 76, 344
    Lleyn Peninsula, 118, 404
    Vale of Clwyd, 272
  Powys, 73
    Ffrwdgrech Falls, near Brecon, 38
    near Brecon, 356
  South, 70, 358
  South Glamorgan, 198
  Y Bala, Llyn Trewelyn, 393
Warwickshire, 365
  Forest of Arden, 162, 358
Welsh/English border, 250
Wessex, 266
West Midland, Malvern Hills, 281
West Sussex, Hallnacker Downs, 303
Wiltshire, 77, 178, 200, 320, 329
Winander (?), 342
Windermere (?), 342
Wye Valley, 351

Yorkshire, 31, 125
  Hull, 253
  North, 79, 85, 197
    Nun-Appleton House, 87
  West, 74, 172, 313
    Haworth, 61
    Heptonstall, 72

Edwin Muir

George Mackay
Brown

Seamus O'Sullivan

W.R. Rodgers

W.B. Yeats

John
Hewitt

Patrick
Kavanagh

John Montague

Seamus
Heaney

John Betjeman

James Clarence
Mangan

Dy

Dafydd ap Gwilym

John Dy

Vernon
Watkins

S.T. Coleridge

Sylvia
Plath

Robert
Herrick

T.S

William
Browne

John
Betjeman

Alfred,
Lord Tenni

Gene
Kemp

Jack Clemo

John
Gray